SHIPWRECK MODERNITY

Shipwreck Modernity

Ecologies of Globalization, 1550–1719

Steve Mentz

MINNESOTA

University of Minnesota Press
Minneapolis
London

Portions of chapter 1 were published as "God's Storms: Shipwreck and the Meanings of Ocean in Early Modern England and America," in *Shipwreck in Art and Literature: Images and Interpretations from Antiquity to the Present Day*, ed. Carl Thompson, 77–91 (London: Routledge, 2014); reprinted by permission of Taylor and Francis Group, a division of Informa.

Portions of chapters 5 and 7 were published as " 'Making the Green One Red': Dynamic Ecologies in *Macbeth*, Edward Barlow's Journal, and *Robinson Crusoe*," *JEMCS* 13, no. 3 (Summer 2013): 66–83.

Portions of chapter 6 were published as "Donne at Sea: The Islands Voyage and Poetic Form," *Forum for Modern Language Studies* 49, no. 4 (2013): 355–68.

Portions of chapter 7 were published as "Shipwreck," in *Inhuman Nature*, ed. Jeffrey Jerome Cohen, 1–15 (Brooklyn, N.Y.: Punctum Books, 2014).

William Carlos Williams, "The Seafarer," from *The Collected Poems, Volume II: 1939–1962* (New York: New Directions Publishing, 1948). Reprinted by permission of New Directions Publishing.

George Oppen, "Of Being Numerous," from *New Collected Poems* (New York: New Directions Publishing, 1968). Copyright 1968 by George Oppen. Reprinted by permission of New Directions Publishing.

Published by the University of Minnesota Press
111 Third Avenue South, Suite 290
Minneapolis, MN 55401-2520
http://www.upress.umn.edu

Library of Congress Cataloging-in-Publication Data

Mentz, Steve.
Shipwreck modernity: ecologies of globalization, 1550–1719 / Steve Mentz.
Includes bibliographical references and index.
ISBN 978-0-8166-9103-6 (hc)
ISBN 978-0-8166-9106-7 (pb)
1. Shipwrecks in literature. 2. Literature and society—History. 3. Ecology in literature. 4. Civilization, Modern, in literature. 5. Shipwreck survival in literature. I. Title.
PN56.S54M46 2015
809'.93355—dc23 2014049432

For Alinor, Ian, Olivia,
and the global ocean

Contents

Two Prefaces

THIS BOOK ABOUT DISASTER starts with a theoretical preface and a narrative preface.

Theory and story together assemble errancy into form. Theory gazes down at catastrophe from above, rearranging chaos into order. Story reassembles the broken pieces through the friction of proximity, piling events upon events. This book's response to disaster employs the perspective of theory and the continuity of story.

If it were possible, I would ask you to read both prefaces at the same time, combining theory and story. It takes the resources of both modes to explain shipwreck's global modernity. But since full simultaneity is not possible, since reading of necessity involves the linear act of moving forward from word to word and page to page, I offer these twin prefaces as Pillars of Hercules framing the entrance into rough seas.

By way of invitation: nec plus ultra.

Theoretical Preface: Epochal Claims and the Age of Shipwreck

The big fish at which the theoretical preface gives up its spear is an ecological theory of historical change. Shipwreck sits at the center of this theory creating disorderly rupture. Crafting a flexible historical language to make sense of continuity and change requires complex, unstable, semipredictable systems. I start with two mutually implicated models for how historical systems alter: theft and composture. I emphasize the second but start with the first.

Theft characterizes the key transaction hidden inside familiar just-so stories about historical breaks. These events are often imagined as productive ruptures out of which some brand-new thing springs, armed and ready for combat. My polemical description of "break history" as theft recalls a long-lived caricature of a modernity that gives birth to itself by stealing from classical antiquity. This familiar story undergirds the basic idea of the Renaissance, the history of which has recently been rehearsed as a "swerve" into modernity.[1] The historiography of the early modern period has, in large part, defined itself through this model, from Burkhardt to Foucault to Greene to Greenblatt.[2] In these stories modernity is a literal Re-naissance, birth and rebirth, novel in the sense of radically distinct from its medieval predecessors and also attached to a distant and idealized past. It may well be time to name this process of cultural transmission for what it is: theft. Petrarch was a tomb robber.

Against this model of radical disruption and new ownership, I offer composture as an ecological metaphor. The past, like the recycling, never goes away. A composting model of historical change recognizes multiple presences in multiple states of decay at all times. Historical change follows the Caribbean poet and theorist Éduoard Glissant's model of history as the "accumulation of sediments."[3] This vision imagines history as a comingling and fecund process, a fertilizing combination of the living and the dead. History as we encounter it in texts and representations is shot through with multiple temporalities. These polychronic systems, as Glissant notes, produce both violence and meaning. The corpses and poems and prose styles that Petrarch robbed from antique graves made new and old things grow.

In critical practice it may not be so easy to distinguish narratives of theft, which propose an absolute difference between historical periods, from narratives of composture, which imagine a productive and disorienting swirl. I draw these two terms from a literary passage, here initiating my practice of using literary models alongside theoretical formulations to help understand historical changes and disasters. A vision of the global ecology in *Timon of Athens* implies that theft represents the dominant visible relationship in the nonhuman environment, but it is buttressed from beneath by composture:

> The sun's a thief, and with his great attraction
> Robs the vast sea; the moon's an arrant thief,
> And her pale fire she snatches from the sun;
> The sea's a thief, whose liquid surge resolves
> The moon into salt tears; the earth's a thief,
> That feeds and breeds by a composture stol'n
> From gen'ral excrement; each thing's a thief.[4]

The five thieves of this passage—sun, moon, sea, earth, and "each thing"—surround a lone composture, but it is the compost that feeds and breeds. An ecological and catastrophic theory of historical change overlooks theft to seek composture. Theft and its struggles over ownership do not disappear from history, but an accumulated layering of exchange and entanglement replaces the baton passing of historical epochs. The history of composture is a history of oceanic fluidity rather than terrestrial separation. We may still need historical periods—we would have trouble organizing the humanities without them—but we need them to be messy and intermingled. To deform a famous critical maxim from Fredric Jameson: "Always periodize—more than twice!"[5]

Being human in an inhuman world means living polychronically, tied inside fraying time knots. As Jonathan Gil Harris demonstrates in his study of "untimely matter," which draws on Nietzsche as well as Jameson, sustained attention to historical materials "suggests the simultaneous agency of past matter and present subject in reworking our conceptions of temporality."[6] The multiply entangled epochal system this preface outlines will be less elegant than the break history it seeks to supplement. The theoretical structures I advance eschew clean transitions for messy turbulence; these historical epochs encompass a plurality that disorients, sometimes drastically. In keeping with my own recent work in the blue humanities, this turbulent historical language supplements terrestrial metaphors with oceanic ones.[7] Thus, the increasingly familiar term Anthropocene must share space with the faceless Homogenocene. Internet-fast visions of globalization must splash into their saltwater substrate, the Thalassocene. All heroic narratives risk the corrosive force of this book's favorite name for the swirl of history, the Naufragocene, Age of Shipwrecks. These names sound out an austere poetry. Amid the turbulence of history, we cling to them, as to life preservers, but we should not trust them too much.

It remains comforting and can be useful to have time parceled out between sonorous syllables, but it is also willfully false. None of the terms we attach to epochs captures the suddenness of lived experience and the feeling of time's passing through and around our animal bodies. Epochal claims falsify by regularizing the thrown-into feeling of entanglement within an always moving historical now. "Everything," says a blind poet, "happens to each of us precisely, precisely *now*."[8] That fluctuating and recurring *now* marks the polyepochal time of shipwreck.

Inside the catastrophe, bodies feel disorder on their skin. Tangible dislocation punctuates both the early modern globalizing process that wiped out so many human and nonhuman populations in the early modern period and our own era of warming oceans and killing storms. The sudden shock and pressure of immersion fractures ships, systems, and alliances. Human history has been enduring these disasters for a long time. Shipwreck, I submit, names the experience of multiple temporalities as clearly as anything.

Reconsidering history through catastrophe requires not one new epochal name but four: Anthropocene, Homogenocene, Thalassocene, and Naufragocene. This four-headed assemblage responds to the difficulty of naming the geologic and cultural now. It may also help clarify the problems cultural and literary historians have surrounding "early modernity," a time of historical transformation variously dated sometime in the vicinity of the early sixteenth century in Europe.[9] The long-held notion of a cultural break dividing the Renaissance from the medieval period, with the more recent era connected to our own day via the mantle of "early modern," tends toward caricature.[10] Scholars have known for some time that these rupture narratives are false, but they die hard.[11] Lee Patterson and David Aers demonstrated conclusively decades ago that claims about "new subjectivity" suddenly emerging after the Middle Ages have always been erroneous.[12] A theory of historical change modeled on composture and ecological multiplicity will not simply ignore or rebut these bad historical fables. The myths of thieving, transformative modernity against which scholars such as Patterson and Aers push err in meaningful ways. Popular and scholarly culture's continued adulation for things like the "birth of modernity" reveals a meaningful pattern in human myth making that is composting on the pile with everything else.[13] Good and bad models compost together, and it is not clear which produces the most fertile soil. Break-driven conceptions of early modernity resemble the Anthropocene in being analytically useful and self-aggrandizing. Epochal claims work better if they are forced to share the spotlight with other models.

It may be that beheading Anthropos is the only way to let real variety in. As Peter Hansen observes in his history of Enlightenment-era mountaineering, epochal claims such as "the birth of modernity," "the Anthropocene," or other revelations of a "new age of man [have] been entangled in a broader time knot."[14] The basic conundrum lies in the attempt to regularize or schematize temporal change, to make sense of the fleeting touch of lived experience. All epochal claims are false in that they force disparate local experience into homogenizing structures, but the desire to categorize experiences, to fix them in place with exact and meaningful names, flowers with each new story about our shared past. We crave transformative elegance: one epoch to name them all. This preface adds new names to the 'cene salad with the dual caveat that I do not fully believe in naming and also do not want to give it up entirely. Hence my turn to turbulent plurality, a disorienting mixture of weak, attenuated, competing epochs.

The case for early modernity emerging within a century on either side of 1500 and the case for a radically new modernity arising after and because of post–eighteenth century industrial capitalism share similar problems. Neither vision of change squares with the evidence of historical continuity. Amid so much novelty, sameness lingers. The supposedly new technological inventions that many scholars, including Francis Bacon, link to the emergence of early modernity, including gunpowder, the printing press, and the magnetic compass, had all previously emerged in China and slowly and erratically traveled from there to Europe.[15] Even objectively new events in global history, such as the ecological reintegration of the Americas with Africa and Eurasia after Columbus, emerged through extensions of medieval practices such as large-scale migration, colonization, trade, and the environmental and human disasters these events caused. The voyage of Pytheas, the Greek sailor who may have reached Ultima Thule around 320 BCE, was not different in kind from those of Columbus and Magellan, to say nothing of the longer trips of Leif Erikson or Zeng He. This book's contribution to interpreting the first age of globalization attempts to avoid spurious claims of novelty while recognizing the dynamic interpenetrations of cultural and ecological changes.[16]

The Renaissance/early modern/medieval terminological and disciplinary knot may resist all efforts at retying, given how much professional and institutional weight sits behind each of the three terms. Rethinking less-fixed ideas of the geologic present may help clarify these problematic historical categories. My epochal claims steer between two imperatives: the need to make sense of the contemporary world's observed ecological instability and the desire to analyze the early modern period without abjecting its medieval predecessor or flattening its historical differences from the present. I propose multiple epochal claims while casting doubt on each of them. Threading this polystructured Scylla and Charybdis, my analysis auditions four alternative terms to describe the past half millennium of Western culture. The analysis seeks a name to characterize a velocity of cultural change that precedes any precise date: 1500 for convenience? 1492 for Columbus? 1522 for Magellan's last ship returning to Spain without its admiral? I offer no magic numbers. Whether we point to Petrarch's fourteenth-century anxiety about his alienation from the classical past, Thomas More's sixteenth-century fantasy about the impact of New World exploration on European politics, or, in the English tradition, the intimations of literary writers from Wyatt to Spenser to Shakespeare to Milton that oceanic exploration would reconfigure the nation's global trajectory, this period increasingly brings maritime meanings to the surface. Particularly in the Anglophone context, the early modern period gets wetter as it gets more modern. What did the ocean mean to English writers, readers, and sailors in the early years of global maritime expansion? This book claims that shipwreck occupies the heart of the human and historical meanings of ocean. This theoretical preface also connects the experience of shipwreck to the names we are using for our own era. Periodizing more than twice, I add Thalassocene and Naufragocene to the epochal names we are currently using. The Age of Shipwreck can productively join, displace, and comingle with these other terms.

Each age conjures a heroic name, an idea of agency, epic or tragic, progressive or destructive, that powers historical change. As I describe in turn my four 'cenes—Anthropocene, Homogenocene, Thalassocene, and Naufragocene—I offer representative figures, showing how each conception of time associates itself with certain human narratives and ideas of agency and change. These figures provide patterns for engaging the violence and disorder of historical change.

Anthropocene

The most popular current term for our unfurling ecowreck fingers as hero and villain Old Man Anthropos, the blunt human force of capital-*M* Man and his industrial production pushing himself onto the dance floor and ruining the party for everyone. The Anthropocene, with an exaggerated sense of novelty, enters contemporary history trumpeting its own importance.[17] The numbers tell the story: four hundred parts per million, measured in the summer of 2013 in Mauna Loa near the heart of Melville's "mysterious, divine Pacific."[18] The massive surge in the production of those gaseous bits of carbon began not long after the New Bedford whale man jumped ship in the South Pacific, roughly a quarter century before petroleum displaced whale oil in nineteenth-century economies.[19] The turn to crude oil and the shift from sails to steam to diesel engines marked fossil fuel's rapid and continuing ascent.[20] Human industrial processes stripped carbon atoms from oil and coal and dispersed them invisibly in the atmosphere. There, these molecules float, trap energy, and patiently, progressively, once slowly, but now rapidly disrupt our human world.[21]

To reconsider the Anthropocene, I offer an early modern literary and historical analogy: the "new" Anthropocene announces its conquest of our era much as Vasco da Gama did the Indian Ocean in 1498, with pomp, ambition, and gunpowder but rather less control than he imagined. To Luis vaz de Camões and his sixteenth-century epic poem the *Lusiads,* this first Carreira da Índia marked sixteenth-century Portugal as the deserving heir of classical epic, sailing beyond the Mediterranean of Ulysses and Aeneas into a cornucopian Indian Ocean of spice and wealth. The bargain Vasco da Gama makes with the global ocean seals his conditional triumph; the epic opens by "[proclaiming] / A New Age and . . . undying fame" for Portugal.[22] The poem, however, also contains a counterdiscourse that recognizes the destructive consequences of maritime expansion. This self-qualifying recursivity might serve to undermine the growing sway of the Anthropocene as well. The poet describes a curse laid on da Gama's fleet by a prophetic Old Man in Lisbon: "You ignore the enemy at the gate / In the search for another so far away" (4.101.1–2). Josiah Blackmore has described this speech as presenting "a negative narrative moment, a type of undertow in the ineluctable and otherwise forward-moving realization of empire . . . an enactment of shipwreck narrative, that is, a discursive moment that counters or disrupts the official discourse of imperialism."[23] Camões's bivalent portrait of da Gama's transoceanic voyage, his literary canonization of this moment as both origin and dissolution of Portugal's global maritime empire, shadows my analysis of shipwreck's role as symbol and foretaste of global ecological crisis. This reading of Camões also provides a way to reconsider the growing sway of the Anthropocene. The ocean of global modernity into which da Gama guided Portugal was neither empty nor simply opulent. The *Lusiads* evokes less an epic of discovery than a new phase of Europe's entanglement in a millennia-old network of trade routes, seasonal monsoons, and mutlicultural networks of exchange. The Portuguese fleet entered the Indian Ocean as ecological disruption as well as imperial or commercial power.

I do not expect my misgivings about the term neither to drive the vast ocean liner *Anthropocene* onto the rocks nor even really to divert it much from its churning course. I do not dispute the fearful pressure and looming heat promised by all those molecules of carbon floating above our heads and in our oceans. But I reject the Anthropos in Anthropocene, the heroic, epic, and tragic centrality of the old man's body, spread now across our watery blue planet. Camões, an East Indies hand who had lived in Asia, recognized what he could not quite admit in verse: da Gama never conquered or "discovered" the Indian Ocean.[24] He went there and became embroiled in it. So it is with Man in the Anthropocene: climate change may be our fault, but it is not only our world. This term, even as tragic lament, continues to place human actors in what Hansen calls the "summit position."[25] We need other options.

Beheading Old Man Anthropos will not liberate us any more than blaming him can provide a satisfying tragic shape to our days. We still must face that great sprawling corpse and its many scattered corpuses, the human, animal, textual, and intellectual flotsam and jetsam circulating through every ocean current in the world. The Carreira da Índia created a global conduit that soon came to transport everything: bodies, texts, viruses, foods, poetry. The price of this expansion, as the cursing Old Man in Camões's epic poem knows, is shipwreck. Maritime disasters are the price of oceanic vistas. "The devil take the man," laments Camões's Old Man, "who first put / Dry wood on the waves with a sail!" (4.102.1–2). Inside the ambivalent triumph and curse of the *Lusiads,* Portuguese expansion into the East Indies looks less like straightforward conquest or mercantile expansion than arrival into an ecologically complex world marked by catastrophe.

Homogenocene

If not Anthropos, then who? Stripping away the tragic vestiges of human epoch making leads to a less emotional but perhaps more sinister conception of our current half-millennial epoch. The era of so-called modernity did not emerge straightforwardly from the voyages out from Europe, whether the Eastern exploits of Vasco da Gama or the virus-filled hand of Columbus in the West. Contact between continents and hemispheres generated an increasingly rapid physical and cultural intermingling, such that human and nonhuman creatures and things that were once isolated in different spots around the globe have promiscuously mixed together. Native American food staples such as maize, tomatoes, and potatoes came to feed China and Europe. The horse cultures of the Great Plains of North America invented themselves atop the descendants of Arab mares and stallions. The global reach of once-isolated human, bacterial, and viral populations decimated living creatures in Africa, Asia, Europe, and especially the Americas. The pattern would repeat itself in the seventeenth century with the belated introduction of Australia to this global network and the repetition there of the massive die-off of populations with no previous experience of Afro-Eurasian diseases.[26]

The Homogenocene tells a story of catastrophic cultural change without heroes. Columbus plants his flag for Isabella, but malaria and smallpox clear the New World for European settlement. The unfinished pressure of this mixing process throws every global thing into every corner of our connected world. Ride a slow boat up the Mahakam River in eastern Borneo for four days, as I did in 1990, and at the headwaters you will find people wearing New York Yankees T-shirts. Globalization names the propulsive force behind this project, homogenization its inevitable consequence.

The Homogenocene imagines a future of sameness in which every ocean in the world ends up another Mediterranean Sea, enclosed by human culture and labors.[27] In the five hundred–year history of European fishing in the North Atlantic, as Jeffrey Bolster has recently shown, ecological depletion follows a mimetic pattern: the western waters of the North Atlantic became by 2000 as depleted as the eastern waters had already been by 1500.[28] Swimming in this Homogenized ocean, we seek visions of difference.

This name scares me more than Anthropocene. I am afraid of losing differences and distinctions into sameness. If recasting the Anthropocene requires dethroning Man from either the heroic or the tragic position, the challenge of the Homogenocene is a world without heroes, villains, or memorable figures of any kind. Its symbol may be the jellyfish that are thriving in today's warming acidified oceans. The coming era of these jellies exerts an increasing pressure, insinuating itself into our practices and understandings. It beheads Anthropos, but at great cost. In a heat death of supercomposture, everything becomes the same as everything else.

Thalassocene

Floating with the jellies lurks a possible oceanic turn. Global modernity and the capitalist project of endless expansion might, as Hegel once claimed, float on the sea.[29] The philosopher Peter Sloterdijk names this vision of modernity after the sphere: "Globalization or sphereepoise is the fundamental event in European thought, one that has not ceased to provoke revolutions . . . for two and a half thousand years."[30] A less human-centered idea of the global might focus on the largest object on the surface of our planet, the World Ocean.

A proposed Thalassic or Oceanic Age in the West might stretch from Henry the Navigator, who never went to sea himself, through harrowing and sometimes doomed voyages—shipwreck, as Hans Blumenberg tells the story, is the price sailors willingly pay for the propulsive gift of the winds—up until the Wright brothers colonized the sea of air.[31] But the increase in blue-water voyaging during the early modern period should not displace legendary foresailors such as the fifteenth-century Chinese admiral Zheng He or the nameless Phoenician who may have sailed around Africa in the fifth century BCE, to say nothing of the transpacific voyages of prehistoric Polynesian navigators. Less obviously historical figures such as Sinbad or Ulysses further indicate that the oceanic turn, while pronounced in European culture after the mid-fifteenth century, was neither isolated nor new. The Thalassocene as oceanic epoch might not be properly historical in the sense of emerging at a particular time but rather a fundamental precondition of our littoral species, as John Gillis has recently argued in *The Human Shore*. In Gillis's reconsideration of the long narrative of human history, the shoreline becomes "humankind's first Eden," the source of physical nourishment and cultural inspiration.[32] The World Ocean wraps its immense salty arms around all terrestrial settlements and civilizations, making islands of the vastest empires. The Thalassocene might be better understood not as an epochal designation but as a recurrent material counterforce, a pressure the inhuman ocean exerts on all histories, inimical to the human lives it helps structure. To be oceanic remains the coastal curse of our species and our planet. Ocean-borne weather reaches its blue fingers deep into all human habitations.

This oceanic countermovement, source and fuel of shipwrecks, undergirds the thalassic poetics this book explores. Images of deep-sea fecundity and excess mark the poetics of ocean, from sunken treasure to biotic opulence.[33] Literary forms strain to comprehend saltwater vastness, and efforts to craft linguistic vessels adequate to this task become explicit meditations on the limits and powers of poetry itself. The "endlesse work" of "[counting] the seas abundant progency" in book 4 of Spenser's *Faerie Queene* combines wonder at oceanic vastness and a poet's plea that his project match his ambition.[34] Marine excess becomes the ultimate groundless ground of poetic metaphor, so that a saltwater subject licenses the most vaulting ambition—"So fertile be the flouds in generation, / So huge their numbers, and so numberlesse their nation" (4.12.1.8–9)—and also excuses mortal inadequacy—"Then blame me not, if I haue err'd in count / Of Gods, of Nymphs, of riuers yet unred" (4.12.2.6–7). Being oceanic expresses a condition and ambition of literary culture more than a particular historical period, even as the "maritime turn" of European culture after the fifteenth century seems to have emphasized and recognized its oceanic entanglement.[35]

Naufragocene

The hubristic poetics of naming carries a potent charge, and I believe in these names only as tactics, not permanent labels. But if I had to pick, I think *shipwreck* names it best. Shipwreck was not new to the first age of globalization; these disasters are as old as sea travel itself. The metaphoric structures associated with shipwreck cling like lampreys to all ships navigating the global ocean. For Western cultures increasingly fascinated with oceanic totality, shipwreck became, as this book shows, an ecological parable. Ancient stories about human encounters with divine wrath would become increasingly topical representations of the fates of men, goods, and voyages by sea. Global trade produced feedback loops in Western understandings of their own places in world culture, such that the microgenre of shipwreck—a swirling loss of direction that is also a redirection, a sudden shock, a violent encounter with disorder—became a central metaphor for historical change. Wetness no longer seeps in but floods. Shipwreck resonantly names an epoch whose contours precede but also prestructure the arrival of fully global capitalist exchange. An era that saw American silver and Far Eastern spices circle the globe in European ships hurls bodies and ships and other hybrids into unevenly wet realms. Reconceived as a single interconnected saltwater space, what modern scientists call the World Ocean unifies human societies while subjecting individual humans to watery peril.[36] The heroic thefts of transoceanic imperialism conceal the rich composture produced in an era of shipwreck.

As I have argued about the Thalassocene, the Naufragocene marks less a radically new epoch than a reemphasis, reinscribing onto vaster and less-known spaces classical and medieval tropes of doomed ships and misdirected sailors. Shipwreck becomes less the exception than the rule. We sail to Tarshish with Jonah; to Marseilles with Mary Magdalene; to Hispaniola with Columbus. Shipwreck takes us everywhere—all around the world. No oceanic straights are free from its risks and anxieties.

The globalizing vision of early modern shipwreck speaks to contemporary theoretical concerns that explore the planet as a single conceptual unity. Perhaps the most insightful philosophical exegesis of the global appears in Peter Sloterdijk, whose massive three-volume work *Spheres* treats the spherical form as Western intellectual history's most powerful and enduring invention. Starting with classical Greek geometers and moving to the geometric globes of early modern navigation, Sloterdijk finds in "the theory of the sphere . . . the first analysis of power" (33). In a more recent book, *In the World Interior of Capital,* Sloterdijk has emphasized the oceanic nature of European globalization. "Only the sea," he writes in an impassioned moment, doubtless aware that he is paraphrasing Hegel, "[offers] a foundation for universal thoughts . . . [and] a true Modern Age."[37] Locating the elusive turning point into modernity in an entry in Antonio Pigafetta's journal that relates "three months and twenty days" of constant smooth sailing with Magellan across the Pacific, Sloterdijk emphasizes the shocking moment in which early modern sailors realized, contra Ptolemaic and other classical geographies, that our planet is mostly ocean, not earth (41). My reading of early modern shipwreck narratives as responses to ecological globalization adds saltwater details to Sloterdijk's philosophical geometry. The key figure in my reading of watery globalization is neither the philosopher nor the cartographer but the sailor.

Many other contemporary theories of the global differ from Sloterdijk's massive project in their relative inattention to oceanic structures.[38] Jean-Luc Nancy's *The Creation of the World or Globalization* explores capitalist flattening and counterglobal *mondailisation,* or world forming, but with little attention to watery concerns.[39] Gayatri Chakravorty Spivak offers "planetarity" as a counterpressure to globalization, but also without sustained attention to the physical nature of the blue planet.[40] Ecotheorist Ursula Heise adds a "sense of planet" to environmental thinking, but again with scant attention to salt water.[41] These global thinkers all explore what we might describe as globalization from above, an air- and airplane-driven concept of planetary unity that has as its emblem *The Blue Marble,* a photograph taken from space by Apollo 17, rather than the blue environment experienced by oceanic sailors. As Sloterdijk's historical exploration of ideas of the globe in classical Greece and early modern Europe show, however, the ocean constitutes history's first global substrate, not perhaps as undifferentiated as the sea of air but for many centuries the only truly global pathway for human exchange. Even today, the vast majority of mercantile goods travel by sea, although most humans circle the globe by air.[42] This book argues that our global thinking, in order to be meaningfully ecological, must become oceanic rather than merely terrestrial. Any global ecology worthy of the name must include the ocean and recognize that world history emerges through land–sea hybrids.

Everyone knows the original sailor of the Age of Shipwreck, that man of constant sorrow who endures wet dislocation. I want to sidle up to him indirectly, lyrically, not in Greek hexameters but in twentieth-century Russian verse, in the lines of Osip Mandelshtam as translated into English by James Greene. He is the hero of the Naufragocene and of this book. He appears in these pages in many forms and under many names. He knows what it feels like to live in shipwreck:

> But breathing the smell
> Of resinous tears oozing through planks,
> Admiring the boards of bulkheads riveted
> Not by the peaceful Bethlehem carpenter but by that other—
> Father of journeys, friend of seafarers—[43]

Mandelshtam's Ulysses, with his "unbridled thirst for space" (47), builds ships, fathers journeys, befriends mariners. He lives inside disorder, in "air dark like water, [where] everything alive swims like fish" (47). In a chaos where "everything pitches and splits," the mariner survives not by building structures like a Bethlehem carpenter but by riveting bulkheads to keep the flood at bay. Breathing "resinous tears," the mariner assembles an alliance between human and wooden bodies. In Bruno Latour's terms, he makes a composition—though Latour, like so many of his theoretical peers, subsumes the ocean in his analysis.[44] Visions of ship–man–fish hybrids like Mandelshtam's appear throughout this book, marking strained assemblages that make possible, if only temporarily, survival amid immersion.[45] The oceanic globe into which the Naufragocene plunges human sailors is not a friendly place. In this inhospitable environment, the essential tool is Ulyssean *metis,* cunning or craft, through which the wily mariner employs tools, weapons, words, and allies to extend his long voyage home.

Placing an early twentieth-century poetic version of Ulysses at the opening of my study of the early modern Age of Shipwreck emphasizes that I make no firm claims for chronological consistency. Many moments in this book will appear out of time as I shuttle between early modern texts and suggestive parallels from modern and cotemporary poetry. The nongrounded, nonepic, constantly changing world-that-is-ocean becomes particularly visible during the age of Europe's first global maritime voyages, but its contours present themselves whenever and wherever keels plough waves. To live with shipwreck was the particular fate of many Western mariners in the centuries following the so-called discovery of the New World. These disasters limn today's oceanic encounters and panhistorical figures such as Ulysses as well. Shipwreck, to modify a poet's phrase, is history, but history without chronology.[46] Its patterns entangle themselves in ways that resist or rupture narratives of historical progression. Against the felt experience of rupture and the twinned historical realities of continuity and change, narratives of modernity, from Petrarch to Burkhardt to Greenblatt, offer elegant but implausible solutions. Against the experience of environmental catastrophe, the Anthropocene proffers one more—one last?—master narrative. The Naufragocene and its 'cene-ic companions, by contrast, reject elegance, advance disorder, and remain alert to complex narrative patterns that organize the human experience of the nonhuman environment. Living in the Age of Shipwreck requires both the masthead perspective of a navigator and the wet entanglements of a laboring sailor. In this world we must work before we can see.

In the shipwreck of history, we need tools, labor, and metis together. Also, poetry—a swimmer's poetics of feel, endurance, and mortal limits. We might not make it through the Naufragocene or any of these other 'cenes, but it helps to recognize and multiply to name the disorder that we are in.

Narrative Preface: Ulysses and the Global Ecology

The narrative preface begins in Auschwitz with Primo Levi. Trapped inside the greatest human disaster of twentieth-century Europe, the chemist and writer uses shipwreck to imagine a possible future. During thirty precious unobserved minutes walking between a worksite and the main camp, Levi narrates to Jean, a fellow prisoner, the story of Ulysses in canto 26 of Dante's *Inferno* in order "not to waste this hour." Levi claims not to know "how or why [the canto] comes into [his] mind" (112) and further emphasizes that his memory of the poem and his translation of it into French to retell it to Jean is "disastrous—poor Dante and poor French!" (112).[47] The classical hero's afterlife in Hell resonates with the experience of Auschwitz, but as Levi retells the story, Ulysses's shipwreck becomes a future-driven catastrophe. The hero's fatal decision to leave Ithaca and sail beyond the Pillars of Hercules models human ambition in a hostile world. Seeking knowledge and experience, the mariner motivates his men by celebrating humanity: "Think of your breed; for brutish ignorance / Your mettle was not made; you were made men, / To follow after knowledge and excellence" (113). Like Columbus and Magellan, Ulysses sails west and south into an imagined future that would include, in the global ecology, the worldwide circulation of goods, peoples, and catastrophes.[48] In Levi's half-garbled telling, the driving lure is saltwater globalization, "the open sea . . . when the horizon closes in on itself, free, straight ahead and simple, and there is nothing but the smell of the sea; sweet things, ferociously far away" (113). This vision of ocean as utopian no-place, escape and refuge even in land-locked Auschwitz, opens up the underlying thalassophilia of shipwreck narratives, a frightened but powerful longing for the destructive element. To sail out on that open sea, for

Ulysses as for Levi, means casting your body into a global system of catastrophe and freedom. The global ecology of open ocean represents a possible future even, or perhaps especially, in Auschwitz.

The catastrophic futurity of shipwreck enables these stories to represent a global ecology that disorients and transforms. Shipwreck recalls in history and in literature Northrop Frye's resonant joke that names maritime disaster as the "standard means of transportation" in literary romance.[49] For early modern sailors as for Ulysses, shipwreck leads to forbidden and deadly places, including Hispaniola, where Columbus made landfall; Cebu, where Magellan died; and Mount Purgatory in the southern hemisphere, where Ulysses and his shipmates encounter the whirlpool. These New Worlds are inseparable from shipwreck; there is no global expansion without catastrophe. In risk-dense waters mariners survive for a time through luck, maritime skills, or divine protection, but in the end they cannot endure the oceanic encounter. Dante's portrayal of shipwreck speaks through Levi in Auschwitz "as if [he] also was hearing it for the first time: like the blast of a trumpet, like the voice of God" (113). Levi forgets several stanzas of Dante's poem, remembers stray phrases, and times the ending of his narration to match the pair's return to the camp. Ulysses's shipwreck represents the heart of European civilization for Levi because it captures the disaster-filled trajectory of global expansion. The hero's encounter with the unknown ocean exposes the nonhuman limits of the human encounter with our alien globe. It is a story that for Levi contains the key to all stories: "I must tell him, I must explain to him about the Middle Ages, about the so human and so necessary and yet unexpected anachronism, but still more, something gigantic that I myself have only just seen, in a flash of intuition, perhaps the reason for our fate, for our being here today" (115). In the split instant of narration, in Auschwitz and with Ulysses in the Southern Ocean, Levi finds understanding in the great waters.

Levi's retelling emphasizes Dante's portrait of local human ambition entangled with global control. Levi quotes the canto's last full terza rima stanza, which describes Ulysses's ship sucked down into the whirlpool: "And three times round she went in roaring smother / With all the waters; at the fourth the poop / Rose, and the prow went down, as pleased Another." The ship's destruction pleases the divine power that the pre-Christian hero cannot name; Ulysses understands the Christian god only as "Another" ("Altrui" in Italian). The horror of an all-powerful deity who is pleased by human misery lingers in Dante's poem, as it does in many literary and historical depictions of shipwreck. For Levi the story of Ulysses's death belongs in Auschwitz because it measures the gap between divine order and human failure. We tell and retell stories like this one, he suggests, because they capture the precariousness of mankind in an indecipherable world. Against human fragility, Levi opposes narrative. "Perhaps," he comments, "despite the wan translation and the pedestrian, rushed commentary, he has received the message, he has felt that it has to do with him, that it has to do with all men who toil, and with us in particular; and that it has to do with us two, who dare to reason of these things with the poles for the soup on our shoulders" (114). Daring to reason is daring to narrate, to retell Dante and enter into the ocean of literary culture. Levi's chapter ends with the words that conclude Dante's canto—"And over our heads the hollow seas closed up"—and he frames Auschwitz as containing both Ulysses's death and Dante's narration, shipwrecked sailor and inspired poet.

Levi selected this shipwreck story twice, both that afternoon in Auschwitz and again in 1947 when he wrote the first volume of his memoirs, published under the title *Se questo è un uomo* (*If This Is a Man*). The story speaks for him to the dark vision of Auschwitz and the crisis of twentieth-century modernity it represents. By drawing on a twelfth-century poem for his key example, however, Levi locates the human fascination with shipwreck outside the twentieth century. Levi insists we must read Dante's canto differently after (and in) Auschwitz. But Levi's retelling also insists that shipwreck is historically mobile as a trope for the conflict between human bodies and nonhuman power. Facing the whirlpool in the ocean or in Auschwitz, the human response is narrative.

This book explores shipwreck stories largely but not exclusively in early modern Europe, with its historical focus ranging between roughly 1550 and the publication of Daniel Defoe's *Robinson Crusoe* in 1719. These stories unfold the representative logic of the emerging global ecology that recalls Levi's experience: they narrate catastrophe in order to endure catastrophe. Shipwreck stories represent the human experience of natural hostility, narrating humankind's failed attempts to navigate an uncertain world. By using shipwreck to examine the ecological crises occasioned by the early stages of globalization, this book aims to reconsider the cultural changes associated with early modernity. Shipwreck, a story we fear repeating but cannot resist retelling, captures a crisis of cultural authority. Planetary globalization split wide growing tensions among the expanding claims of empiricism and the still-dominant belief in supernatural powers. Encounters with alien cultures and ecosystems forced Europeans to recognize the variety of the planet's natural and human structures. Stories of maritime disaster provided ways to think through changing views of humanity and the natural world.

Shipwreck narratives respond to this crisis of authority by aestheticizing rupture. The world viewed through shipwreck is already broken, divided between lost hopes for fair passage—Levi's "open sea" (113)—and the flotsam that washes up on the beach. In telling and retelling these stories, shipwreck narrators present a disoriented vision of human experience. Claims for human expertise and power get balanced by the unanswerable counterclaims of killing storms, behind which stand inscrutable God and the unknowable Ocean. Shipwrecks can fit into schemes of universal Providence, as the canto of Ulysses fits into Dante's *Commedia.* In this recuperative view, shipwreck represents God's chastising hand. Wrecked ships were meant to sink, and Ulysses and his men were meant to drown. But against the mortal costs of shipwreck, claims of divine justice seem inadequate. God's pleasure offers no consolation for Ulysses and, perhaps, little enough for Dante. Levi, caught inside human tragedy, finds meager consolation. The human response to shipwreck is narrative: stories to memorialize disaster. These narratives can protest against mortality, celebrate the complex plans of an all-controlling God, or, often, do both at once while opening up tensions between these interpretive poles. Early modern readers and writers latched onto these stories for the same reasons Levi did in Auschwitz and for the same reasons American teenagers flocked to James Cameron's *Titanic* in the summer of 1997: shipwreck makes palpable the stark contradiction between human desires and mortal limits. These stories were, and remain, equipment for thinking in a world of ecological catastrophe: they balance our hopes for an ordered universe against our knowledge of the costs the disorienting world exacts from its inhabitants.

Magellan's Globalization

As a physical fact, globalization in the West began with Magellan. The most resonant moment of his voyage, however, was not the homecoming of one ship after three years at sea but the explorer's violent death in the Pacific island of Cebu five months earlier. The Age of Discovery was an Age of Disaster. Thinking about early globalization requires calling attention to lost ships, drowned sailors, and massive disruptions of European and non-European societies. The so-called Columbian Exchange, which might be less anthropocentrically called "ecological globalization," brought together the ecologies of Eurasia, Africa, and the Americas for the first time since the continents split apart. Saltwater connections between these ecosystems generated worldwide maritime trade networks and some of the most disruptive events in recorded history. Putting wooden girdles round about the globe produced the catastrophic clashes of cultures, peoples, viruses, and ecosystems we now describe as the early modern period. Long-cherished fables about rebirth and the origins of modernity should not occlude the violent reality captured in Magellan's death. Through these human encounters with the World Ocean, globalization created ecological disasters. This book interrogates those disasters under the name of *shipwreck*.

Stories of shipwreck epitomize the ecological, economic, and human costs of the first global ecology. During this period England and her early colonies embraced the transoceanic exploration, trade, and settlement that would shape the next four centuries of Anglo-American history. In many genres and forms, including Providential sermons, mercantile propaganda, private journals, and lyric poems, writers and sailors grappled with the new centrality of deep-sea voyaging to English culture. Writers reshaped the ancient narrative paradigm of shipwreck into an early modern ecopoetics of the maritime encounter. From Shakespeare and Defoe to humanist scholars and common sailors, early modern shipwreck writers struggled to reconcile the mysterious god-sea of ancient and biblical sources with the navigable spaces of the early modern globe. Narratives of shipwreck tell resonant but unfamiliar stories of the cultural changes central to emerging modernity.

This book treats representations of shipwreck as literary responses to the disruptive new world of global connectedness, which the pioneering environmental historian Alfred Crosby famously called the "Columbian Exchange."[50] Rather than extending Crosby's semicelebration of the influence of Columbus, however, I interrogate the integration of the continents and oceans under the term *global ecology*. The ecological reunion of the formerly isolated plant and animal populations of the Americas, Africa, and Eurasia radically altered human and nonhuman life on earth. Crosby calls the exchange of flora, fauna, diseases, and knowledge a "trend toward biological homogeneity," which has the comforting ring of scientific understatement, but he also emphasizes that this global exchange constituted "one of the most important aspects of the history of life on this planet since the retreat of the continental glaciers" (3). The human disasters that ensued, from the collapse of the native American population to the concentration of wealth and power in Europe after the plundering of Peru and Mexico and later the worldwide trade in African slaves, emerged alongside and through this ecological crisis. Columbus's arrival on Hispaniola may not have been a shipwreck, but it was a disaster.

European global expansion did not always feel disastrous, at least not to Europeans. The eruption of global maritime trade and the integration of European, American, African, and Asian economies and ecologies created wealth and poverty, winners and losers, but what Amerigo Vespucci called the New World most often was understood in Providential terms as an opportunity to spread the Gospel while enriching European monarchies.[51] This book explores English and other European accounts of shipwreck in historical records and literary topoi in order to reconsider the cultural meanings of early globalization. Reimagining the supposed break of early modernity as an ecological shipwreck qualifies Renaissance triumphalism and displaces human "discoveries" from the center of the narrative. The planet's oceans and winds generate shipwrecks, and this master plot epitomizes human struggles within an unfriendly environment.

This book's reading of shipwreck narratives extends what I have previously termed blue cultural studies into a blue ecological humanities that supplements land-based cultural histories with oceanic perspective.[52] Building on multiple currents in oceanic history, including Atlantic history, Mediterranean-centered new thalassology, and global maritime ecostudies, this new project explores the human–ocean encounter at its most violent and intimate, when ships split and mariners plunge into hostile waters. The threat of the ocean, realized most vividly when sailors become swimmers, reflects the larger transformations accompanying England's global expansion. *Shipwreck Modernity* uses narratives of maritime disaster to articulate how the blue World Ocean can revise our ideas about literary and environmental history.

This book contributes several new terms to scholarly discourse.

Wet globalization. Cultural analyses of early modern globalization, trade, colonialism, and imperialism need to pay closer attention to the challenges and disruptions of maritime and navigational labor in the early modern. The ocean was never a frictionless medium, particularly not in the early age of sail. This book explores the challenges and practices of early modern seamanship in close detail rather than relying on the view from shore. I proffer *wet globalization* as a reminder that the instantaneous globe of international finance—the globe that, as Gayatri Spivak says, "lives on our computers"—has always contained the ocean as its material substrate and mechanism.[53] Hegel, as previously noted, famously argued that the World Ocean provides the material base for global capitalism. Numerous marine biologists and Arthur C. Clarke have extended this claim by noting that "earth is a misnomer; the name of this planet should be Ocean."

Blue ecology. The sea's overwhelming presence in the natural environment reminds us that this element, long marginalized by ecocritical perspectives that privilege terrestrial spaces, can help correct lingering pastoral or Romantic fantasies about Nature. Thinking with the two-thirds of the earth's surface covered by the sea can develop a "blue" corrective to "green" environmental criticism. Ecocriticism has so far focused largely on what Aldo Leopold calls a "land ethic."[54] As Dan Brayton and others have recently argued, these conversations need to pay more attention to salt water.[55]

Shipwreck modernity. Early modernity has long been understood as an era of rapid transformation, but this book's focus on the master trope of shipwreck recasts traditional images of the radical break that has been central to the historiography of early modernity from Burkhardt to Foucault. Disaster

> narratives replace the familiar story of the once-and-for-all epistemological rupture with a disorienting but sometimes survivable disaster. The resulting history of early modernity resonates with the felt experience of radical change without insisting upon final separation from the past.

These three strains of argument together articulate an accumulative and disorienting model of early modern cultural change, one better described through composture than progress. Stories of maritime disaster layer themselves atop and exchange forms with more familiar narratives about early modernity, such as Max Weber's disenchanting of the world, in which intellectual constructs like history and science displace ancient magical forces like Fortune and Providence. The sediments on the ocean floor represent the global ecology as a process of disorienting agglomeration. In this model the mixed mode of shipwreck narratives—punctuated by allusions to classical literature, appeals to Christian Providence, anticipations of empiricist critique, and attacks on human folly—presents an uneven process of cultural accumulation. Literary accounts of maritime disasters from Shakespeare through Defoe reveal the Janus-faced ambivalence of early modernity, in which Providential and protomodern explanatory systems accumulate atop each other.

My analysis of these narratives traces three elements that together comprise a shipwreck as recognizable literary microgenre: melodramatic presentation, epistemological crisis, and recuperative metaphysics. These three features allegorize shipwreck as a master topos for cultural change. The story begins by performing the radical break, deepens the crisis through physical and conceptual instability, and then often concludes with a tantalizing promise of Providential recuperation, in this world or the next. This three-stage formula presents a picture of cultural transformation richer than the simple binary of the break. Modernity as the Renaissance experienced it and we still inhabit it balances an "incomplete project" of cultural rationalization, analyzed from Marx and Weber through Habermas, against the still-potent metaphysical claims of religion and other supernatural systems.

Since most of the records we have of shipwreck come from survivors or onlookers, the central experience, death by drowning, is more often alluded to than experienced. Tales of survival only gesture toward the full cultural nightmare of shipwreck. So as not to lose sight of the catastrophic and uneven nature of early modern globalization, my chapters include multiple interruptions, often in the form of brief records of losses at sea. As the example of Magellan shows, death at sea constantly intrudes on the historical record and on my analysis. These deaths implicitly contest the semicomforting Providentialism of literary and theological shipwreck stories. The tension between literary fictions such as *The Tempest* and *Robinson Crusoe* and the unnarratable horror of maritime catastrophe resonates across each subsequent chapter.

Locating shipwreck at the metaphorical center of an ecology of saltwater globalization, this book explores European mariners' historical shift from coastal and Mediterranean voyaging to worldwide bluewater networks. In a broader sense this study joins current efforts in oceanic literary studies to unpack the diverse cultural and psychological meanings of the sea. The ocean itself becomes an essential actor in the drama of globalization. Joining posthuman critics from Bruno Latour to Timothy Morton in an attempt to think past and across the nature/culture divide, I offer a shipwrecked vision of English literary culture that brings together literary invention, ecological crisis, and the human experience of disruptive historical change.

In shipwreck the stormy sea represents two things at once: the direct hand of God intervening in human events and the ultimate hostility of the oceanic environment. Sailing on global seas entails a violent ecological encounter and harrowing theological risk. The hostile ocean represents the opposite of the human-formed garden, and shipwreck narratives elaborate a thoroughly antipastoral view of the human relationship with its environment.[56] Shipwreck narratives were both theological parables and opportunities to explore changing ideas about the natural environment. During this period shipwreck also became an increasingly common and reported historical phenomenon, with especially deadly routes including the Portuguese Carreira da Índia and the transpacific passage. Tales of shipwreck register the intense conflict between ideas of divine presence in history and increasingly empirical notions about how and why catastrophes occur. When English ships went down, reports echoed the narrative habits of Homer, Virgil, and Ovid even when they described these events in largely human terms. Shipwreck narratives comprise in their multiplicity a microcosm of cultural change and dislocation.

Early modern writers who took up the shipwreck trope recognized it as a classical topos, a theological paradox, and a resonant description of human vulnerability in the world. These writers form a countertradition in which disaster unfolds a new story of human experience and isolation. As Primo Levi says of his shipwreck story in Auschwitz, "It is vitally necessary and urgent that he listen, that he understand . . . before it is too late" (115). This study turns to shipwreck to unfold that urgency and transformative power.

The Shipwreck That Is This Book

This book's chapters follow the narrative arc of shipwreck from crisis to immersion to salvage. This two-headed preface models the plural methodologies of subsequent sections of this book. The first three chapters that follow proceed analytically to determine the primary forms and meanings of the shipwreck microgenre. The next two chapters adopt a narrative mode by closely engaging the manuscript journals of two seventeenth-century English sailors. The final two chapters return to analysis in an attempt to salvage form from disorder. The study as a whole argues that shipwreck models and responds to global ecological crisis. Focusing on the physical encounter between human bodies and deep oceans provides a way to reframe our understandings of historical change and discontinuity as felt experiences. These disasters wet bodies to the skin and hurl tidy conceptions of the natural environment into disarray.

The first chapter, "The Wet and the Dry," lays out the book's analytical method by emphasizing the distinction between the wet shock of immersion and the drying-out accomplished by intellectual understanding. Stories of shipwreck present episodes of immersion and disorderly wetness, followed by attempts, with varying success, to return to conceptual dryness. The next two chapters explore the first phase of the microgenre, the initial crisis. Chapter 2, "Angry Gods," takes the archetypical hostility of Poseidon and Juno in classical epic to represent a pattern in shipwreck narratives in which supernatural rage causes oceanic suffering. Looking at sermons and theological treatises alongside classical literature and historical sources clarifies the theological backdrop against which shipwreck unfolds. Chapter 3, "Isle of Tempests," explores in detail the wreck of the *Sea-Venture* in Bermuda in 1609, reading this event as an example of how oceanic meanings infiltrated English literary and cultural habits of thought. These early chapters are followed by a short interchapter, "Pearls That Were His Eyes," which imagines the uneasy cohabitation of human flesh and oceanic depth.

The next two chapters of my shipwreck story take a narrative turn toward *metis*, a Homeric Greek term that means "cunning and skill" and that I associate with seamanship. Mariners respond to shipwreck with skilled work, and these two chapters show how maritime labor provides a language for understanding crisis. The in-the-moment perspective of laboring mariners, I argue, should inform our understanding of ecological catastrophes historically and today. The first metis chapter explores the journals of Jeremy Roch, a seventeenth-century English naval officer who was also an amateur poet and astrologer, in dialogue with the legal theories of Hugo Grotius. The second chapter in this section examines the massive manuscript diary of Edward Barlow, a self-educated seaman who began writing his journal while a prisoner in Batavia during the Third Anglo–Dutch War. These two chapters about the perspective of early modern sailors precede another short interchapter, "Philosopher at the Masthead," which ventriloquizes Herman Melville's Ishmael, lazing high above the sea on the *Pequod*'s mast, his poetic inattention engaging the World Ocean very differently from the manic drive of his captain.

The last section of the book returns to analytical mode and aims toward salvage and survival after the wreck. Chapter 6, "We Split," uses the early modern maritime poetry of John Donne, William Diaper, and Phineas Fletcher, in dialogue with modern sea poems by Melville, Wallace Stevens, and Thomas Hardy, to interrogate the forms of English literature's oceanic turn. The final chapter, "Castaways," blends analytical and narrative modes to provide an allegorical retelling of the shipwrecked heart of Daniel Defoe's *Robinson Crusoe*. Reading Crusoe's landfall on his island as an ecoparable about the competing pressures of land and sea suggests that Defoe's novel uses shipwreck to unpack the global maritime experience that in the early eighteenth century had become central to English national identity.

Last of all, "Three Short Epilogues" draws conclusions about ecological crisis, historical change, and fractured continuity. The first epilogue reimagines maritime disaster through the phrase "the bright light of shipwreck" from the Vietnam-era American poet George Oppen.

The second epilogue takes up the resonant image of *The Bookfish,* a seventeenth-century printed illustration of a cut-open North Sea codfish with holy treatises inside its belly. This saltwater image, I claim, models a fully oceanic literary criticism. Taking up the challenge that *The Bookfish* represents, the last epilogue presents seven ecomaxims to guide future thinking and scholarship. Moving from catastrophe to pleasure, from sailors to swimmers, and from mobility to distortion, these maxims aim to stimulate future thought about the sometimes-overlooked oceanic substrate of global culture. Shipwreck defines the direct encounter between human bodies and the World Ocean, the moment when sailors become swimmers, when ecological disorder makes itself felt on flesh. The vision of the future it provides is neither comforting nor stable. It speaks to our oceanic globe and its dynamic, catastrophic ecology.

· CHAPTER 1 ·

The Wet and the Dry

Shipwreck Hermeneutics

The disaster ruins everything, all the while leaving everything intact. It does not touch anyone in particular; "I" am not threatened by it, but spared, left aside.

Maurice Blanchot, *The Writing of the Disaster*

SHIPWRECKS ARE WET CATASTROPHES. Shipwreck narratives seek ways to dry them out. The progression of shock, immersion, and salvage epitomizes the cultural representations that this book explores.

The primary analytic paradigm for this process is the conflict between the wet and the dry. Wet representations emphasize the shock of immersion and its threat to human understanding and survival. The primary literary mode of this phase is melodrama. Moments such as the opening stage direction of *The Tempest* (1611), "A tempestuous noise of thunder and lightning heard," highlight the shock of wetness.[1] The sight, sound, and feeling of wetness produce radical critiques of accepted norms, such as the Boatswain's mocking "the name of king" (1.1.17) later in this scene. Immersion, the middle stage, puts all forms of order in suspension. This radical openness and disorientation, however, cannot last. In response to oceanic immersion, writers deploy various ways of drying out human experience. Shipwreck fictions such as Sidney's *New Arcadia* (1590), in which Pyrocles calls a sinking ship "that little all we were," present maritime disaster as a microcosm of humanity's plight in a hostile environment.[2] Dry Providential metaphysics ameliorates the fear that the human condition is always and only a shipwreck. These happy drying fictions float uneasily in the inhospitable ocean. The last words of the Elizabethan explorer Sir Humphrey Gilbert on board his ship in 1583, "We are as near to heaven by sea as by land," insist that shipwreck creates a place of privileged double vision in which the doomed mariner glimpses land and sea, life and death, at the same time.[3] Composting wet and dry trajectories together makes shipwreck a microgenre for catastrophic ecological encounters.

Shipwreck lurks at the metaphorical heart of the ecology of saltwater globalization. The global maritime networks of early modern European expansion have ancient roots but radically expanded after the fifteenth century. As worldwide blue-water trade routes became essential to European economies, the cultural resonance of voyaging changed. This book joins current scholarship in oceanic studies to unpack the diverse historical, cultural, and psychological meanings of the transoceanic turn of early modern European culture. My central innovation claims that, beyond its economic and human consequences, early globalization was fundamentally ecological in nature. Oceangoing ships and voyages generated the global ecology in which all material things in the world—animals, plants, viruses, cultures—were distributed around the globe. The threat of shipwreck makes the ocean itself an essential actor in this historical drama. Covering more than two-thirds of the earth, the inhospitable sea represents the most powerful nonhuman actor in world history. Attending to the global force of the sea applies posthuman ecological pressure to the historical experiences of globalization. I offer a shipwrecked vision of Anglophone global literary culture that brings together literary invention, ecological crisis, and the human experience of disruptive historical change. The wet and dry patterns of shipwreck reveal the structures through which fragile bodies encounter destructive elements.

Sometime around 1560, the poet, courtier, and mariner Luis vaz de Camões plunged into salt water off the Mekong Delta in Southeast Asia. An experienced East Indies hand and a strong swimmer, he reached shore despite the loss of his ship. According to legend, he carried with him, in his mouth, the only manuscript copy of his then-unpublished verse epic the *Lusiads,* which would be printed in Lisbon in 1572 and assume its place in the canon of Portuguese literature. Some poems survive shipwreck.[4]

• • •

Not all the texts this book explores are literary, but my method of close textual analysis seeks out a poetics of shipwreck across multiple genres. The formal logic of poetic structures informs my analysis, whether I consider the lyrics of Donne and Shakespeare, Elizabethan sermons, or the amateur prose and verse of officers and sailors in the Restoration navy. The poetics of shipwreck creates a shared pattern through which human subjects encounter the oceanic globe. The texts that emerge from these real and metaphoric encounters operate through a logic of self-invention that the German philosopher Peter Sloterdijk calls "anthropotechnics."[5] Exploring human efforts to create "a symbolic framework," Sloterdijk asserts that a human is above all a creature who "struggles with itself in concern for its form" (10). Anthropotechnic efforts to imagine order within disorder, or to reconceive disorderly experience within orderly frames, illuminate the struggles of premodern writers, thinkers, and mariners to comprehend their encounters with the global ocean. Saltwater reality presented a shocking challenge to humans who splashed into it.

Wetness and the Ship-Body

There is a voice that insists that human bodies and wooden ships occupy the same space. It comes from Richard Younge, in his broadsheet *The State of a Christian,* a single-page work that also appeared later as a preface to Henry Mainwaring's *Sea-man's Dictionary* (1644). Its mania suggests how intensely and how physically the oceanic encounter stimulated the early modern imagination:

> My Body is the Hull; the Keele my Back; my Neck the Stem; the Sides are my Ribbes; the Beames my Bones; my flesh the plankes; Gristles and ligaments are the Pintells and knee-timbers; Arteries, veines and sinews the serverall seames of the Ship; my blood is the ballast; my heart the principall hold; my stomack the Cooke-roome; my Liver the Cesterne; my Bowels the sinke; my Lungs the Bellows; my teeth the Chopping-knives; except you divide them, and then they are the 32 points of the Sea-card both agreeing in number.[6]

Younge hurls human body parts, Christian souls, and nautical terms into a single crowded space. The resulting conceptual stew provides a frame through which to consider shipwreck and the dynamic meanings of the ocean. Shipwreck narratives are symbolic performances through which writers tested their own, and their culture's, experiential knowledge of the ocean. When the ship-body crashes into stormy seas, two meanings emerge: first, the wet disorientation of immersion and, then, the slow process of drying out. The tension and exchange between the wet and the dry represents the central ecological pattern of shipwreck; it tells a story that starts with rupture, moves into crisis, and then is followed by a broken or remade continuity. Stories of repeated wetness emphasize that our world remains an unfriendly home, more ocean than firm ground. Human bodies survive this environment only with difficulty, and only temporarily. The drying out of these catastrophes is an incomplete process and cultural fantasy, a safe destination that cannot be finally reached. Recognizing oceanic estrangement is essential to understanding the environmental plight of maritime cultures, from the early modern period to today.[7]

In October 1707 a British fleet led by Sir Cloudesley Shovell crashed into the rocky shores of the Isles of Scilly while returning from service against the French. Four ships were lost and between 1,400 and 2,000 men drowned, including Shovell himself. During the voyage back into the English Channel, the fleet's navigators had lost their course. The catastrophe inspired the 1714 Longitude Prize, eventually awarded to John Harrison for his design of shipboard chronometers that could be used to compute longitude accurately while at sea.[8]

Younge's desire in his broadside to unify ships and bodies emerges from an ancient religious topos in which the believer in the world parallels a ship at sea. Younge was a religious pamphleteer who published over fifty short works, almost all at his own expense, between 1636 and 1673.[9] In this early text, he emphasizes how intimately the ocean touched English bodies. The ship-body fantasy underlines the oceanic turn of seventeenth-century English culture. The broadside contains printed marginal citations of his primary biblical sources: Proverbs, Job, Isaiah, and Revelation.[10] His description moves from the physical focus on ships and bodies to a broader vision of the ethical characteristics that a ship might represent: "The fore-decke is humility; the stearne Charity; active obedience the sailes." The ship at sea combines human bodily form with the ethical features of an upright believer. As the passage nears its end, however, Younge's text divides itself between two different God-driven visions: shipwreck, which punishes sinful behavior, and saving grace, which rescues those who remain true. To be in Younge's ship-body means subjecting oneself to an oceanic divinity that drives all vessels one of these two places. After attacking religious adversaries in both Rome and Amsterdam, Younge places himself in God's care while displaying a sailor's vocabularly, noting that "this silly Pinke having the insurance of Gods omnipresence, findes not only succour from the Stocke of the Churches prayers . . . but likewise that Gods Almighty power and providence is neare at hand as a strong Castle of defence." Sailing in his English "Pinke," a small vessel with a flat bottom, Younge sees divine power countering the sea, providing a vision of rescue rather than hopelessness.[11]

Even more vividly than this salvific vision, Younge emphasizes the horrific terror of the ocean. Citing Psalm 124's vision of flood,[12] Younge ends his broadside with the shipwreck of "this great Gallion . . . when the stormes of Gods wrathe arise, downe she sinkes to desperation, and perisheth in the bottomlesse pit or burning lake of fire and brimstone, where weele leave her to receive a just recompense of reward." The split ending of the pamphlet mirrors the divided vision of the sea in early modern English culture: the great waters led to both success and disaster. Younge positions the Church of England as the sweet spot between Catholic Rome and Calvinist Amsterdam, and in a parenthetical remark, he associates the sinking galleon with England's favorite Spanish punching bag, "that Invincible Armado." But the capstone of Younge's vision is the lake of fire: in the catastrophic half of the story, the ship sinks to hell, not into the ocean. Younge's broadside explores a fantasy ship-body that survives hellish and oceanic immersion. This hybrid is never literally present in the historical and literary accounts this book explores, but Younge's impossibly literal vision creates a touchstone for the tense balance between empirical struggles and Providential rewards.

The mutual entanglement of ecological relations, empirical knowledge, and global understanding in early modern shipwreck narratives is not the structuring framework of the authors I examine. They appeal to a different dominant intellectual discourse for thinking about shipwreck:

Providentialism.[13] As I will show, Providential thinking stands for and to some extent screens away the centrality of shipwreck in global maritime culture.[14] Close attention to representations of shipwreck reveals fault lines, however, in the Providentialist consensus. Stories about shipwreck, preached from pulpits and collected in English-language books on both sides of the Atlantic, reveal the variable shapes of early modern Providentialism under stress. As the intellectual historian Alexandra Walsham describes it, Providence functioned in early modern English culture as "a set of ideological spectacles . . . which helped [individuals] to focus the refractory meanings of both petty and perplexing events."[15] In this interpretive practice, apparent disasters indicate a failure of perspective: Providential events appear erroneous or accidental only because the larger plan remains hidden.[16] The Providentialist vision relies on a hermeneutic process according to which eternal or panhistorical truths exist but lie hidden behind a veil that renders them invisible to human knowledge. Thus, events in the world appear contingent, to mortal eyes, but really are Providential, in terms of God's plan.

The Providentialist mind-set undergirds the repeated invocations of God's pleasure in shipwreck narratives; the phrase "It pleased God" serves as a near refrain in the majority of these accounts. But Providence becomes problematic when bad things happen to good people, and the risks of increased sea travel made Providential control seem both intensely desirable and not entirely comforting.[17] The shipwreck narrative as a literary form, in canonical works from *The Tempest* to *Robinson Crusoe,* in popular narratives, and in other literary and historical forms, positions itself astride this theological dilemma. In these narratives the ancient wonders of the God-sea plunge headlong into disorderly maritime experience. The resultant texts show shipwreck narratives mirroring the disruptions of cultural modernity. Before turning to the two shipwreck accounts that drive this chapter forward, the wreck of the *S. João* in Africa and of Anthony Thacher's ship in Massachusetts, I shall outline my core thesis about shipwreck stories as vehicles for capturing the subjective experience of cultural and ecological disruption.[18] For English writers, readers, and mariners, the master trope of shipwreck captured the essential instability of their increasingly ocean-bound culture.

• • •

In September 1583, Sir Humphrey Gilbert stood on board the homeward-bound HMS *Squirrel* during a storm with a book in his hand. Just before the ship sank with all hands, sailors on nearby vessels heard, or claimed that they heard, the humanist explorer's last words: "We are as near to heaven by sea as by land!" The phrase has become the unofficial motto of Newfoundland, the colony Gilbert had just claimed for Queen Elizabeth.

Shipwreck and the Accumulation of Modernity

The face of the ocean in the early modern period may have been empire, mercantile trade may have been its circulatory system, and slavery its most notorious crime, but its secret human history was shipwreck. Maritime disasters, widely represented in fiction, poetry, drama, and the visual arts, shadowed all oceanic voyages, such that any depiction of an early modern ship at sea contains, embedded, the possibility of a shipwreck story.[19] Disaster was a near story on every voyage, even when it did not happen. As Younge's broadside parable shows, the threat was implicit every time a ship's keel ploughed the waves.[20] Ships were ancient metaphors for cultural stability; the "ship of state" appears in *Antigone,* in Plato's *Republic* (book 6), and in Horace (*Odes* 1.14).[21] Shipwreck narratives were reminders that such stability could rupture at any moment. Michel Foucault has described how the ancient symbology of the ship became increasingly central in the early modern period, as Europeans sailed the World Ocean. In Foucault's analysis ships provided globalizing Europe with a "great instrument of economic development" and also its "greatest reserve of the imagination."[22] Encounters between ships and what Simon Schama calls the "moral geography" of the sea underwrote a transoceanic cultural phenomenon, the deployment of shipwreck narratives as tools for representing humanity in a hostile world.[23]

The largest implications of my analysis recast the traditional image of radical transformation that has been central to the historiography of early modernity from Burkhardt to Greenblatt. As my first preface has shown, I aim to pluralize and therefore weaken, in Vattimo's sense, the familiar story of the once-and-for-all epistemological break known as "early modernity."[24] By connecting this period not with a sudden rupture but instead with an interlocked network of constant changes, as in my fourfold terms, Anthropocene, Homogenocene, Thalassocene, and Naufragocene, my analysis uses shipwreck to represent cultural and ecological changes as disorienting but potentially survivable disasters.[25] These events feel like ruptures but do not fully break with their own past. The past never goes away. The conception of historical change that emerges from shipwreck reflects the felt experience of radical cultural difference without asserting an absolute separation from the past. Sixteenth- to eighteenth-century English maritime narratives combine radical disorientation with strained continuity. These narratives, in which divine power and human ingenuity interpenetrate, show a new cultural imagination emerging less through rejecting ancient or medieval "magical thinking" than by composting ancient discourses with newer ideas.

The shock-immersion-salvage pattern of shipwreck echoes and reformulates familiar but outmoded conceptions of the Renaissance as a cultural break. In the Hegelian reading of history made popular by Burkhardt and Michelet but also anticipated by writers from Petrarch to Bacon, early modernity claims itself as a fortunate shipwreck, in which a birth or rebirth reorients the West's cultural voyage.[26] Shipwreck's Janus-faced narrative structure—its combination of local disaster and global recovery and its intimate portrait of the oceanic environment, which is simultaneously cruel and redemptive—underlines a basic ambivalence about change built into early globalization.[27] The global ecology fractured and reconfigured traditional ideas of order, as it continues to do today. In our current chastened and resistant-to-metanarratives historicist critical discourse, scholars have become wary of heroic visions of the radical break: we no longer accept old narratives in which humanism breaks with scholasticism, capitalism with feudalism, science with superstition, religion with magic.[28] Despite this recognition of historical polysemy, however, we still seek models for understanding the felt experience of cultural change. Early modern writers from Petrarch to Defoe repeatedly testify to their subjective experience of drastic rupture, even though they also continue to employ ancient forms and ideas.[29] Perhaps if we cannot quit stories like the great instauration or transformative modernity, we can use shipwreck to supplement these myths with narratives of violent disorientation. Rebirth is always disruptive. The first "modern" man might resemble Richard Younge as well as Leonardo.

Imagining shipwreck as a master trope can replace the decisive once-

and-for-all historical break with an accelerating process of disruptive accumulation. As narratives of interruption, divine or disastrous, shipwreck stories replace the linear progress of Providential or Hegelian histories with uneven, chaotic episodes of disaster followed, sometimes, by recovery or salvage. In place of familiar understandings of modernity as displacement or disenchantment, shipwreck advances the less orderly image of accumulation and composture. In Glissant's formulation historical modernity builds like the ocean floor with its "accumulation of sediments."[30] Discourses, language, cultures, peoples: everything piles on top of everything else, and everything is simultaneously present in underwater composture. Glissant's critical vocabulary makes global ecological history legible. Accumulation subtends this ecological vision: nothing ever goes away, and all things recombine in new forms. Glissant's sense of history emerges from his distinction between the ancient Mediterranean, "an inner sea surrounded by lands, a sea the concentrates," and the postcolonial Caribbean, "a sea that explodes scattered lands into an arc" (33). This fragmented world, like the edge of the sea, combines "order and chaos," and its development always remains to some extent "illegible" (121–22). Early modern shipwreck narratives suggest that all waters, from the icy depths off Newfoundland where Humphrey Gilbert drowned in 1583 to the warmer waters off Bermuda where the *Sea-Venture* foundered in 1609, share this potential to scatter sailors and their histories. Accounts of maritime disasters from Hakluyt and Shakespeare through Defoe reveal the Janus-faced ambivalence of early modern culture, in which Providential and protoempirical explanatory systems accumulate atop each other.

Glissant's notion of sedimentary accumulation frames my analysis of the oceanic encounter, but his language also recalls the modern origins of American ocean science. The same phrase, "the accumulation of sediments," appears in Rachel Carson's 1951 bestseller *The Sea around Us*:

> When I think of the floor of the deep sea, the single, overwhelming fact that possesses my imagination is the accumulation of sediments. I always see the steady, unremitting downward drift of materials from above, flake upon flake, layer upon layer—a drift that has continued for hundreds of millions of years, that will go on as long as there are seas and

> continents . . . the most stupendous "snowfall" the earth has ever seen.[31]

The accumulation that Carson calls the "epic poem of the earth" (76) articulates in a scientific key what Glissant terms "*creolization*" (34) or "limitless *metissage*" (34). The ecological literary analysis this book undertakes relies on the conceptual overlap shared by the female scientist from Pennsylvania and the male poet from Martinique. Sediments are real things, rocks and silica and "billions of billions of tiny shells and skeletons, the limy or silicious remains of all the minute creatures that once lived in the upper waters" (Carson 76). Sedimented histories also "explode the scattered lands into an arc," as Glissant notes (33). All physical and scientific accumulations have a poetics, and all poetic forms reach toward physical things. The task is to think them together, lyrical science and analytical poem, in the disorienting swirl of a global ecology.

Shipwreck narratives dash early modern European triumphalism onto the rocks and tell a new story of cultural transformation.[32] Representations of these disasters generate something like the experience of the radical present that Walter Benjamin calls "the now," or *Jetztzeit.*[33] The vocabulary Benjamin developed for twentieth-century historiography describes the fracturing pressure catastrophe generates. Like the disasters of the past viewed by his backward-facing Angel of History, the stories told by shipwreck are disruptive. Plunged into salt water, human subjects encounter an unlivable, alien environment. Various discourses surface as barely tenable life buoys, including classical literary forms, Christian Providence, maritime expertise, empiricist critique, and attacks on human folly. Amid the chaos the human experience of saltwater globalization seems less rupture than explosive fragmentation, after which spectators and survivors struggle to assemble coherent visions from debris on the beach.[34] Watched and read from the safety of shore, shipwreck narratives reveal the tenuous place of human bodies in the world. Human beings read shipwrecks as if they were texts and in order to generate texts.[35] If a vision of heaven is the promised end toward which many shipwrecks gesture, a watery grave threatens a nightmarishly final detour. Shipwreck marks the price and establishes the framework of an assertive cultural modernity that passes beyond established limits.[36] These stories emphasize the fragility and multiplicity of unstable, always-changing cultural and ecological orders.

The poetics of shipwreck thus uses its two distinctive modes, the wet and the dry, to represent the subjective experience of historical change. Wet narratives emphasize disorder, disorientation, and rupture; they narrate experiences in which the usual ways of doing things get broken or fragmented. In these moments all forms and fancies of human order dissolve. But narrative cannot bear absolute immersion for long, and nearly all shipwreck stories also contain a dry countermovement that attempts to make sense and meaning out of disaster.[37] Drawing Providential morals about the wages of human sin or practical lessons from navigational errors are two of many tactics through which the immersive shock of shipwreck produces dry truths. Looking at a shipwreck from the safety of shore, as in the famous image from the Roman poet Lucretius, provides a philosophical perspective that uses wet events to create dry wisdom.[38] As Hans Blumenberg has argued about Lucretius's image, the interpretive frame enables shipwreck to become "a didactic drama staged by Providence."[39] But even the most sermonized shipwreck narrative has at its core the wet shock of disorientation and exclusion, even if temporarily, from dry earth. Representations of shipwreck cling to dry interpretive processes like so many spars, holding at bay their final encounter with the ocean. The sudden interchange between dry life and wet immersion drives these narratives and characterizes their ambivalent vision of cultural transformation.

Providence and the Pintles: The *S. João* in 1552

Out of the massive archive of early modern shipwreck narratives, I begin with one of the most famous, the wreck of the Portuguese galleon *S. João* off the coast of southeast Africa in 1552. This well-known story shows how theological language and the technical terms of seamanship combine in a distinctive accumulation of discourses. Entangling human ingenuity with more-than-human power, the microgenre of shipwreck steers frail bodies through deadly seas. In this case the wreck of a wealthy galleon on her way home from India and the subsequent deaths of the aristocratic castaways, the commander Manuel de Sousa Sepulveda and his wife, Leonor, would become one of the most famous tales of early modern Portuguese maritime catastrophe. The tragedy generated at least three sixteenth-century pamphlet histories, the plots of at least two Spanish Golden Age plays, and one full-length poetic epic in Portuguese.[40] The version of the story that I analyze began as a sixteenth-century pamphlet and then became part of the Portuguese literary canon as the first entry in the *História Trágico-Marítima,* the collection of early modern shipwreck narratives that would become "a kind of cultural institution in Portugal."[41] The story of Manuel de Sousa and Leonor also appears briefly in the *Lusiads,* Portugal's national epic.[42] As much as any single wreck, the story of the *S. João* epitomizes the fragility of what Jerry Brotton calls Portugal's "empire built on water."[43] This short narrative epitomizes the Portuguese encounter with the global ecology of ocean.

The historical "Account of the Very Remarkable Loss of the Great Galleon *S. João,*" as told to its anonymous narrator by "one Álvaro Fernandes, boatswain's mate of the galleon" (3), provides a prose distillation of the narrative master plot of early modern shipwreck.[44] Religion and maritime experience coexist uneasily. The story opens with explicit gestures toward a Providentialist frame: "The matter narrated in this shipwreck should make men very much fear God's punishments and become good Christians" (3). The narrative itself, however, multiplies empirical causes for the wreck. Technical explanations crowd out Providentialist tropes, but the narrative does not encourage zero-sum competitions between explanatory systems. Instead, the relatively unstructured account layers each plausible cause on top of the others. The result is less an exposé of Manuel de Sousa's errors or even the dangers of the Carreira da Índia and more a representation of how deeply shipwreck disoriented early modern culture. The story of the *S. João* articulates, as Josiah Blackmore has argued, a "kind of counterhistoriography . . . [to] the hegemonic vision of empire."[45] This story contains disaster rather than explaining it away. The narrative lacks the commitment to progress built into verse epics like the *Lusiads* and mercantalist histories like Hakluyt's *Principal Navigations.*[46] The account's multiple overdetermined causes for its single drastic consequence highlight a narrative asymmetry typical of representations of maritime disaster. Shipwreck stories have disproportion built into them; they are fundamentally about the mismatch between terrestrial humanity and the oceanic globe. Small errors create vast disasters. Human decisions, foolish or foolhardy, never correspond to the enormity of events. Shipwreck narratives uneasily intermingle historical accuracy and literary resonance.[47] On a broad level it is literary form—in this case an attenuated form of tragedy—that organizes these accounts. Shipwreck authors attempt to salvage their culture's expansionist enterprise while censuring its failures and excesses. The resulting narratives produce and respond to maritime disorientation: like being at sea, shipwreck makes you uncertain of where you are.

At the center of the cultural poetics of early modern shipwreck lies the vexed but essential question of causation, of why this ship and not that one ends up wrecked.[48] "Tell me the cause, O Muse," sings Virgil in the background.[49] In addition to conventional invocations of God's will and the wages of human sins, the *S. João*'s wreck teems with causes and potential causes. The result is a confusing accumulation of apparently insufficient reasons, a hostile, wet, and disorderly portrait of life at (and in) the sea. Many distinct moments within the opening pages of this short narrative compete to represent the key failure of Manuel de Sousa's ship. This compilation of mutually redundant but coexistent causes was typical of many early modern shipwreck narratives, though the *S. João* provides an extreme case in terms of its compact relation. Living at sea, this narrative makes clear, requires a radical surrender to contingency. My textual analysis locates no fewer than thirteen different causes of the wreck in the space of six pages in the modern edition. I outline these causes here, as a summary of the disaster.

Thirteen Ways of Wrecking the *S. João*

1. *The Date*: They leave India "on the third of February" (4).
2. *The Cargo*: The ship held "seven thousand *quintais*" (4) of pepper.
3. *The Sails*: The "poor condition of their sails" was "one of the causes—indeed, the main one, of their destruction" (4, 6).[50]
4. *The Storm*: On May 11, "they were hit by a wind from the west and west-northwest accompanied by many lightning bolts" (5).
5. *No Extra Sails*: "They had no sails other than those already on the yards, as the other set of sails had been through a storm on the Equator and was torn and could not be trusted" (5).
6. *Repairs*: "One of the reasons they had not already rounded

the Cape by this time was the time spent in striking the sails in order to repair them" (5).

7. *The Pintles*: As the storms continued for three days, "the ship laboured so much that it lost three pintles from the rudder, that is, the part of it on which the entire perdition or salvation of a ship depends" (5).
8. *The Second Storm*: "The storm broke out in all its fury. Then it seemed to please God to make an end of them, as later happened" (6).
9. *The Mast*: "The crew, axes in hand, began chopping at the mast when all of a sudden it snapped above the pulleys as if it had been felled by a single stroke" (6).
10. *Winds*: "Then, the wind tore off the mainsail and the stormsail" (7).
11. *Waves*: "A wave broke the rotten rudder in two and carried away half of it, leaving the pintles in the stern-post gudgeons" (7). "A wave struck the ship so violently that it uprooted the mast and threw it into the sea" (7).
12. *Failure to Make Landfall*: "And so they went at the mercy of the sea and the wind, rolling now to this side, now to that. The ship could not be steered, and there were more than fifteen spans of water below the deck" (8).
13. *Fate*: "But since it was already written on high that this captain, his family, and all of his company would meet their end, anything they might try to accomplish would be overturned by fate" (9).

This point-by-point summary highlights the multiple overlapping errors that contributed to the disaster. The sheer variety of these causes makes an instructive contrast with Younge's fantasy of union between ship and body. The thirteen causes fall into five mostly distinct categories: failures of foresight, failures of seamanship, failures of technology, dangers of the ocean, and the control of fate. These categories structure the tension between navigational experience and Providential control. Many shipwreck narratives include multiple potential causes, though few elaborate each as fully as the tale of the *S. João*. The first scene of *The Tempest* provides a control case: the ocean and Providentialism both appear prominently, but Shakespeare's play does not distinguish clearly between errors of foresight, seamanship, and technology.[51] The more modern case of the *Titanic* provides another example, which emphasizes errors of foresight and technology more than Providential order, except in literary representations like Thomas Hardy's "The Convergence of the Twain" or, with different emphasis, James Cameron's 1997 film *Titanic.* In the narrative of the *S. João,* the four empirical categories—foresight, seamanship, technology, and the ocean—partially displace Providential control from the center of the story. The core narrative emphasizes a struggle between seamanship and ocean, with foresight and technology serving as handmaidens to human skill. Fate assumes final control, as it always does, but the liminal place of references to fate—they appear only in the prologue and the conclusion—suggests that seamanship in crisis fuels the story more directly than Providentialist habits of thought. It seems important, in this context, that the narrative source was the boatswain's mate, not a poet or a playwright. In this account, more clearly than in the highly polished rhetoric of Camões or Shakespeare, the fragmentary and fractured nature of the text reflects a physical encounter with oceanic disorder.

Two early failures of foresight frame the narrative, but without making the disaster entirely a referendum on human error. Manuel de Sousa sails home a bit too late in the year (way of wrecking no. 1), thereby making it likely that he will not have rounded the Cape of Good Hope before the storms of May.[52] He also overloads his ship (no. 2), as many merchants did on the homeward voyage; individual mariners often tried to enrich themselves with personal cargos.[53] These errors prompt the editorial observation that "ships so overladen must take extreme cautions since they run great risks" (4). Risk, of course, was endemic to sea travel, and merchants needed to load their ships to turn a profit. Many ships returned safely to the Atlantic despite leaving India as late as April.[54] These failures of foresight frame the difficulty of this ship's voyage, but they do not themselves condemn the passage to failure. Shipwreck looms as risk not as necessity.

The tale focuses more on the relationship between seamanship, the proper performance of maritime labor, and technology, the proper response of maritime tools to seamanlike use. Together, these factors produce viable tactics that humanity can use to survive oceanic disruption. Among the thirteen causes, poor seamanship underlies at least three. The time spent on repairing the sails (no. 6) delays the ship. The repairs were also ineffectual; the sails remained weak and fail during the storm (no. 3). Arguably, the loss of the mast (no. 9) can be attributed in part to a failure of seamanship, since a more skilled or quick-working crew might have been able to preserve it. The mariners do, however, repair this error by making a new mast "from the remaining stump . . . [and] a section of spar, nailing it down and securing it with lines as best they could" (6). The jury-rigged mast does not function very well—it was "so makeshift and shaky that any strong wind would have destroyed it" (6)—but it demonstrates how seamanship can redress failures of maritime technology.

Technological failures challenge seamanship's resourcefulness. The allegorical crux of nearly all shipwreck stories, in which human labor fails and divine forces assume control, makes itself felt through multiple ruptures of human and technological abilities. In fact, if seamanship is considered primarily a way of using technology, as the first iteration of maritime labor in Western literature—the metis of Odysseus—suggests, then the separation between technology and seamanship may seem artificial. Two clear failures of technology—the tattered sails (no. 3) and the lack of a spare set of canvas (no. 5)—pose problems for seamanlike labor. But it is only after technology fails and the ships floats "at the mercy of the sea and wind," (8) despite being near "a beach quite suitable for landing if they could reach it" (8), that the mariners seem truly alone in the sea. Neither seamanship nor technology intercedes between them and the ocean. The narrative emphasizes their helplessness: "Truly, men ought to think on this, for it causes great fear!" (8). Seamanship saves many survivors, including Manuel de Sousa and his wife, but when the lifeboat finally "broke in two" (10), it was not maritime skill that saved the rest: "Many of those on board struggled to cling to the boxes and pieces of wood in order to get to land. More than forty Portuguese and seventy slaves died this way. The rest came to land as God pleased: some on top of the waves, and some under, and many were wounded by nails and wood" (10). Human skill fails, leaving divine power—"as God pleased"—in total control. Seamanship cannot endure naked encounters with the sea.

The most dramatic failure of technology and seamanship involves the pintles (no. 7). Pintles, as modern sailors know, are small rods that slide into eye-shaped gudgeons in order to fasten the rudder to the stern. They highlight in a concentrated way the dependency of all maritime labor upon precise technology. Pintles are small devices on which navigation depends utterly. These finely crafted tools cannot be rebuilt or repaired at sea under ordinary circumstances. When functioning, they articulate the key connection between pilot's hand and ship's stem. Thus, the narrator's apparently excessive description of the pintles as "the part on which the entire perdition or salvation of a ship depends" describes the physical and spiritual fates of the six hundred souls on board the galleon and is also literally, technically true. Without pintles the ship cannot steer; these missing pieces fracture the relationship between helmsman and ship. The narrator's language insists that the pintles were the most important technological failure on the voyage, even though comparable claims appear elsewhere. Of all the broken tools on board, however, it was only the pintles whose failure was kept secret, "to avoid inciting terror and fear in everyone" (6). The fate of the pintles, in a telling variation on the Providential plan, must be kept hidden, but by human experts not divine opacity. Maritime technology creates a hidden order known to initiates like the master and the carpenter but not spread widely. These specialists bridge the generic labor of the crew and the arcane workings of the vessel. They function as quasi priests of a hidden technical order. Maritime expertise functions as a secular form of insight into the more-than-human oceanic environment.

Against three forms of human ingenuity—the foresight of the captain, the labor of the crew, and the know-how of the officers—stands the inhuman ocean. Natural forces are the most numerous causes of the wreck, although they also seem the most ordinary. The storm that first hits the ship on May 11 (no. 4) seems typical of fall storms in the southern hemisphere near the African cape. The second storm, which hits three days later (no. 8), calls up a starker explanation: "Then it seemed to please God to make an end of them" (6), but even so, the storm is not unusual. The winds that destroy the remaining sails (no. 10), and the waves that carry away the rudder and then the mast (no. 11) create familiar damage. The narrative suggests, albeit without directly stating it, that a more competent performance of the human tasks—more foresight or better seamanship or more durable technology—might have made these events survivable.

As the prologue had already emphasized, however, God had marked out the *S. João* for disaster. The controlling force of fate, of what "was already written on high" (no. 13), preemptively frames the narrative as a series of inevitable failures. Neither labor nor technology can alter God's decree. The presence of divine will in the narrative, as in other shipwreck narratives, brackets the conflict between humanity and the sea, turning mortal struggles into might-have-beens. From the point of view of the reader, however, fate does not resolve the tension so much as push the problem aside. Readers remain embroiled in questions of foresight—"Should the *S. João* have shipped less cargo?"—of seamanship—"Could the master have steered her onto the beach?"—and of technology—"What if the pintles had not broken?" Fate provides a global hermeneutic solution that fails to address the specific details of the drama at hand. Like Poseidon in the *Odyssey* or Juno in the *Aeneid,* fate controls but does not clarify. In the technical world of seafaring labor, pintles seem as important as Providence. The narrative of the *S. João* appears deeply wet in its discursive mode, albeit framed by the dry language of theological control.

Shipwreck and Loss: Anthony Thacher in 1635

Anthony Thacher, like Manuel de Sousa and his wife, survived shipwreck. Thacher's story, however, reveals the inverse relationship between maritime experience and theological consolation. Thacher, who was not himself a sailor, shows in his first-person account the insufficiency of theological rhetoric to face maritime catastrophe. He cannot fully dry out his wet narration. After being caught in a hurricane off Massachusetts in 1635, Thacher wrote a letter to his brother that tried to describe his survival in conventional language about God's "great mercy and wonderfull deliverance."[55] Thacher's losses in the storm, however, included his cousin and all five of his children. His oceanic experience strains his recourse to Providentialist rhetoric. When God's pleasure drowns innocents, it is hard to accept that Providence rules the waves.

The moments of greatest emotional intensity in Thacher's letter come when he describes his children's "untimely" (59) deaths. The word "untimely" captures his letter's half-articulated protest against Providential control. Thacher recognizes the heretical implications of this word and nearly erases it as he writes, "mine owne poor Children So untimely (if I may so tearme it without offence) before mine eyes halfe drownded and ready to be swollowed up" (59). In a Providential universe in which all things happen by God's pleasure—Thacher repeats the refrain "It pleased God" twice (58)—any wish that things happen otherwise can feel blasphemous. Though Thacher never questions his own suffering or his cousin's death, the word "untimely" protests against a God who drowns children. When Thacher describes his family and fellow passengers "drowned in the mercyless Seas" (61), he invokes no divinity behind the waves. For the moment, at least, the deaths are "untimely" and the ocean "mercyless." Wet hints of antitheological chaos float in the surf.

Thacher's anguished relation of his experience nearly unravels the Providential hermeneutic from inside. His final conversation with his cousin John Avery, a minister, reveals shipwreck as a theological conundrum about the opacity of God. The two men's dialogue functions as a call-and-response. Thacher tells Avery that "the Lord is able to helpe and deliver us," and Avery replies, "What his Pleasure is we know not" (60). Avery asserts that God "hath promised to deliver us from Sinne and Condemnation through the all Sufficient Satisfaction of Jesus Christ," and Thacher provides the orthodox reply, "That is all the deliverance I now desier and expect" (60). But at exactly this point, when the two debate eternal things, the physical reality of the ocean interrupts them: "Which words I had no sooner Spoken but by a mighty wave, I was with a peece of the Barke washed out upon part of the Rock where the wave left me almost drowned but recovering my feet" (60). Avery's declaration of faith defies the sea to reveal God's hand behind it—"This [spiritual redemption] therefore we may Chalenge," he insists—but the ocean replies to Thacher without words.[56] Waves crash over the consolations of theology, flooding Providence with salt wetness.

Sir Hugh Willoughby and the crew of the *Bona Esperanza* spent the winter of 1553–54 in a bay near the borders of modern Russia and Finland, their vessel immobilized by sea ice. Their frozen bodies were discovered by Russian fishermen in the spring.[57]

Prayers like Avery's represent conceptual responses to maritime disorientation; he employs neither foresight nor seamanship nor maritime labor. This language of theological surrender is not limited to clerics. Thacher describes a sailor who has been washed overboard abandoning labor for prayer: "Oh we are all Cast away, Lord have mercy on us" (59). *The Tempest*'s opening scene presents a comparable abandonment of labor for despair: "We split, we split, we split" (1.1.58). Thacher's response to the unruly sea differs from his cousin's in that he attempts to link prayer to physical effort. At crucial moments, he joins his strength with Providence: "The Lord directed my toes into a Joint in the rockes side as also the topes of Some of my fingers with my right hand by meanes whereof the waves Leaving mee I remained so, having only my head above the water" (61). Thacher's position, like that of the mariners on the *S. João* or the Boatswain in *The Tempest,* requires both divine guidance—the Lord directs his toes and dismisses the waves—and physical skill.[58] His survival story has its supernatural moments, in particular when he stands "boult upright as if I stood upon my feete but I felt no bottom" (61), but remains poised between natural and supernatural forces.

The tangled syntax of one of Thacher's sentences reveals the fractured structure of the shipwreck hermeneutic in oceanic crisis. He explains his survival strangely: "Wee were by the violence of the waves and fury of the windes by the Lords permission Lifted up upon a rocke" (59). The repetitive grammar frames divine permission as both necessary and extraneous to human survival. Thacher provides empirical causes—"by the violence of the waves and fury of the windes"—that might suffice to explain the wreck, but when he then adds the phrase "by the Lords permission," he supplements this natural description without displacing it. The syntactically parallel phrases "by the violence of the waves" and "by the Lords permission" present opposite causes for the storm, either natural or divine. These opposite forces, however, occupy the same grammatical position. Rather than displacing each other, these explanatory systems accumulate alongside each other. The Lord's permission may underwrite the waves' violence—such would be the orthodox reading—but Thacher's anguished description suggests that he recognizes, and nearly articulates, how hard it is to unify a merciful God and the hungry ocean.

The letter as a whole uses the conventional rhetoric of the sea-deliverance narrative to reorient Thacher after the disaster. When Increase Mather turned the story into a sermon and later included it in *Illustrious Providences* (Boston, 1684), the conventional frames would become even clearer.[59] Walking the beach, Thacher blames himself:

"Then it Came into my mynde how I had accationed the death of my Children, who had accasioned them out of their native Land" (62). Like his protest against their "untimely" deaths, his guilt over his children's fate implicitly places human choices against God's Providence. His final paragraphs return to "Gods goodnesse unto mee" (63), but they also highlight his own efforts and those of his fellow New Englanders to re-create order after disaster. Like Robinson Crusoe, he salvages items from the wreck, including steel and flint, a dead goat, and "my Sonne Willes Coat" (63). He accepts God's mercy and offers prayers. He also socializes and memorializes the disaster by writing the letter to his brother in England and by giving names to the island and the rock: "That desolate Island . . . I named after my own Name Thachers Woe. And the Rocke I named Avary his fall" (63). The biblical cadences seem crucial: Thacher like Adam gives order to his maritime landscape through language. His woe and his cousin's fall get engraved on dry land. Language gives human meaning to a deadly coastline. These names still appear on maps of Massachusetts, off Cape Ann. Thacher's anguished Providentialism reveals a rupture in the oceanic encounter that shipwreck narratives would strain to fill.[60]

Wet and Dry Together: The Wreck of the Amsterdam (circa 1630)

Framing my study of the poetics of shipwreck between the overloaded causality of the *S. João* and the Providentialist straining of Anthony Thacher locates these narratives on a continuum between disorienting wet and consoling dry. This binary frame, however, should not imply that the wet and the dry exist in isolation. Instead, these opposed tendencies function inside each individual articulation of the shipwreck microgenre. As early modern Europe became flooded with maritime stories in multiple forms, the imperative to mix modes and represent both the shock of immersion and the relief of salvation increased. Caught between navigational expertise and theological belief, between empirical and supernatural explanatory systems, shipwreck writers felt pressure from both sides. As an example of a richly unified presentation of wet and dry together, I choose *The Wreck of the Amsterdam,* a seventeenth-century oil painting currently hanging in the National Maritime Museum in Greenwich (Figure 1).[61] This painting, made by an anonymous Flemish master sometime around 1630, portrays a ship in crisis off a rocky shore in dazzlingly accurate technical detail. It also functions symbolically as another version of Younge's *The State of a Christian,* with the sailor climbing the mainmast below the crosstrees in the lower center of the image representing both skilled mariner and endangered believer. The painting's combination of empirical details and theological meaning was typical of Low Countries maritime painting in the seventeenth century.[62] This image provides a visual summary of my claim that early modern shipwreck narratives generate an accumulative modernity in which supernatural and empirical world views overlap.

The most striking visual features of the painting are its wet details, in particular the dramatic portside heeling of the *Amsterdam* herself. The ship has not yet foundered, unlike her companion vessel to the lower left, but her deck balances perilously near the water. With the visual precision that was already a hallmark of seventeenth-century Dutch maritime painting, the canvas displays the terror of impending shipwreck. Multiple bodies swirl in the water near the already-down ship, whose stern bears an image of the Virgin Mary. A few survivors have managed to reach shore, and in the upper left a single figure prays, perhaps for the salvation of the threatened vessel or for the souls of the perished, or more sinisterly, perhaps he and his fellows on shore are hoping to salvage treasure from the wrecks.[63] The central ship, which bears the coat of arms of the city of Amsterdam on her stern, appears in danger, but even in crisis the vessel appears carefully balanced: the mainsail has torn free and flutters in the gale, but the main topsail above it has been carefully furled. The *Amsterdam* balances on the cusp of disaster.

A later shipwrecked *Amsterdam,* a Dutch merchant ship, came to rest on the coast of England in early 1749.[64] The huge East Indiaman was a top-of-the-line ship, displacing over seven hundred tons and carrying more than three hundred souls. Her remains lie in the tidal sands off Hastings in southern England and are visible today at low tide. The disaster never fully disappears.

The painting's composition suggests several allegorical schemes that might produce suitably dry interpretations. If the central ship represents the city of Amsterdam and the broken vessel on the left, the Catholic Church, then the painting becomes an allegory of Protestant

FIGURE 1. Balanced between a rocky coast and devil ships, the *Amsterdam* represents shipwreck's wet and dry core. Anonymous, circa 1630. Copyright the National Maritime Museum, Greenwich, London.

resistance to the Spanish Empire. The flame-shrouded demon ships to the upper right add to this symbolic pattern, so that Amsterdam must sail a perilous path between shipwrecked Catholicism and demonic fire. Given that Amsterdam was one of the last Dutch cities to join the revolt against Spain, the painting may also have a topical political meaning. It may additionally refer to a specific event, perhaps the demise of the ship *Amsterdam* on its return from the East Indies in 1597, though that ship was burnt intentionally rather than sinking in a storm. The painting may even simply be a parable about the precariousness of human life—or it may be some combination of all those things.[65]

Much of the painting's emotional energy swirls around the enigmatic figure on the mainmast of the *Amsterdam*. The cross-like mast on which he perches points up and toward the light piercing the clouds on the top of the canvas, as if gesturing toward salvation. His own direction, however, is less clear. The perfectly furled sail above him suggests that he is not heading up toward the light but climbing back down, after having furled the topsail.[66] If he is moving downward, the visual relationship between maritime labor and theological allegory is perfectly inverted: religious meaning strains upward toward heaven, whereas maritime labor climbs back down toward the deck. The interface of these explanatory systems gets written onto the endangered body of the sailor clinging to the rigging in the storm. This unnamed sailor hangs near the heart of *Shipwreck Modernity.* He holds himself astride the competing symbolic claims of religion and seamanship, enduring crisis as competing interpretive systems accumulate beneath and around him. He is wet but, at least potentially, getting dry.

· CHAPTER 2 ·

Angry Gods

Theologies of the Ocean

Is the shipwrack then a harvest, does the tempest carry the grain for Thee?

Gerard Manley Hopkins, *The Wreck of the Deutschland*

ANGRY GODS WRECK SHIPS. Oceanic voyaging places human bodies directly at risk of encountering divine wrath in the form of a tempest. The clearest explanation for maritime catastrophes has always been divine displeasure. Shipwreck's function as theological parable has ancient roots, from the wrath of Poseidon in the *Odyssey* to Yahweh's anger with Jonah. As told and retold, the shipwreck master plot combines supernatural violence with a longer-term Providentialist plan: in the end Odysseus returns home, and Jonah redeems Ninevah. John Dryden's memorable opening couplet in his translation of the *Aeneid* links the two essential elements of divine anger and divine plan; the hero encounters the storm "forc'd by Fate, / And haughty Juno's unrelenting hate."[1] The fate/hate couplet that opens Dryden's English version of classical epic connects divine control with catastrophe. The poet asks the reader to imagine divine hatred as a form of supernatural planning. What feels like hatred is actually Fate. For Christian writers, as well as in the Christianized reading of Virgil that emerged in the middle ages, Juno's anger and Fate together represent humanity's partial experience and knowledge of Providence. In suffering shipwreck Aeneas sacrifices his body to the divine plan. Swimming with Angry Gods in tempestuous seas creates a theo-ecological encounter as the hero plunges into the depths of the world. Commentators from James Janeway to Richard Hakluyt cite Psalm 107: "Those who go down to the sea in ships, that do business in great waters; / These see the works of Lord, and his wonders in the deep" (23–24).[2] Shipwreck extends the neutral-sounding "business" of the mariner into a direct physical encounter with wet wonders. For preachers and theological thinkers, the oceanic encounter epitomizes the relationship between human weakness and divine power. Angry Gods initiate the disaster, and suffering humans begin by looking to the heavens.

Interpretive responses to divine wrath comprise an "oceanic theology" that seeks to dry out the immersion of shipwreck. In the desire to look past shipwreck, sermon makers follow a pattern that they adapt from Virgil and other classical poets of shipwreck. The *Aeneid* connects the reward of Rome with ships foundering in the Mediterranean, which means that the reader must think past the saltwater present of the poem's opening shipwreck. Virgil's hero appears trapped in a catastrophic present but must be educated into a future-oriented Providential scheme. This drying out happens through poetic form. The opening book of Virgil's epic creates a dual template. Neptune emphasizes oceanic disorder even as he dispels it. Chastising the winds, the sea god asserts divine control over his environment:

> Is it for you to ravage Seas and Land,
> Unauthoriz'd by my supream Command?
> To raise such Mountains on the troubl'd Main?
> Whom I—But first 'tis fit, the Billows to restrain,
> And then you shall be taught obedience to my Reign. (1.190–94)

As Neptune asserts his control, the wild ocean recedes. The direct encounter is too wet, too stark, and too chaotic for easy comprehension. In order to speak, the god first calms the sea.

Traditionally, this moment of crisis has been read in terms of the hero's Roman reward. The first epic simile in Virgil's poem, which analogizes Neptune's calming of the seas to the political authority of "some Grave and Pious man" (1.217), serves to dry out the wetness of shipwreck. The city and the land, tools and legacies of empire, organize our reading of disorder at sea.[3] In a meaningful sense, sailors cross seas in order to get to land; the vast early modern English literature of maritime discovery, from Hakluyt forward, spends much more time describing foreign lands than alien seas. But as saltwater travel expanded outside the

Mediterranean basin and sea voyages became longer and more distant from known spaces, early modern writers and thinkers came to realize that the ocean was more than simply a blank space between different lands. Encounters with the ocean changed sailors' lives and habits. These men and women could not live entirely at sea, but their intimacy with the watery element marked them as semiaquatic, set apart from their terrestrial fellows. The cultural obsession with sailor-heroes is as old as Odysseus, but the expansion of global sea travel after the fifteenth century increased this figure's resonance. The rise of the sailor-hero finds in Melville's *Moby-Dick* an epic apotheosis, and in this book I often use Melville as an imaginative theorist of oceanic meanings, in order to draw out the implications of early modern maritime narratives. Melville's most famous sailor is Ishmael, who seeks the sea to cure the "damp, drizzly November in my soul" (18), but the novel's wettest hero may be Bulkington, mentioned only twice in the early pages of *Moby-Dick.* Bulkington appears alongside Ishmael in the Spouter-Inn in New Bedford having "in midwinter just landed from a four years' dangerous voyage" (96). After so long a sea journey, the shadow hero immediately joins the *Pequod* and "unresistingly push[es] off again for still another tempestuous term" (96). Bulkington epitomizes the radical separation of sailor from landed humanity: he appears unable to remain on land, and he remains so opaque as scarcely to figure in Melville's novel. He represents the theological mystery that only sailors approach: that "in landlessness alone resides the highest truth, shoreless, indefinite as God" (97). Bulkington, the only figure other than Queequeg who Ishmael calls "comrade" (29), loves only the sea. He models the doomed love of human for ocean. Along with Aeneas and Jonah, he symbolizes this chapter's narrative theology of shipwreck.

Shipwrecks have been representative narratives of divine power since Homer, and the global expansion of European sailors after the fifteenth century emphasizes this motif's theological conundra. Bulkington's focusing example reveals the underlying thalassophilia of wreck-risking embarkation. More intimate than most discovery narratives, stories of shipwreck present the shock of saltwater immersion. This contact speaks directly to theological and ecological concerns. The sermons and Providential narratives this chapter explores range in date from the 1590s to 1690s and in geography from England to Jamaica and Florida, but they share a basic effort to respond to the oceanic encounter through Christian theology. Like Thacher off the coast of Massachusetts, these writers grappled with the divine meanings behind maritime catastrophes. As Gerard Manley Hopkins phrases it in this chapter's epigraph, the firm presumption of Providential control insists that shipwreck be a "harvest," in which certain ships and sailors are reaped for the greater good. If the tempest "carries the grain" for God's pleasure, the shipwrecked sailor becomes ballast, carried along in the belly of the storm. Ballast's proper task is transport, not resistance.

Conventional interpretations of biblical sea narratives in which Noah represents righteousness or Jonah repentance fail to do justice to the disorienting nature of the oceanic encounter. By emphasizing that the global experience of shipwreck was fundamentally ecological, I suggest that typical habits of interpretive displacement, in which shipwreck represents the cost of empire, or mercantile expansion, or the spreading of the Gospel, need to be supplemented with something wetter and more physical. Sermons dry out maritime experience, but they also contain traces of their prior wetness. Making better sense of the cultural force of shipwreck narratives requires reconsidering the place of the sea itself in poetic and religious culture. Here, I turn to contemporary theologian Catherine Keller's "tehomic theology," which argues that the book of Genesis contains a long-misunderstood celebration of oceanic chaos, which appears to preexist God's creation of the world. For Keller the words of Genesis 2—"And the Spirit of God moved upon the face of the waters"—identify the ocean as the preexisting profundity out of which God created the universe.[4] Against understandings of creation *ex nihilo,* which became standard Christian doctrine by the fourth century, Keller places an alternative ocean-driven vision of creation *ex profundis,* out of the depths. She argues that the land-centered fantasy of *ex nihilo* "taught the West to shun the *depths* of the creation" (xvi). Returning *tehom* (the sea) to its full share in universal creation, Keller argues, can counterbalance some of Western culture's destructive impulses. Many Western religions, including but not limited to Christianity, imagine a primal *Chaoskampf* between a usually male God of the Sky who conquers a usually female Goddess of the Sea.[5] Keller invokes a paradox, "the face of the deep," to gesture toward richer and more sympathetic collaborations between these two spaces. She further argues that the phrase "face of the deep," with its reflection turned back onto itself, serves to "belie the dichotomy of surface and depth"

(163). Keller's vision of tehomic or oceanic wisdom represents an attempt to think wetly, to modify traditional ways of drying out human understandings. It means embracing shipwreck not as a temporary detour on the road to Rome but as momentary vision of deeper and more fundamental truths. Even eternal cities do not span all of human history as the ocean does.

Using tehomic theology to reconsider shipwreck helps reframe the seaward turn in early modern English culture. This chapter begins with perhaps the most popular English consideration of the theological implications of shipwreck, John King's oft-reprinted *Lectures upon Jonas,* first delivered in York in 1594. It then moves through several works of theologically inflected early modern shipwreck stories in English, including Anthony Pet's representative story of surviving a shipwreck off the English coast in 1613; Jonathan Dickinson's account of his shipwreck in Florida in the 1690s, *Gods Protecting Providence,* which was first published in Philadelphia in 1699; and the English preacher James Janeway's oft-reprinted *Legacy for his Friends* (1674). Throughout my readings of these texts, I recast straightforwardly Providentialist interpretations in favor of more tehomic understandings that emphasize the physical engagement of humans with the sea. As Richard Younge's broadside has shown, the lessons of the oceanic encounter were not simply the familiar virtues of faith and sympathy but more radical truths about shared catastrophe and endurance. I advance an ecological reading of shipwreck theology by interpreting these narratives through the physical mixing of bodies and ocean. Encounters between land mammals and vast oceans would come to define the global ecology. The ecotheology of shipwreck requires an embrace of what Hopkins calls a "harvest" from the point of view of the grain, not the reaper.

In addition to Keller's tehomic theology and its preexistent material Ocean, another guiding interpretive spirit of this chapter is Epeli Hau'ofa, the Fijian anthropologist and activist whose transformative essay "Our Sea of Islands," first published in 1993, reimagines the Pacific through oceanic connection rather than separation. Invoking the long history of transpacific navigation by non-Western mariners, Hau'ofa describes "Oceania" as positive space rather than immense nullity. In his view intimacy with the ocean generates maximum mobility and human power: "Oceania is vast, Oceania is expanding, Oceania is hospitable and generous, Oceania is humanity rising from the depths of brine and regions of fire deeper still, Oceania is us."[6] In rejecting the separation he associates with European colonial rule, Hau'ofa inspires a more sympathetic, even utopic, conception of the relationship between humans and ocean. The struggle of the shipwrecked sailor does not always match the activist's plea for liberty, but the sense of the ocean as human as well as alien space informs my reading of the ecological encounter between European sailors and global waters. Bringing with them mariners' tools and the conceptual resources of early modern Christianity, these sailors were ill prepared to face the depths of Keller's tehomic theology or the ecstatic mobility of Hau'ofa's "sea of islands." The wet pressure of shipwreck forced these things to the surface.

In the Hyperobjects's Belly: John King's *Lectures upon Jonas* (1597)

No one has ever hit the sea harder than Jonah. In a story of shipwreck and redemption, which forms a basic template for the catastrophic encounter between humans and the ocean, the book of Jonah occupies the spiritual center of early modern Christian ideas about the oceanic globe. John King's monumental volume *Lectures upon Jonas,* printed in 1597 and reprinted five times before 1618, contains his yearlong cycle of sermons on the Old Testament parable, originally given at York in 1594.[7] King, who went on to become Bishop of London and was appointed by Archbishop Whitgift to give the first Sunday sermon at court after Queen Elizabeth's death, preached Jonah as an imperative for religious reform.[8] Beyond King's sectarian agenda, however, his sermons on Jonah reveal an awareness of the immense cultural stakes in the developing relationship between England and the sea. As Melville's Father Mapple would show much later, the hidden spiritual truth of Jonah's encounter with the whale contains an attack on land-based ideas of order. "Woe to him," cries Mapple, expressing the dilemma inside which all theological interpreters of shipwreck find themselves, "who seeks to pour oil on the waters when God has brewed them into a gale!" (53).[9] King's sermons attempt not to calm the sea nor even survive the storm but to find theological meaning within the disaster. Out of chaos, the preacher finds meaning.

My reading of King's Jonah suggests the salt vastness the prophet touches represents the ecological force Timothy Morton calls "the hyperobject." Comprising objects that exceed human scales and subtending today's age of catastrophes both physically and metaphorically, Morton's hyperobjects challenge human perceptions. His concept responds to global warming, but it has oceanic resonance. One of his phrases for the impact of hyperobjects on modern culture, in fact, employs shipwreck as its central metaphor: "The Titanic of modernity hits the iceberg of hyperobjects."[10] The fracture that hyperobjects generate in human conceptions of the world—Morton's introduction calls their advent "a quake in being" (1–24)—requires that human bodies accept a deeper ecological engagement inside what Morton elsewhere terms "the mesh," a nonhierarchical, nonanthropocentric understanding of physical ecology.[11] While Morton is more attached than I am to the term Anthropocene and while his post-Romantic focus tends to obscure pre-1800 elements of human history, the hyperobject provides a productive way to think about the ocean in its relationship to human subjects. In fact, many of the elements Morton sees as essential qualities of the hyperobject—it must be viscous, nonlocal, interobjective, phasing, and temporally undulating, and it must reveal human hypocrisy, lameness, and weakness—seem analogous to the ecocultural resonance of the ocean.[12] If the ocean is the hyperobject par excellence of human history, then shipwreck represents the most intimate encounter of human body and oceanic force. After Odysseus, Jonah occupies this human heart more deeply than perhaps any other figure.

At the center of Jonah's tale, the prophet who Melville calls "God-fugitive" accepts that he must be cast into the sea and thereby embrace maritime disorder. In King's telling, this sympathetic embrace of the deeps comes after a sustained elaboration of the prophet's terrestrial nature. To Jonah the earth is proper to humans, whereas the sea is God's domain. Like Shakespeare's Boatswain, he would have preferred a dry death. "And though the sea hath no mercy at all," Jonah says in King's sermon, "threating both heaven and hel with the billowes thereof at this time, and bearing a countance of nothing but destruction, & it had beene a blessing unto me, to haue died on land in some better sort, or to have gained the favor of a more mercifull death, yet *cast me into the sea,* and let the barbarous creature glut itself."[13] This sacrificial turn, which King treats as Jonah's typological anticipation of Christ (192–93), launches Jonah into marine depths. This moment of discovery, of verticality, in which the human body leaves its proper domains and abandons even the provisional home of the ship, literalizes shipwreck on both human and oceanic scales. A body goes into the ocean, and in that encounter, as King interprets Jonah, a national drama of repentance and purification begins. King, who knew John Donne when both men were attached to the household of Thomas Egerton in the late 1590s and whose sermons may have influenced Donne's maritime poetry, sees in Jonah's descent not just the Christian typological metaphor that is the overt content of his sermon but also a physical encounter that becomes spiritual:

> The world is a sea, as I find it compared, swelling with pride; & vanglory the winde to heave it up; blew and divide with envy, boiling with wrath, deepe with coventousness, swallowing and drinking in al by oppression, dangerful for the rockes of presumption and desperation, rising with the waves of passions and perterbations, ebbing and flowing with constancie, brinish and salte with inquitie, and finally *Mare amarum,* a bitter and unsavory sea with all kinde of miserie. (209)

Like Younge, King locates his essential self, and his nation's, in salt water. Like Melville, the preacher looks into the waters for "the image of the ungraspable phantom of life" (20). Jonah's shipless wreck isolates the theological kernel of all shipwreck stories: going into the ocean makes it possible, sometimes, to emerge changed.

As he enters the water, Jonah represents sailor as much as prophet. King, thinking of the increasing visibility of English sailors and sea travel in his own lifetime, assimilates Jonah to the mariner who puts his life in oceanic peril: "to put his life within four inches of death, & what safety is it, in comparison, to see the raging of the waters from the sea banckes" (47). Referring to Lucretius's celebrated injunction about the philosophic pleasures of watching a shipwreck from a safe vantage point on land, King describes Jonah as sailor and prophet on the maritime vanguard of English culture.[14] "Sailors and adventurors," says King, "are neither amongst the living, nor amongst the dead: they hang between both, ready to offer up their soules to every flawe of winde, and billow of water" (58). This medial position gestures toward an ecological openness in sailors, as in King's description of their bodies "offer[ed] up" to wind and water. Jonah the shipwrecked sailor combines theological and ecological awareness; his plight performs the orthodox typology of Christ's sacrifice and embraces the physical discontinuities of transoceanic travel. Although he never reaches the far end of the Mediterranean, King's Jonah epitomizes blue ecological experience. He does not sail on the full oceanic globe of Drake or Cavendish, but his transformative encounter with salt water provides a powerful symbol of wet ecological globalization.

The ecology that dooms Jonah speaks the language of storm-filled sea. To the sailors on board, the only legible message is hostility: "The sea is in armes against the mariners themselves" (173). King, however, emphasizes that the stormy waters issue a command to repent and deliver God's message: "The sea went, it had a charge for Ionas, as Ionas had for Niniveh" (172). These two positions—the sea as opaque hostility, as the sailors see it, and the sea as divine command, as King interprets it—together create an indecipherable paradox. The interpretive task set before Jonah requires him to untangle theological message from environmental chaos. Faced with this near-impossible task, the first response is, in Melville's phrase, "hideous sleep" (51). King, like Melville, sees this sleep as a refusal of God's assigned task:

> The sleep of Ionas is a strange, prodigious, and brutish kind of sleepe, as ever I hearde of. The windes rage, the sea roareth, the ship tottereth and groaneth, the mariners fear, and pray, and cry, every soule in the ship, so many persons unto so many Gods . . . Ionas in the meantime . . . sleepeth (78).

Sleep, an utter lack of human attention and reversion to a semivegetative existence, here represents willful ecological and interpersonal blindness. (In refusing to act in response to our age of ecological crises, perhaps the twenty-first century sleeps Jonah's sleep?) Jonah refuses sea, wind, ship, and mariners. He also refuses the ocean's lesson in mutability. King later insists that to be in the ocean entails embracing instability: "Our liues are nothing but uncertaintie. . . . We are tumbled and tossed in a vessel as fraile as the ship was, which everie streame of calamitie is readie to breake in shivers, where neither anchor nor rudder is lefte, neither head, nor hand, nor stomacke is in case to give us comfort" (266). Again paralleling Younge's ship-body, King imagines Jonah in the depths as a body without stays. His descent is the core ecological and theological experience, going down to meet his God.

Finding the whale deep below the surface, Jonah represents the sinner at his nadir. King emphasizes that the prayer from the whale's belly epitomizes an ideal of reaching out to God from moral alienation: "Ionas might truly say in a double sense *de profundis clamavi, & abyssus abyssu, invocat, out of the deep haue I cried, & one depth calleth upon another,* who lay both in the bottom of a mo[n]ster and in the lowest gulf of affliction that every soule was plunged into" (309). The whale doubles the sea: both represent supreme exile from God's heaven and human existence. Describing Jonah as archetypical shipwrecked sailor, King locates him in a supremely alien space. With neither ship nor coast in sight, "he was not onely in the sea, but in the midst, the heart, the inwardst secretes and celles of it, as the heart of a living thing is midmost, and inwardst unto it" (345). Like the whaleship *Essex,* whose encounter with a sperm whale in 1821 would help shape *Moby-Dick,* Jonah has been given access to the "heart of the sea."[15] As King imagines his plight, Jonah encounters the full seething force of the World Ocean: "Hee was not onelye in the hearte of the sea, but of the *seas.* There is but one universal and maine sea, which is the girdle to the dry land" (345). Recognizing that the unity of the oceans overwrites the grammatical distinction between singular and plural—all oceans are one ocean—King imagines Jonah directly encountering the wet globalization that was reshaping English culture at the end of the sixteenth century. Even more than Ulysses in the surf, Jonah in the abyss receives the full force of the ocean. It changes him.

The ultimate form of Jonah's change may be spiritual, but the impact makes itself felt first through his emotions. The surrounding waters seep into the prophet's body, making manifest the strains that global forces put on human flesh. At this moment Jonah is an ecological prophet, feeling on his bare skin the inchoate vastness of the ocean's global unity. If the central claim of Morton's hyperobjects is that these massively distributed assemblages, such as climate change itself, cannot be felt directly by humans, Jonah's extreme immersion describes how it would feel to touch the hyperobject. The waters and the whale speak to him: "There is no agony nor passion of the sea but Ionas feels it. The disquietmentes of that element, are either the meetinge of the freshe and salt waters together, or the ebbing and flowing of it; [/] or the waves and surges that arise, either by windes in the aire, or by flaws and expirations from the caverns of the earth; with all these is Ionas acquainted" (345–46). Coming to know the abyssal depths, becoming "acquainted" with this least hospitable part of the planet, remakes Jonah from fugitive to redemptive preacher. His triumph in Nineveh will come from his close identification with God's private truth: "They *believed* GOD not Ionas, although in meaninge it is all one, they believed GOD as the author, Ionas as the minister. GOD in Ionas, or Ionas from GOD, and for GODS sake" (461). This supernatural union was born at sea.

Jonah's version of the story of the shipwrecked sailor plunges deep into the wetness of global ecology. As King carefully unwinds the biblical language, he cites Ovid's description of Ceyx's shipwreck (*Metamorphoses* 11) to emphasize that, from the human point of view, ocean waves during a storm appear to be warring with each other: "The Poet notably expresseth them in the shipwracke of Caeix that they played upon the shippe, as engines and brakes of warre play upons castles" (347). Alongside Jonah's confinement, however, the sermons that describe the depths include hints of fantastical freedom. King repeatedly notes that Jonah's voyage is confined to the Mediterranean, "the Mid-land sea" (346). His whale-borne voyage from Jaffa through the Hellespont and Bosporus to the Euxine Sea was "often encumbred with straightes, and never had cause to complaine overmuch of liberty" (362). But alongside this land-encircled navigation appear hints of the larger transoceanic voyages that English sailors had recently begun. "If," King speculates, "he had past through the Ocean, where he had gained more sea roum, and the continent being farther off, would haue yelded a liberal current, and lesse haue endaungered him" (362). Oddly recalling boosters of transatlantic settlement such as Richard Hakluyt, King's fleeting vision of a "liberal" ocean does not displace the horror of Jonah's abyssal descent. Instead, it briefly flies a liberating flag, gesturing toward an oceanic expansion of English culture. Releasing Jonah and his whale into vast oceanic sea room, with the Boatswain's line, "Blow till thou burst they wind, if room enough!" (*Tempest,* 1.1.7–8), echoing in our ears, anticipates the global experiences of English sailors and fleets. As King recognizes, there is a partial safety in landlessness, paid for by supreme disorientation and deterratorialization. Even Jonah, the deepest-diving shipwrecked sailor, cannot abide that full sea.

Bare Survival: Edmond Pet in 1613

Discounting Jonah's supernatural deliverance as unrepeatable, the shipwreck microgenre follows two basic narratives: survival and catastrophe. A short pamphlet published in London in 1613 unfolds the happier possibility by emphasizing the anthropotechnic skills of the mariner in alliance with divine opacity. The anonymous text frames Edmond Pet's story doubly as lamentable tragedy and wonderful deliverance. The full title names the event both triumph and disaster: *Lamentable Newes, Shewing the wonderfull de-liuerance of Maister Edmond Pet Sayler, and Maister of a Ship, dwelling in Seething Lane in London, neere Barking Church. With other strange things late-ly hapned concerning these great windes and tempestuous wea-ther, both at Sea and Lande.* The pamphlet orients the reader toward religion in its opening sentences. "Good reader," it begins, "I haue here set downe unto thy view, and for thy example to amendment, the great hurt and losses that hath beene both at Sea and Land, but especially the wonderful preseruation of one Maister Edmond Pet Sayler, and Maister of a ship, and part owner."[16] The tension between wet loss and dry preservation produces a multiple readerly awareness, in which Pet's exemplary experience stands out above his peers'. Survival is not just a theological reward for good behavior; it emerges through human endurance, political and religious affinity, and even a familiar classical poetic model. The narrative uses these tools to dry out its wet core. It displays versatile multimodel anthropotechnics and suggests the possible affiliation of the sailor with the believer.

When God's storm strikes Pet's ship, the narrative moves quickly past familiar invocations of God's will to the multiplicity and confusion of Benjamin's "now-time." Lacking a clear depiction of technical maritime labor—the author knows what a mast is but cannot distinguish among "certaine cords or lines" (4)—the storm scene provides four distinct explanations for the ship's survival. These present themselves, perhaps in order of importance, as follows: first, "Gods prouidence"; then, "the great care of this Maister Pet"; then, "sore labour" by others on board; and finally, "earnest praier unto the Lord, night and day of those in the ship" (3). These four causes fall neatly into two pairs of divine and human efforts, with providence and prayer on the divine side and the cares and labors of Pet and the crew on humanity's. Pet's nautical expertise, however, builds a bridge between things human and divine. His skill facilitates Providential resolution better than the less ordered labors and prayers of the crew; out of disorder, the Master and the Lord produce order. As the storm worsens, however, the human component of that order, Pet's seamanship, gets overmatched, and he and the other sailors assume the same passive position, "so that then they did wholy relie upon Gods mercy, ceasing from their labours" (3). The narrative progression from confused activity to passive resignation measures the human engagement with the storm. The narrative's oscillation between these forms reveals its hybrid poetics. The story it tells is both God's and the sailor's.

After nautical efforts fail, Pet switches tactics and gives a "godly speech" (3). Pet's prayer is fairly typical of the shipwreck genre; he asks God "to deliver us from this great danger" (3) and cites the Old Testament examples of Jonah, Susannah, and Daniel as well as several New Testament miracles as hopeful parallels. In political terms Pet's speech unifies; now that the crew no longer functions as working sailors, Pet binds them together as a community of believers. "Let us kneele downe," (3) he admonishes the crew. Pet here parallels Aeneas unifying his crew during the storm that wrecks them in Carthage (*Aeneid* 1.113–21).[17] Pet, however, cannot quite accomplish Aeneas's task. The ship's subsequent failure ruptures his fragile political body: "The ship began to sinke deeper and deeper into the Sea, whereupon euery one began to shift for himself in laying hold some upon one thing, and some upon another" (4). From orderly "labour" and Pet's "care," the ship of state becomes chaos—which is to say, ocean. To work at sea means living in this undifferentiated state, what King describes as the "uncertain and variable lives" of all seamen.[18] In this mutable world all the crewmembers and passengers except Pet perish. To encounter the ocean means being alone in God's wet hands.

To survive the inrush of the sea requires Pet to devise a way to distinguish himself from oceanic disorder. He sets himself above the crew literally and symbolically. First clearing away the now-useless ship's tackle, Pet climbs the mainmast where, modeling himself after an earlier classical hero, "he tied himself, for feare least by the strength of the winde and raine, he should be blowne off into the Sea" (5). Pet lashes himself to the mast to avoid the hostile ocean rather than enticing Sirens, but like Odysseus he uses maritime tools—rope and the mast—to preserve himself alone. The resonant image of Pet on the mast, where he survives for the remaining forty-eight hours of the storm, represents a combination of skilled human labor—Pet "made shift to get up to the top of the Mast" (5)—and divine forbearance. The narrative creates in Pet's position a two-sided symbol, gesturing both toward the value of maritime skills and the abjection of the human subject before God. The Master, now linked to his ship, remains above the sea, but barely so.

This bifurcated allegorical structure, in which events in the world are legible in themselves and also coded references to Providential meaning, extends through the sailor's deliverance. Two ships pass him by, the first English and coldhearted and the second Dutch, warlike, and full of "kindness and mercy . . . like the good *Samaritane*" (6). The second ship, which may represent the Dutch Reformed Church, saves Pet and brings him to shore in Harwich, where even his wife and friends do not recognize him, "by reason he was swelled of such bignes, and so changed with sitting, as I told you before 48. hours in the winde and raine" (6). Out of the ordeal emerges a physically changed and theologically purged Master.[19] The pamphlet concludes that these catastrophes represent the wages of an angry God "for our sinnes" (8). Pet's narrative itself, however, focuses on the subjective experience of human suffering, with attention to the scant resources, especially seamanship and prayer, on which human beings can depend at sea. The bifurcation of *Lamentable Newes* and *wonderfull deliuerance* provides a vision of early modern historical experience at odds with itself. The hybrid human-and-divine poetics toward which Pet grasps at once eludes the reader and transforms the Master.

"Our Sea of Islands"

Epeli Hau'ofa's hymn to oceanic connectedness sits oddly alongside Pet's struggles with a hostile ocean, but both present visceral, physical connections between human and oceanic bodies. The warm waters of Fiji and the Pacific have, in Hau'ofa's depiction, a more sympathetic feel than the cold North Sea above which Pet lashes himself to the mast, but both writers imagine human and oceanic bodies united. The fear that Pet and his men share of sinking "deeper into the sea" represents a vertical allegory, which contrasts the power of God in the heavens against hellish oceanic depths. In this context Pet on the mast strains away from sea toward sky. Against this religiously inflected verticality, I juxtapose Hau'ofa's expansiveness. His world view combines supernatural verticality with immense horizontal reach. Writing of Pacific navigators before the arrival of European ships, he explains that "their universe comprised not only land surfaces, but the surrounding ocean as far as they could traverse and exploit it, the underworld with its fire-controlling and earth-shaking denizens, and the heavens above with their hierarchies of powerful gods and named stars and constellations that people could count on to guide their ways across the seas" (31). To this open, mobile, oceanic space, Hau'ofa argues, Europeans brought confining lines, right angles, and property divisions: "It was continental men, Europeans and Americans, who drew imaginary lines across the sea, making colonial boundaries that, for the first time, confined ocean peoples to tiny spaces" (31). Had Pet been looking for ecological openness, rather than terrestrial safety, in his encounter with the North Sea, he might have seen the waters differently.

In practical terms, however, Pet's dilemma, like his crew's, is the threat of drowning. As the fate of Thacher's cousin Avery has already shown, at the bottom of the oceanic encounter lies death. The rhetorical and theological efforts to dry out Pet's experience suggest that the basic Providentialist narrative structure fears wetness. Like Thacher, King, and other theological writers, for Pet the ocean represents a divine alterity that exceeds human endurance. Had Pet chosen Hau'ofa's conception of the sea–human relationship, he might have tried swimming or, perhaps, casting himself into the rough waters in a small boat. My ecological analysis does not suggest new ways for sailors to survive stormy seas but instead attaches different meanings to their efforts to do so. Being adrift in a storm like Pet, shrinking away from cold hostile waters, puts the shipwrecked sailor in an impossible position. This dilemma, however, better represents oceanic reality than do fantasies of Dutch rescue. All shipwrecked sailors crave rescue, even those who, like Robinson Crusoe, manage to survive on their own. The lesson of ecological globalization and the Naufragocene is that rescue never lasts. Landfalls are temporary.

Jonathan Dickinson and the Gulf Stream: *Gods Protecting Providence*

Hau'ofa's sense of maritime connectedness among Pacific islanders also speaks to the life and writing of Quaker merchant Jonathan Dickinson. Dickinson, who was born in Jamaica, was shipwrecked when relocating to the mainland in 1696. His account of his adventures, which was first published in Philadelphia in 1699, describes a life richly saturated by the symbolic and physical presence of the sea. Dickinson details his survival of a wreck on the Florida coast near Jupiter Island in September 1696 and his voyage north from there to Saint Augustine, where he arrived in November. (The account also describes his subsequent journey to Charlestown and eventually Philadelphia, where his party joined the sizable Quaker population). Dickinson's memoir translates the ancient theological parable of shipwreck into the idiom of early modern Providential history. The narrative, which went through multiple editions in late seventeenth-century Philadelphia and London and was also published in Dutch and German, has recently been mined by historians for its portrait of shifting relationships among English, Spanish, and Native American communities. The most sustained recent critical engagement with the text, by the historian Amy Turner Bushnell, shows how modern understandings of Native American culture can help us read through Dickinson's own prejudices and blindness.[20] My reading of Dickinson's narrative departs from this historical focus on multicultural encounters, and as a result it sidesteps what historians such as Bushnell consider the most interesting parts of the story. Instead, I explore the text's tantalizingly brief depictions of oceanic space, including the shipwreck itself and the voyage up Florida's coastline. Rather than focusing on Dickinson's engagements with Native Americans, I ask what he found in the sea. His story includes castaways and cannibals but is also about coming to terms with the ocean.

Representations of the ocean in early modern and even modern culture often treat the sea as an image of hostile nature.[21] The ocean for Dickinson, as more broadly for early modern culture, represents an unstable confluence of theological mysteries, physical challenges, and narrative variety. My analysis of the early modern sea in Dickinson's text suggests how the fluid element can help restructure traditional borders and borderlands. The ocean facilitates movement and destabilizes structures. It threatens to dissolve all things. Thinking about the ocean as a space of profound and inhuman meaning, rather than an emptiness to be crossed, transforms a narrative of maritime disaster into a parable about humanity's encounter with an inhuman world.

I begin by looking closely at the title page of Dickinson's first edition, published in Philadelphia just two years after his party's arrival there. The main title, *God's Protecting Providence,* links the book to an established seventeenth-century genre of "remarkable providences" that includes collections by James Janeway in London (1674) and Increase Mather in Boston (1684). Looking down the page, however, reveals two distinct versions of the dangers undergone. The first threat, as the full title reveals, was *the devouring Waves of the Sea, amongst which they Suffered Shipwrack.* It is the second threat, however, that has attracted attention from modern critical readers: *the cruelly devouring jawes of the inhumane CANIBALS of FLORIDA.* The typesetter, perhaps anticipating the market, used capital letters to emphasize the human threats, but even so, the ocean precedes the cannibals. The two biblical quotations on the bottom of the page also reflect this human-or-ocean duality. Psalm 93, cited first, emphasizes the power of the Lord to dominate "the noise of many Waters . . . the mighty Waves of the Sea." Psalm 74, cited second, describes "habitations of Cruelty" in the "dark places of the earth." My focus is on the waters, and I suggest that Dickinson's narrative, though it lacks Younge's manic focus on physicality and seamanship, also represents a fantasy of sympathetic union between the ocean and divine power. Dickinson does not quite share Younge's belief in a ship-body, but his narrative repeatedly hints at a saltwater poetics of ecological alliances.

The story of *God's Protecting Providence* entails transoceanic relocation. Dickinson's decision to leave Jamaica in 1696, where he had been born and where he, along with his fellow merchants, suffered devastating losses following the 1692 earthquake, appears to have been motivated by the desire to open a branch of the family business in Philadelphia. He was not destitute, since he carried £1,500 worth of cargo on the barketine *Reformation* when she set sail, but he also carried his wife and their five-month-old infant son, so he was presumably planning to stay on the mainland. The party that survived the shipwreck included eight mariners plus the master Joseph Kirle; Dickinson's family; another Quaker merchant; the well-known Quaker missionary Robert Barrow, who would expire upon reaching Philadelphia and whose fame in Quaker circles probably motivated the publication of the narrative; and Dickinson's eleven slaves. This hybrid composite of race, class, and gender differences formed an ungainly whole, as was typical of the polyglot maritime periphery of settlements such as Jamaica.

The tale's oceanic entanglements first appear only to comprise the wreck itself. Except for the title page, little in the opening section of the journal emphasizes the ocean as such. The first entry begins matter-of-factly: on August 23, "Being in company with twelve or thirteen sail of merchant-men under the convoy of the *Hampshire* Frigate . . . [we] sailed from Port Royal in Jamaica . . . being bound for Philadelphia" (3). Perhaps Dickinson was no sailor, or was not interested in navigation, because the early entries are short and straightforward: "We lost sight of the *Hampshire* Frigate," on August 31, as well as, "Made the table-land of the Havana," on September 14. Before coming to Havana, they received what surely must have seemed, at least in retrospect, an ill omen: "This afternoon came a tornado from the land; and our master being on the quarterdeck, our boom jibing knocked him down and broke his leg: which accident was grevious to him and us: but I having things suitable, with a little experience set it" (4). The injury to Joseph Kirle left Dickinson the de facto leader of the party, and this brief episode, which represents a key moment in his assumption of leadership, also emphasizes the sudden destructive power of wind and sea. In the face of the tornado, Kirle's skill in seamanship could not avoid a jibing boom, though Dickinson's own "little experience" in medicine proved valuable. This skill introduces an anthropotechnic element to the narrative, though his expertise appears largely to exclude maritime matters.

The real disaster came with the arrival of oceanic power on September 23, after the frigate had started following the Gulf Stream up the Florida coast. A northeast storm had begun two days previously, but the shipwreck struck with as little warning as the breaking of Kirle's leg: "About one o'clock in the morning we felt our vessel strike some few strokes, and then she floated again for five or six minutes before she ran fast aground, where she beat violently at first" (5). Suddenly stopped, the ship became vulnerable: "The seas broke over us that we were in a quarter of an hour floating in the cabin" (5). Unwilling to attempt to abandon ship in the darkness, they waited until the sun rose, at which time God's providence also appeared: "And at daylight we perceived we were upon the shore, on a beach lying in the breach of the sea which at times as the surges of the sea reversed was dry" (5). As in Younge's pamphlet, the story of the wreck bifurcates itself into happy and sad tales: "We rejoiced at this our preservation from the raging seas; but at the same instant feared the sad consequences that followed" (5). Dickinson presents the sudden, shocking shipwreck with no sustained consideration of its causes or meaning—it just happens and, then, quickly gives way to the first encounter with Native Americans on shore. The arrival of these figures, and their "very furious and bloody" countenances (6), structures the bulk of the narrative, as the party passes through a series of different native groups, pretending unconvincingly to be Spanish in hopes that they would then be passed on to the Spanish settlement at St. Augustine.

Dickinson's turn to human social relations on the Florida coast, however, should not overshadow his abrupt oceanic encounter. Like other religious memoirists, he attributes his party's preservation to "the Lord in whom we trusted" (7), but his minimal description of the crew's management of the vessel does not allow the reader to infer any sort of human errancy on the part of the sailors. His lack of technical detail inverts the expertise displayed by the boatswain's mate who narrates the sinking of the *S. João*. Maritime disaster instead appears to be the basic state of human existence; to strike aground suddenly in the middle of the night in a storm comprises, to borrow Younge's title, "the state of a Christian." Unlike the theological morals drawn by Increase Mather or James Janeway, however, Dickinson's story does not explicitly call attention to the hand of God. Rather, shipwreck on the Florida coast appears as a simple, stark reality. Perhaps a man born in Jamaica who lived through the 1692 earthquake expected such experiences.

The two months the party spent traveling up the coast of Florida saw complex cultural interactions, and Dickinson appears largely at a loss to explain the motivations or understandings of his native interlocutors. Often, Dickinson's infant son, who was repeatedly saved from starvation by being nursed by a Native American woman (26, 33, 36–37), serves as a kind of interface or bridge between the groups. It is also possible, however, to cull from the party's adventures a few examples of how maritime skills and technologies help to orient them. In the mosquito- and sand-fly-infested wilderness of Florida, it was the sea, not the land, that was relatively familiar. Traveling north, they made better time by sea than by land. The survival of Dickinson's party was largely the product of their engagement with native Americans, but they also needed their maritime skills.

Among the items that the castaways salvaged from the wreck were the basic tools of maritime orientation: "one of the master's quadrants, and seamen's calendar, with two other books" (11). These items enabled "our mate . . . [to take] an observation, and we found ourselves to be in the latitude of twenty-seven degrees and eight minutes" (11). By fixing their location through maritime technology, the party created conceptual as well as geographic stability. Dickinson emphasizes that "some of the Indians were offended at [the observation] . . . [and] one would draw an arrow to shoot [the mate]" (11). The symbolic tension seems clear: the tools of celestial navigation countered the party's dependence on Native American helpers. Though Dickinson does not say so, the logic of his narrative implies that using these tools gave some notional independence to the shipwrecked party. When the master made another observation toward the end of the month that showed the party to have traveled thirty-seven minutes north (roughly forty-three miles), this knowledge reestablished some sense of order for the group.

It also seems significant that the bulk of the northward progress toward St. Augustine was accomplished by sea, not land. Dickinson's party depended upon Native American help for canoes and paddlers, but the sea was the most viable passageway for most of the trip. The party could not sleep on the small boats, so each night brought them back to threatening land, but in Dickinson's description the sea sometimes becomes a place of divine harmony. When they left the Indian town of Jece (near today's Vero Beach), where they spent most of October, they rowed north with supernatural inspiration: "It pleased God to strengthen us in this our condition, so that we rowed all this day without ceasing until three hours after it was dark, by which time we got to an Indian town" (44). The farther north they traveled, the more essential it became that they travel by sea, so that when they were just "five or six leagues to Augustine," they begged for passage in a Spanish canoe, "being all of us lamed and stiff" (57). The narrative continually emphasizes what the Spanish governor of St. Augustine finally termed "the poverty of the country" (61), that the land in Florida was inhospitable, but Dickinson also describes, while he did not always emphasize it, the relative hospitality of the ocean.

Dickinson never suggests that the ocean's practical value emerges from its divine essence. The theological key to his narrative is instead the aged and sick missionary Robert Barrow. In the narrative's most explicit theological reference, Barrow expounds to the castaways a verse from Revelations 3:10: "Because thou hast kept the word of my patience, I also will keep thee." (14). To Barrow, the Lord's promise to preserve his faithful implies that his party will survive being "cast among a barbarous and heathenish people, if that it was His blessed will, he would preserve and deliver us from amongst them, that our names might not be buried in oblivion" (14). Barrow's prayer, then, directly counteracts the cannibals on the book's title page; the Quaker celebrates God's power to preserve the faithful amid human hostility.

Alongside Barrow's Providentialist understanding of their plight, however, Dickinson himself describes what he calls his "secret hope" that the party will be preserved. This hope springs forth at the sea. Dickinson relates that their maritime labor created this hidden faith on November 13, two days before the party staggered into St. Augustine: "Thus striving in a deep exercise of body and mind we traveled on, admiring God's goodness in preserving us thus far through so many eminent dangers. In the sense of which a secret hope would arise (though involved with human doubts and fear) that the Lord would yet preserve us" (53). The contrast between Dickinson's "secret hope" that emerges from maritime travail and mobility and Barrow's more passive theological plea for divine rescue uncovers a half-articulated maritime anthropotechnic logic underlying Dickinson's narrative, in which the sea appears more amenable for human agency than does the land. The apparent hospitality of the sea had clear limits; the party still feared for survival during a fierce storm in which they "imagined that the sea was broke in upon the land, and that [they] should be drowned" (32). But while the wild coast of Florida was foreign and inhospitable, the warm waters offshore presented a space on which Dickinson and the crew and passengers of the *Reformation* could help themselves.

Dickinson's implied construction of the sea as a space for human agency helps add blue ecological meaning to his narrative of cultural contact. Especially in the context of contact narratives, there is a strong tendency, visible in early modern writers such as Dickinson and also in modern critics, to view the ocean as a means of transport that recedes in importance once the shore has been reached. A narrative like Dickinson's, if read carefully, suggests that the ocean is an abiding presence and, for Europeans in the New World, a dangerous but productive reservoir of knowledge and agency. The maritime skills of Native Americans, among those of other marginalized peoples, should not be overlooked, though Dickinson does not emphasize them in his narrative.[22] The back-and-forth oscillation between land and sea structures *God's Protecting Providence* in symbolic as well as narrative terms.

On a broader scale, placing Dickinson's journal in the context of early modern theological writings about maritime experience, from John King through the seventeenth-century compilations of Mather and Janeway, clarifies the theology of the maritime encounter. This theology is not only a historical phenomenon. Just as Younge's broadside posits a deep and intimate connection between human bodies and salt water, so Dickinson's narrative unfolds their necessary entanglement in the adventures of a seventeenth-century merchant. Dickinson may not have loved the sea, but he depended on it for wealth and mobility in ways that connect him to the oceanic celebrations of Hau'ofa. The religious core of Dickinson's Providence may in fact contain tehomic insights, in Keller's sense, in that his preservation emerges from sea more than land. Settled among the Quakers in riverside Philadelphia, Dickinson may seem an odd choice as apostle for an oceanic ecology. But his story, read against its orthodox grain, reveals the controlling force of the ocean in mercantile and theological expansion.

"Many Famous and Wonderful Instances": James Janeway's Legacy

The Nonconformist minister James Janeway is most famous for his account of children being converted to true religion, but his *Legacy to his Friends* (1674) contains a series of sea deliverances that offer comparable consolations. These moral tales, later republished under the title *A Token for Mariners* (1711) with expanded front matter, use the leverage of maritime disaster to promote theological comfort. Like Thacher's letter, the publication of which in Increase Mather's *Essay for the Recording of Illustrious Providences* (1684) helped establish the sea providence subgenre, Janeway's book emphasizes God's special care of his faithful in extremis. To be at sea in this context means to be disoriented in a spiritual and also protoecological sense, to be alienated from the place God has provided for humankind. In this place divine aid is essential.

The 1711 expanded edition of Janeway's compilation emphasizes the tension between maritime skill and theological faith. Unlike Pet or even Dickinson, Janeway insists that faith alone must define the believer's attitude toward the sea. This split, more than the sometimes repetitive elements of the volume's twenty-seven narratives, registers the intellectual and theological dilemma the sea posed for orthodox writers. Especially in Janeway's prefatory prose, he sought to subordinate professional maritime practices, with their imperative for skilled labor, to orthodox theological doctrine. In a "Preface to the Reader; and Particularly to Mariners, and other Seafaring Men" added to the 1711 edition, the distinction between faith and seamanship looms large. A paraphrase of Psalm 107 implies that sailors occupy a privileged theological position: "Though God's Wonders are every where visible . . . yet more particularly are they Evident to Seafaring-Men, whose Business is in the Great Waters, and their Lives exposed more than Others to innumerable Hazards and Dangers."[23] The solution for these men, who "as it were, carry their Lives in their Hands," is to use "their best security . . . wholly to rely on the Providence and Protection of him whose Power the Winds and Waves obey" (A3). As if refereeing a contest between God and seamanship, Janeway the editor presses his case for the divine via the example of Saint Paul, whose ship wrecked on Malta but whose fellow passengers were saved. The example of this deliverance, which was provided "for a praying Paul's sake" (A3v), as Janeway claims, displaces seamanship in favor of faith: "A steadfast Reliance on God in all their Dangers, nay, at all times, . . . is the best and surest Anchor-hold and Security that recourse to can be had" (A4). The narratives he presents, which often include detailed descriptions of seamanlike labor, sometimes work at cross-purposes to this editorial declaration. The inclusion of a series of special "Prayers to be Used by Seafaring Men" (149–60), however, all of which exclude specific mention of maritime skills and labor, reinforce the primacy of theological control.

The frontispiece illustration of the *Token for Mariners* lays out the human dilemma of Janeway's God-only stance (Figure 2). At the center of the woodcut sits a ship at sea, tossed at a slight angle by the waves, with sailors on deck laboring to keep control. The dominant figure is a glowing eye, the light from which streams down in five distinct beams toward the ship. This divine light intersects with a lightning bolt just above the ship's mainmast, so that the mast itself appears struck both by God's care and the storm's rage. Orthodox belief requires the unity of divine love and the storm, and this particular overlap, sitting just above the center of the image, draws together three sets of lines—the vertically descending rays of God's love, the jagged violence of the lightning, and the fragile upwardness of the mainmast—in a complex figuration of human dependence, divine control, and ecological instability. Left out of this allegorical structure, however, are three Jonah-like shipwreck victims who cling to flotsam in the water at the bottom center of the image. These three sailors, whose sparsely rendered faces turn toward the viewer, make an ethical appeal beyond the emblematic qualities of the struggling ship. The light of divine love seems not to touch them as they float in a wild sea. They represent the limits, or perhaps the necessary costs, of Janeway's orthodox view of God and the ocean. Castaway by God's storms, these mariners need the anthropotechnic skills that Janeway's editorial labors dismiss.

Aesthetic Storms

The solution to Janeway's dilemma lies not in orthodoxy but poetry. Janeway's miracle tales attempt to exclude human labors, but his Christian vision also obliquely connects to Hau'ofa's pan-Pacific connectivism. The Pacific Islander and the seventeenth-century English minister both imagine that it may be possible for humans to engage directly with oceanic pressures. For Hau'ofa oceanic navigators can glimpse a more-than-human order, whereas for Janeway only divine revelation can glimpse such truths. Oceanic engagement for both leads either to rescue, for fortunate sailors, or to watery death. From an ecological point of view, however, entanglement itself is the main story. Touching the World Ocean and not recoiling from its vastness entails feeling the wet globe in a physical way.

For literary writers this maritime awareness would become an aesthetic value. Joseph Conrad, who describes sailing as an "elemental moral beauty" (Mack 134), treats the sea storm as an occasion for divine awareness:

> If you would know the age of the earth, look upon the sea in a storm. The grayness of the whole immense surface, the wind furrows upon the faces of the waves, the great masses of foam, tossed about and waving, like matted white locks, give to the sea in a gale the appearance of hoary age, lusterless, dull, without gleams, as though it had been created before light itself.[24]

Conrad's aesthetic storm recalls Keller's "face of the deep" before the arrival of God's creating light. The storm precedes vision; it represents a preelemental, prefundamental—no fundament lies beneath it—picture of being in the world. Amid this chaos human fictions of order

FIGURE 2. A Providentialist view of shipwreck: the ship is in danger, men cling to a broken mast, but the eye of God looks down unblinking. *A Token for Mariners.* By permission of the Folger Shakespeare Library.

get tossed about. Plunging into the surging waters, it may be possible, for a moment, to take pleasure in dynamism.

Intimations of the possibilities of human–ocean alliance may appear tangential in early modern theological writings. The widely appreciated pleasures of the seashore may be, as Alain Corbin has noted, a product of eighteenth-century historical developments.[25] But as I have previously argued with reference to Shakespeare, the aesthetic virtues of oceanic variety were not lost upon pre-Enlightenment thinkers.[26] W. H. Auden's famous pronouncement that Romanticism "invented" the modern conception of the sea seems massively overstated.[27] Immersion may not be comfortable, but it is transformative. The deep sea, home of monsters and storms, nonetheless appears enticing to desperate sailors such as Jonah or Bulkington. Maritime theologies of Angry Gods ensured that the ocean remained an alien space and also a place of power and mystery.

· CHAPTER 3 ·

Isle of Tempests

Bermuda in the Early Modern Imagination

NO ISLAND IS AN ISLAND.

They are undeniably real things, out there in the ocean, but they do not mean what we want them to mean. These visible structures of coral, rock, dirt, and vegetation assert stability amid the tumult of great waters. Over human lifetimes, islands remain fixed. But they are never isolate, not since the oceans became trade's highways. Isolation is impossible on the global ocean. The symbolic force of islands, their role as havens and homes, never tells the full story. Islands appear as wished-for sanctuaries for shipwrecked sailors, but as in the *The Tempest* and *Robinson Crusoe,* they often prove as treacherous as the waters themselves. According to John Donne, "no man is an island," because there is no separation of any human from the divinely ordained whole: "Every man is a piece of the continent, a part of the main. If a clod be washed away by the sea, Europe is the less."[1] Donne's famous phrase describes human coextension as a landed, continental phenomenon, in which human belonging to a divine whole fashions a corporate "Europe" matched against the "washing" pressure of the sea. The sailor in the poet perhaps recognized an oceanic countermeaning, in which isolate existence founders not just on continental unity but on thalassic interconnection. The geographic and cultural histories of islands insist that these remote places cannot remain isolated. The pressure to connect that characterizes maritime space, which Mediterranean historians Peregrin Horden and Nicholas Purcell describe through the term "ready connectivity," helps reimagine oceanic vastness as a system of nodes and spokes.[2] Islands in the deep oceans, their locations mapped onto shipping lanes by the patterns of the trade winds, become connected points when considered in transoceanic context. Isolated and connected, islands cause shipwrecks and rescue survivors.

No location in early modern English history reveals the paradox of the oceanic island more clearly than Bermuda. It appears in historical and poetic records less as island than as sea-land, a collection of rocks that is also part of the ocean. The imaginative history of these islands, from their poorly documented entry into the European record in the early sixteenth century to their status as long-lived English colony in and after the early seventeenth century, produces a literalized metaphor of dual connection to sea and land. As English sailors expanded onto the Atlantic rim, writers and propagandists extolled the supposedly fertile soil of the New World. Bermuda's beaches and reefs provide an oceanic counterpoint to this fantasy. The history of Bermuda adds saltwater particularity to England's early colonial experience, supplementing land-based legends with a story that was disoriented by the ocean, marked by shipwreck, and never straightforwardly progressive. A mid-Atlantic chain of islands and reefs geographically separate from both the connected arcs of the Caribbean islands and the river-fed hinterlands of the North American continent, Bermuda sat near the heart of the early English experience of the Atlantic. It was the land-sea on which England's North American ventures first wrecked and the strand on which they salvaged themselves.

A Bermuda-inflected analysis of early English settlement on the North Atlantic rim emphasizes the power of oceanic disorientation. As the shipwrecked arrival of the first English settlers shows, this island in the ocean confounded expectations, resembling neither the utopian fantasies of Virginia Company propaganda nor the riches of Spanish Mexico. Bare sand beaches and a gentle climate sheltered the survivors of the *Sea-Venture* wreck in 1609, and Bermuda even provided the wrecked men with enough provisions to rescue the starving colonists at Jamestown when they arrived there, nine months later. But the redemptive narrative that the Virginia Company would trumpet in subsequent years overlooks the alien qualities of the island. Bermuda would become England's second New World colony, and it remains today the United Kingdom's oldest colonial possession, but it never produced the bounty the company wanted. As Michael Jarvis puts it in the opening pages of his award-winning history *In the Eye of All Trade,* Bermuda's perspective on the Atlantic system was comparable to the view "from the deck of a ship."[3] From this unstable platform, the Americas appear as oceanic as continental. Bermuda's maritime connections and its short-lived prosperity during the tobacco boom of the 1620s connected the island to the English economy, but it remained a wet, disorienting outlier.[4]

The idea of insularity, a place that is apart, alone, and unconnected to the wider world, is a fiction derived from geographic observation. Thinking with islands is at least as old as the *Odyssey,* but as European sailors began to move out into the deep ocean during the late-medieval period, islands assumed new symbolic importance. Tiny rocks distributed across the vast Atlantic imply a world less cohesive than the close-knit archipelagoes of the eastern Mediterranean. Simone Pinet describes the growth of late-medieval island thinking as the meeting of many cultural and cartographic strains. Chief among these were the transfer of the idea of sacred wilderness from forest to sea after St. Columba's missionary voyages to the Irish and North Seas in the sixth century. New "idea[s] of isolation" also emerged from changes in landholding practices such as enclosure. Island thinking contributed to the late-medieval vogue of *isolaria,* or island books, after the fifteenth century.[5] Pinet's assertion that in the late-medieval period "insularity [was] a new way of interrogating the real" (155) matches John Gillis's broader claim that "islomania in its many different guises is a central feature of Western culture."[6] Both Pinet and Gillis see the love of islands assuming a fictional trajectory. For Pinet this mania develops out of affinities between chivalric romance and the *isolario* tradition, which eventually produced new hybrid forms, including *Don Quixote* and the early modern atlas. Gillis, by contrast, explores a longer history from the *Odyssey* to the late twentieth century in which the island is a privileged locus of imagination, exploration, and change. Premodern English mariners shared the European islo-obsession that both Pinet and Gillis explore; sixteenth-century English sailors charted the Greek archipelago and touched the island landmarks of the emerging Atlantic system, including the Canaries, the Azores, the Cape Verde Islands, and St. Helena. From St. Columba's mission to Iona forward, also, the archipelagic nature of England became increasingly visible and integrated into public life.[7] Already in possession of an island culture, the English sailors who wrecked on Bermuda in 1609 were primed to interpret its strange land- and seascapes and to integrate them into their emerging view of the oceanic globe.

Like early modern sailing ships, which often encountered Bermuda by chance or, in the case of shipwreck, against their will, this chapter engages the island through repeated shocks of disorientation. The chapter follows two parallel histories of early modern Bermuda. The more fragmented story leads from first contact in 1503 through to the British colony's founding in 1612. This story gets told in brief historical interruptions that emphasize the constant recurrence of Bermudan pressure on the larger story of European exploration of the early modern Atlantic world. The second, better-documented story begins with the *Sea-Venture* wreck in 1609 and advances via multiple histories of this event forward to the rival poetic responses to Bermuda of Edmund Waller and Andrew Marvell in the mid-seventeenth century. Together, these two stories reflect the disoriented image of the Atlantic that Bermuda provided to seventeenth-century English writers and readers. As Ariel notes in *The Tempest,* these islands were "still-vexed" (1.2.229), troubled by storms and troubling to mariners. They provide perhaps our most deeply maritime vision of the interaction between humans and the sea in the early days of English transoceanic settlement.

1503. Juan Bermudez, who sailed with Columbus on his second voyage, appears to have "discovered" the islands named after him as early as 1503 while returning from a voyage to resupply the Spanish colony planted on Hispaniola.[8] Early Spanish records sometimes call the island "La Garza," after the name of Bermudez's ship. Neither at this time nor on a later documented voyage did Bermudez set foot on the islands. For him they were rocks and reefs, seen from sea.

The *Sea-Venture*: 1609

Famed for storms and shipwrecks, Bermuda represented to English sailors and writers a maximally oceanic space, an island that barely seemed to be land at all. Its storms were part of its disruptive force; they were more notable to most sailors than its soil, since most ships that passed these islands before 1612 would not have stopped on the land. Charted early in the sixteenth century, this isolated chain of islands and submerged reefs came to occupy a key node in the emerging Atlantic system. From the English point of view, Bermuda arrived through shipwreck: in June 1609 the *Sea-Venture,* flagship of a fleet attempting to resupply Jamestown, wrecked on a Bermudan reef. After spending nine months stranded on the island, the crew built two pinnaces, the

Deliverance and the *Patience,* out of Bermuda cedar and rigging salvaged from the wreck. These vessels sailed to Jamestown in time to rescue the starving colonists, including their former fleet-mates.[9] In 1612 the Somers Isles Company—named for the Virginia Company official General George Somers, but the allusion to Bermuda's summery climate would become proverbial—established the second permanent English colony after Jamestown. Over six hundred miles offshore and part of no larger island chain, the colony remained an outpost in mid-ocean. The colonial seal, with its image of the *Sea-Venture* wreck and Virgilian motto "qua fata ferunt" (wherever the fates may lead), captures the island's tenuous maritime dependency.[10] Bermuda was, paradoxically, both England's first successful colony and also an economic failure by the middle of the seventeenth century.[11] The mild climate and lack of competing native population enabled the shipwreck survivors, led by Sir Thomas Gates and Somers, to lay in enough provisions in nine months to relieve starving Jamestown.[12] By 1625, in part because of a landfall find of ambergris in the early days of the colony, Bermuda was more prosperous than Virginia.[13] The collapse of the tobacco market in the later 1620s and the island's inability to find another export crop, however, along with conflict between local Bermudians and the profit-seeking company in London, contributed to slow growth later in the seventeenth century.[14]

Descriptions of Bermuda as paradise began as Virginia Company propaganda but also contained hymns to oceanic peculiarity. Storm-circled Bermuda became the part of the English maritime world that, despite being land, was most deeply infused with sea. Unlike later Caribbean plantations such as Jamaica and Barbados, which were integrated into the brutal slave and sugar economy of the later seventeenth and eighteenth centuries, Bermuda remained relatively isolated. Efforts to dry out this wet place included historical records, starting with narratives by William Strachey and Sylvester Jordan that Shakespeare may have seen before writing *The Tempest*; maps, including Richard Norwood's 1614 survey of the island; and multiple histories of the island and the Somers Isles Company. None of these texts, however, could eliminate the salt taste from the islands' history.

1515. The Spanish historian Gonzalo Ferdinandez d'Oviedo y Valdes records that while sailing with Bermudez they sighted Bermuda but were unable to make landfall. Oviedo reported that he wanted to go ashore "to leave in the island certaine hogs for increase" but was prevented by "contrarie winds." While offshore, he noted "a strife and combat betweene these flying fishes, and the fishes named giltheads, and the fowles called sea mewes, and cormorants, which surely seemed unto me a thing of as great pleasure and solace as could be devised."[15] Oviedo's view of the islands as a site of strife and pleasure would be often repeated across the centuries of early European contact.

Ariel's Islands

The most famous reference to Bermuda in early modern English literature comes in Ariel's offhand description of the "still-vexed Bermoothes" (1.2.229) in *The Tempest.*[16] While the geographical contexts of Shakespeare's play have been expanded lately, with arguments advanced for New World and Mediterranean contexts, as well as for the relevance of Africa, Ireland, and even Ovid's exile on the Black Sea, the so-called Bermuda pamphlets remain central to the play's historical context.[17] Accepting that Shakespeare knew, at least obliquely, some early descriptions of the 1609 wreck and that he invokes this story in Ariel's words, the symbolic force of this chain of Atlantic islands provides context for the play's portrayal of the early modern maritime globe.[18] What is important about Bermuda both for *The Tempest* and for my analysis of the global ecology of shipwreck does not depend on whether Shakespeare's language draws on Strachey, Jordan, or some other account. Rather, early modern ideas about the ocean, in which Bermuda maintains a privileged space, underlie *The Tempest*'s, and seventeenth-century England's, engagement with maritime globe. Numerous sixteenth- and early seventeenth-century narratives paint the Bermudas as a stormy and deeply unsettling island chain. It was a key landmark for European sailors returning from the Caribbean and also a constant danger to navigation. The islands represent a maximally oceanic space. While New Historicist scholarship has valuably explored *The Tempest* as a protocolonial play through Bermuda's connection to the Virginia Company, these islands and this play also speak directly to the global ecology of the early modern ocean.

Ariel's elliptical comment may be too brief to repay elaborate exegesis, but the notion that Bermuda represents a maximally mobile and fluid space fits with the larger oceanic register of *The Tempest*.[19] The spirit's reference to the islands contrasts their volatility to the safe "harbor" (1.2.225) where he has deposited the king's ship. The two notions of maritime space Ariel invokes—harbor or ocean, safety or hazard—characterize Shakespeare's Bermuda thinking. The errand on which Prospero has previously sent Ariel to Bermuda, "to fetch dew" (1.2.228), gestures toward the island's historical later role as facilitator of trade, though perhaps "dew" is more parody of a valuable maritime cargo than symbol of it. The "tricksy spirit" resembles these oceanic islands in being both radically different from human life and also strangely hospitable.[20] Like Bermuda and like the early modern ocean itself, Ariel exists at or just beyond the borders of the known or knowable human globe. As an oceanic supplement to Prospero's control, the spirit produces a productive disorientation that resolves into deliverance.

Isle of Storms: Humanism in Strachey's "True Reportary"

William Strachey's account "A True Reportary of the Wracke and Redemption of Sir Thomas Gates," which appears to have circulated in manuscript before being printed by Samuel Purchas in 1625, represents a thoroughly humanist representation of shipwreck. As a narrative it functions as an act of settlement, making the alien sea-land hospitable for English mariners. While later writers would extend Strachey's vision and imagine Bermuda as potential colony, Strachey's initial humanist transformation accomplished the essential conversion of the alien to the familiar. For Strachey, wrecking on Bermuda represents falling victim to supernatural horror, but the isle's horror assumes recognizable classical forms. No voices from the depths impede his narrative. His letter is addressed, in courtly fashion, to an "Excellent Lady" (perhaps, according to Louis B. Wright, Sara, the wife of Sir Thomas Smith, a prominent backer of the Virginia Company); Strachey cites Horace's *Odes* several times; and he invokes the herald of the Greek army at Troy when struggling to depict the storm.[21] "It is impossible for me," Strachey writes, "had I the voice of Stentor and expression of as many tongues as his throat of voices, to express the outcries and miseries" (6). Purchas's marginal comment in the 1625 edition seems apt: "Swelling sea set forth in a swelling style" (7n). Strachey, like other humanists, uses the dry container of a familiar literary style to make his wet oceanic voyages comprehensible to his landed audience.

Applying that intellectual drying mechanism to the chaos at the center of shipwreck, however, requires more stylistic effort. The storm begins with "the cloudes gathering thicke upon us, and the windes singing, and whistling most unusually." These forces apply more-than-human pressure to the ship, so that Strachey's situation appears more like Jonah's than Odysseus's: "A dreadfull storme and hideous began to blow from out the North-east, which swelling and roaring as it were by fits, some houres with more violence then others, at length did beate all light from heaven; which like an hell of darknesse turned blacke upon us, so much the more fuller of horror, as in such cases horror and feare use to overrunne the troubled, and overmastered sences of all."[22] Strachey's language borrows terms and forms from the Latin rhetorical tradition of shipwreck descriptions in Ovid, Virgil, and, in the early modern period, Erasmus's *Naufragium* or Alberti's *Intercenales* to structure his maritime experience.[23] As in these models, Strachey's ocean represents an alien space, but the literary examples help humanize the sea for his readers. The "True Reportary" is a deeply literary shipwreck narrative. Seeing supernatural forces behind the storm produced an amalgam of Virgilian narrative tropes with the growing tradition of Christian sea deliverance narratives. One element of Strachey's fully conventional description that identifies Bermuda as hybrid sea-land is his insistence that ship and crew are beyond hope in the ocean. "For surely (Noble Lady)," he writes, "as death comes not so sodaine nor apparent, so he comes not so elvish and painfull (to men especially even then in health and perfect habitudes of body) as at Sea. . . . For indeed death is accompanied at no time, nor place with circumstances every way so uncapable of particularities of goodnesse and inward comforts, as at Sea" (289). As in Janeway's narratives or King's sermons, the sea marks the bounds of mortality. Strachey's "sea-storm," to borrow the apposite compound term from Shakespeare's Miranda (1.2.177), locates alienation in the sea. He uses the rhetorical resources of classical poetry and humanist prose to describe the waters around Bermuda as a maximally inhuman space, a threatening, death-imbued waterscape.[24] For Strachey the storm off Bermuda delivered the *Sea-Venture* to the inhuman embrace of the sea.

Moving from storm to island barely changes Strachey's sense of being at sea. If the storm was a Sea of Death, Bermuda was, he recalls, "called commonly, *The Devils Ilands,* and are feared and avoided of all sea travelers alive, above any other place in the world" (293). For Strachey, however, the inhospitality of this part of the Atlantic works in large part as rhetorical effect, as his next sentence reveals the castaways' happy fate: "Yet it pleased our merciful God, to make even this hideous and hateful place, both the place of our safetie, and meanes of our deliverance" (293). Bermuda in his description spans opposite types: hideous and idyllic, devilish and Providential, sea and land. Virginia Company propaganda would emphasize the irony of being delivered by the Devil's Islands, but Strachey's writing continuously shows oceanic ambivalence in these remote islands. Drawing on Oviedo's history, which he names, he imagines Bermuda as a storm center in which ocean and land exchange forms:

> These Ilands are often afflicted and rent with tempests, great strokes of thunder, lightning and raine in the extremity of violence: which (and it may well be) hath so sundered and torne down the Rockes, and whurried whole quarters of Ilands into the maine sea (some sixe, some seven leagues, and is like in time to swallow them all) so as even in that distance from the shore there is no small danger of them and with them, of the stormes continually raging from them, which once in the full and change commonly of every Moone (Winter or Summer) keepe their unchangeable round, and rather thunder then blow from every corner about them, sometimes fortie eight houres together. (294)

In this description, which precedes the portrait of the terrain, Bermuda is not so much land as temporary outcropping peeking above the "maine sea," to which it must return. The question of "the commodities of the other Western Ilands" (294) were immediately on the minds of the Virginia Company officers cast away on Bermuda, but even though the islands would, at least for a few decades, support a tobacco export industry, few crops thrived in what Strachey accurately describes as "dark, red, sandie, dry" soil (294). The island had little fresh water but an abundance of hogs, presumably cast away on the island by a Spanish ship, as was a fairly common practice among sixteenth-century sailors, in an effort to provide food to future shipwrecked survivors. Bermuda did provide abundant seafood: "Crevises oftentimes greater than any of our best *English* Lobsters; and likewise abundance of Crabbes, Oyster, and Wilkes" (296). The island was alien, savoring of salt water. Starting with the nine months' stay by the *Sea-Venture* crew, however, Bermuda would over the course of the seventeenth century become distinctively English, becoming, along with slightly older Virginia, the first permanent North American colonies. Bermuda remains a member of the Commonwealth to this day. Imaginative acts of settlement, starting with Strachey's letter, would attempt, over decades and centuries, to dry out these wet islands. They would never really succeed.

1527. Hernando Camelo, a Spanish subject from the Azores, petitioned King Charles V that he be allowed to colonize Bermuda. He argued that since the islands were "made for by all the fleets and vessels coming from the Indies, it was desirable it should be inhabited, so that there could be found a roadstead and also assistance for so long a voyage." Camelo also wished "to ascertain if, with the peopling of it, a remedy could be found for the tempests there encountered."[25] King Charles granted the request, but no Spanish colony seems to have been planted. An inscription with the date "1543" and a cross remain barely visible on the southern shore of the island, perhaps indicating that an attempt was made.

Island in the Ocean

The most oceanic qualities of Bermuda were not visible from the deck of the doomed *Sea-Venture* nor even from the fine sand beaches. Rather, Bermuda's geographical isolation distinguishes it from its Caribbean and continental peers among early European settlements in the New World. The first printed European map that names Bermuda, which appeared in 1511 in a collection by Peter Martyr, shows how out of place the Bermudas were in the Caribbean-centric Spanish New World. As Figure 3 shows, Bermuda was out of place in the early Spanish New World. For early explorers such as Bermudez, Oviedo, and Camelo, this island was more isolated and less hospitable than any other.

Bermuda's eventual importance to the early modern Atlantic system, first in the Spanish-dominated sixteenth century and later for England, flowed, first and foremost, from geography. The islands soon

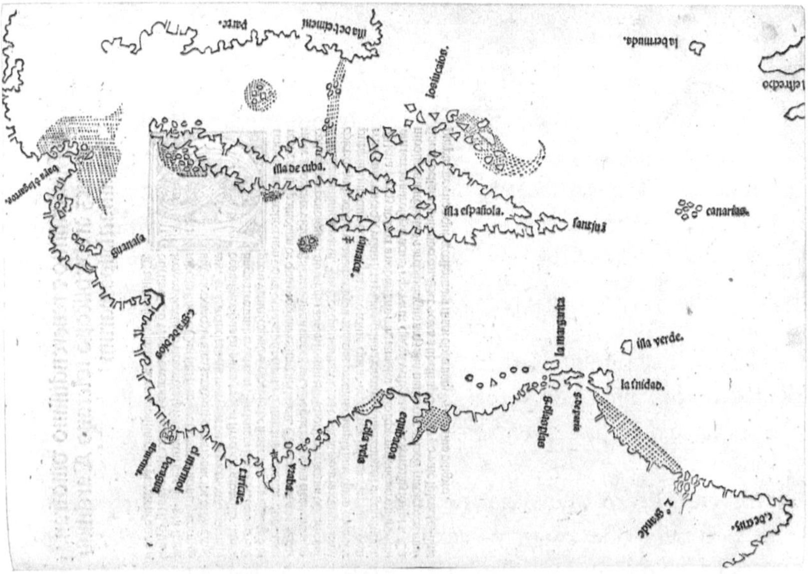

FIGURE 3. The earliest image of Bermuda on a printed map reveals the visual disparity between Bermuda, in the upper-right corner, and the better-known islands of the Caribbean. Courtesy of the John Carter Brown Library at Brown University.

became part of a common eastward passage back to Europe from the Caribbean; ships followed the Gulf Stream around the tip of Florida and up the coast of North America before heading east with the prevailing winds. This voyage became the standard route for the Spanish *flota,* and according to D. B. Quinn, it was the route "followed by almost all shipping coming from the Caribbean" in the sixteenth and seventeenth centuries.[26] On this route the Bermudas served as both guidepost and trap: ships were instructed to sail north past the islands before turning east, but since this part of the voyage often encountered northerly headwinds, the temptation to cut the corner and sail close to the reefs on Bermuda's northern side often proved too much. When bad weather struck, shipwrecks were common; the number of European wrecks on the Bermudas is "estimated cautiously at over thirty before 1600."[27] Thus, the island group was a useful haven for French and English privateers and a threat to unlucky mariners. French pirates may have attempted a settlement in the mid-sixteenth century, and the English privateer Richard Grenville, after dropping off Ralph Lane's colony on the Outer Banks, captured Spain's *Santa Maria de San Vicente* near Bermuda in August 1589. On this scaffold of geographical and navigational facts, legends of the Isle of Devils grew.

To invoke Bermuda in early seventeenth-century England, then, was to name a very different New World from Virginia, Peru, or Newfoundland. The Bermuda islands were strange, isolated, and as yet unconnected to any imperial or mercantile settlements. The nine-month stay of the crew of the *Sea-Venture* in 1609 was hardly the first visit to Bermuda by shipwrecked Europeans, though it may have been the longest to date.[28] To transform these islands into a colonizable space entailed a symbolic reordering of oceanic chaos. But it was precisely chaos—oceanic space—that had defined these islands in European eyes since their first discovery.

1563. Don Pedro Menendez de Avila petitioned Philip II for permission to sail to Bermuda to seek his son, missing and presumed shipwrecked. No record survives of Menendez's visit to the islands, though it seems possible that his crew may have left wild hogs on the island, as Oviedo had wanted to do in 1515. On the same voyage, Menendez and his fleet would massacre a Huguenot colony that had planted itself near St. Augustine in Florida, killing the settlers "not as Frenchmen, but as Lutherans."[29]

From Hell to Summer: Jourdain's Two Islands

When the Isle of Devils was renamed Somers Isle and the Somers Isles Company took formal possession in 1612, something changed in English culture's understanding of the sea. The colony's name came from its founder, Sir George Somers, but the imagined turn away from devilry was pointed and partly intended to lure colonists across the sea. The new name explicitly inverted earlier reports of Bermuda's inhospitable nature. The cumulative effect of many parallel descriptions represents these islands and their surrounding waters as a focal point for the supernatural powers of the sea. Samuel Champlain wrote that "the sea is very tempestuous about the said island, and the waves as high as mountains" (1610–11).[30] By contrast, Richard Norwood's map, published in 1626 but made from a 1618 survey of the island, parcels Bermuda into a series of English settlements, thus effectively, in D. K.

Smith's phrase, providing "the image of a domesticated Bermuda."[31] When the *Sea-Venture* and her 150 souls arrived on the Isle of Devils in June 1609, the islands' unique geography and isolation within the early modern maritime world controlled their symbolic charge.

1571. Job Hortop, an English sailor returning to Europe with the Spanish treasure fleet, reports that when the ships reached the latitude of the Bermudas, Hortop saw "a monster in the sea, who shewed himselfe, three times unto us from the middle upwards, in which parts he was proportioned like a man, of the complection of a Mulliato, or tawny Indian."[32]

If Strachey's "True Repertory" represents a perfectly humanist epistolary response to the isle of tempests, Sylvester Jourdain's near-simultaneous *Discovery of the Bermudas, Otherwise Called the Isle of Devils,* initially published in London in 1610, paints a more complex picture. Jourdain's book in the 1610 and 1613 editions engages the incipient colonial project and Bermuda's function as symbol of the untamed ocean.[33] Like Strachey, Jourdain was connected to the Virginia Company, and both of their narratives suggest that, while these islands were difficult to colonize, colonial enterprise aimed precisely to transform such places. Like Strachey, Jourdain used humanist tropes to displace Bermuda's oceanic meanings.

The two editions of Jourdain's history describe through their titles the changing status of the islands in the English imagination. In 1610 he published *A Discovery of the Barmudas, Otherwise Called the Isle of Devils.* In 1613 he reprinted substantially the same text under the title *A Plaine Description of the Barmudas, Now Called Sommer Ilands,* with the new name referring to the new colony. Jourdain, like Strachey, used Homer and the humanist tradition to describe the islands as ripe for transformation: "For the islands of the Bermudas . . . were never inhabited by any Christian or heathen people but ever esteemed and reputed a most prodigious and enchanted place, affording nothing but gusts, storms, and foul weather, which made every navigator and mariner to avoid them as Scylla and Charybdis, or as they would shun the Devil himself."[34] Jourdain depicts the islands as traps for classical heroism, flattering the heroic self-image of early modern explorers, including armchair explorers, and making the exotic locale comprehensible for English readers.

Like Strachey, Jourdain balanced his classical allusions against Christian topoi. The turn in his narrative to God's power, however, is not external; rather, in their accounts the island itself acquires quasi-Christian virtue. For Strachey the preservation of the crew reveals the hand of God in the world and God's power to cleanse the Devil's Islands. "They be called commonly the Devil's Islands," he writes, "and are feared and avoided of all travelers alive above any other place in the world. Yet it pleased our merciful God to make even this hideous and hated place both the place of our safety and the means of our deliverance" (16). For Strachey, as for Jourdain, the assumption that Bermuda was not inhabitable is a "foul and general error" (16). Jourdain, while still using the phrase "Isle of Devils" in the title of his 1610 first edition, goes farther than Strachey in advertising the healthfulness of the islands: "Whereof my opinion sincerely of this island is that whereas it hath been and is still accounted the most dangerous, infortunate, and most forlorn place of the world, it is in truth the richest, healthfullest, and [most] pleasing land (the quantity and bigness thereof considered) and merely natural, as ever man set foot upon" (109). The second edition of Jourdain's pamphlet, published in 1613, makes the point explicit in a new title, *A Plaine Description of the Barmudas, now called Sommer Ilands.* The name refers to Sir George Somers, who guided the castaways through their order, but the islands now also recall the sun. The next logical step was colonization.

1577. Sir Humphrey Gilbert, the first major backer of English colonization of the Americas, proposed to Queen Elizabeth that a colony on Bermuda would be ideally suited for raiding Spanish shipping. Nothing came of this suggestion, though Gilbert was issued a patent to plant a colony in any lands not currently settled by a Christian power in 1578. His fleet left England in 1582 for Newfoundland, which Gilbert claimed for England before drowning when his ship foundered in the North Atlantic on the return voyage.

Mapping the Ocean: Richard Norwood

Remaking the Devil's Islands into a colonizable earthly paradise entailed reconceiving this fragment of the Atlantic rim in the early modern English imagination. No single Englishman did more toward this effort than Richard Norwood. Sailor, surveyor, mathematician, author, and resident of early modern Bermuda, Norwood's intellectual projects were essential to making Bermuda meaningful to England, for both settlers on the island and readers in London and Virginia. His project required skipping over six hundred miles of open ocean to connect Bermuda to the colony on Virginia. The earliest description of the colony that was planted in Bermuda in 1612 was written by Norwood, who described the islands "as it were the Key, [for] opening a passage, and making the way more safe to many parts of this new World, and especially to Virginia."[35] The ideological work of reimagining the islands as paradise had been begun by Strachey and Jourdain, with their emphasis on Providential delivery facilitated by the island's natural hospitality, but Norwood's work connected Bermuda to English America.

Norwood's map, made after his survey of the island in 1616–17, remains one of the iconic images of the Somers Isles Colony. The rectilinear arrangement of property lines and the names of English landowners domesticate this alien space (Figure 4). Norwood himself was a less orderly character than his map might make him seem. While he was best known for his mathematical books and for the often-reprinted how-to manual *The Sea-Man's Practice* (1694), his journal of his early years on Bermuda, which was drafted in 1639 but mainly describes his stay on the island from 1613 to 1617, tells a story of religious curiosity and geographic variety. Early travels to the continent inclined him toward Catholicism, but in Bermuda he was converted by evangelical protestants. When he later returned to the colony as schoolmaster in 1638, his religious teachings became controversial. He abandoned that post in 1649, briefly returned to it in 1661, and finally became a private teacher on the island until his death in 1675.[36]

A brief maritime episode in Norwood's journal highlights the oceanic impress on his sense of order. Sometime in 1615, when the new colony was low on supplies, Norwood devised a plan to seek "palmetto berries for relief" from a farther point on the island. Hollowing out a small tree, he made a boat, "but so small it was that one man alone could not go in it but it would overset."[37] In this minimal craft, which he made more seaworthy by fashioning rough outriggers with a pole and small logs, Norwood sailed to one of the smaller islands in the Bermudas, harvested berries, and prepared to return to the settlement. The wind having shifted, he was stranded for five days alone, and having

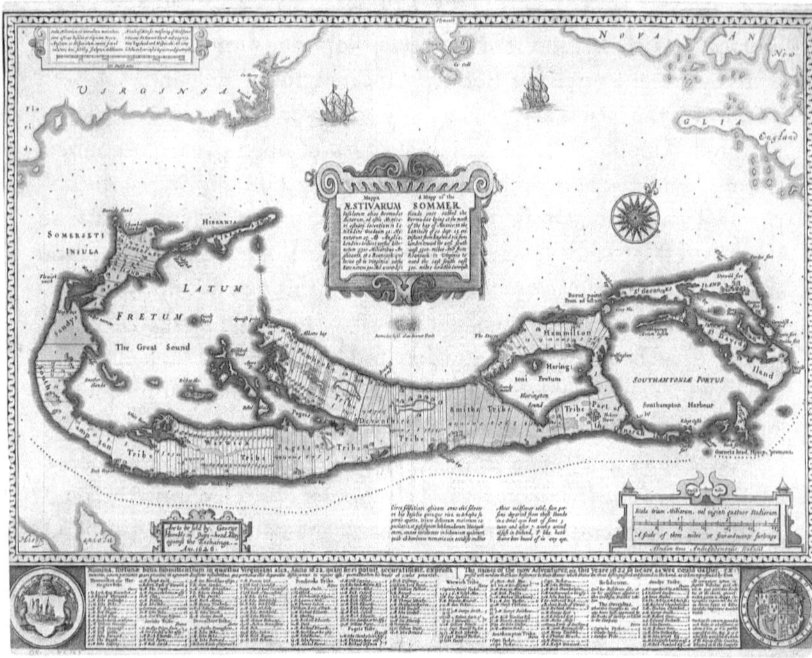

FIGURE 4. Richard Norwood's detailed map of Bermuda, made following his survey of the island in 1616. Courtesy of the John Carter Brown Library at Brown University.

grown desperate during his solitude, he put out to sea in the hope of a favorable breeze. One of his makeshift outriggers being lost, he patched the boat with his body: "So as to supply the want of it I was fain to counterpoise the other by my weight on the other side" (55). In this delicate position, offshore in a hard breeze and rough seas, Norwood risked shipwreck in order to return to his fellow settlers. "During which time," he continues, "I think some three hours, my life was as it were hanging all that while by a little string" (55). Like Robinson Crusoe, Norwood interprets his watery peril as divine judgment and recognizes that in putting out to sea he had made himself vulnerable: "I conceived I had and did grievously tempt God in going so desperately in such a boat as was scarce worth to adventure a dog in: yet to put to shore I had no mind, and besides was far off" (55). Both mariner and believer, Norwood here isolates the contrast between those positions. As sailor he has "no mind" to put to shore, but as believer he fears for his life in "such a boat." Like Bermuda itself, he wavers between landed hopes and oceanic anxieties.

Unlike the *Sea-Venture,* however, Norwood's ship did not wreck, though he did resolve not to put out to sea again in such a weak vessel. When he returned to the colony, he was treated as a magician by the people, who could not believe he successfully voyaged in such a craft: "Whereupon some suspected I could not have gone in her but I must practice some unlawful art" (56). Norwood's art, however, was less a counterpart to Prospero's than a form of technical skill, seamanship built out of the same tool kit as his surveying. His near wreck provides a model for surviving Bermuda different from the humanist narrative practices of Strachey and Jourdain. For Richard Norwood the way to survive on oceanic islands is through skilled labor.

1587. Pedro de Aspide, a Spanish subject, petitioned Philip II to launch a pearl fishery on the Bermudas. The king proposed an inquiry into whether the islands should be settled, but it appears no investigation was made.[38]

Bermuda from America: Richard Rich's *Newes from Virginia*

Richard Rich's pamphlet-length poem of twenty-two stanzas *Newes from Virginia* (1610) emphasizes the ideological connection between Bermuda and Virginia and reveals how the historical proximity to the mainland colony has overwritten the local history of Bermuda. Rich's pamphlet, like Strachey's and Jourdain's, uses its title to signal its overarching interest: if the key word for Strachey's letter is "wrack" and for Jourdain's pamphlet is "Bermudas," then for Rich's poem it is "Virginia." The story of (as the title continues) *The Lost Flock Triumphant* assimilates Thomas Gates's and George Somers's survival with their subsequent rescue of the Virginia settlement.[39] Rich's poem stakes out the humanist claims of poetry to exceed narrative description or private letters: "It is no idle fabulous tayle, / nor is it fayned newes: / For Truth herself is here arriu'd" (sig. A4). Like Strachey and Jourdain, Rich imputes the crew's survival to God—"heauen was Pylotte in this storme," he writes (sig. A4v). His relation of their survival, which, like Jourdain's account, omits the internal political strife among the shipwreck survivors that Strachey included and which may have prevented Strachey's account from being published before 1625, accents the formal balance between the deaths of "Two only of their men" against two new births on the island: "And for the losse of those two soules, / which were accounted deere: / A Sonne and Daughter then was born, / and were Baptized there" (sig. B). The final appeal of Rich's poem is for more settlers for Virginia: "There is no feare of hunger here," he writes, "for Corne much store here growes" (sig. B2). Bermuda's hospitality has been subsumed into the larger narrative of the colony. Rich clearly values the landed Virginia colony more than the oceanic disorder of Bermuda, and careful reading of the pamphlets in maritime context can recover the conceptual labor needed to salvage Bermuda from the unknown sea.

For literary scholars and readers of *The Tempest,* Rich's narrative, in which colonial interests and Christian triumphalism counteract the oceanic disorientation that Bermuda once represented, provides a rich backdrop for characterizing Shakespeare's understanding of the Virginia enterprise, the *Sea-Venture*'s wreck, and oceanic space. Competing depictions of the sea and the Bermuda islands in these texts encourage us to consider not simply the opening storm but also *The Tempest*'s other depictions of social order and government in a maritime context. The shifting nature of the Bermudas, from Devil's Islands to "Sommer Isles" to the newest adjunct of the Virginia settlement, shadows the play's interest in multiple forms of government, from Alonso's monarchy to Prospero's (and Antonio's) dukedom. The tension between classical and Christian interpretive frames in these texts also informs Shakespeare's play and its tension between licit and illicit magic. Finally, the sense of Bermuda as a navigational "key" (to use Norwood's word) asks us to reconsider the apparent location of the island in Shakespeare's play, astride a different, but also crucial, sea route between Algiers and Naples. Shakespeare clearly did not intend his island to be Bermuda, but the shifting meanings of Bermuda indicate how islands themselves were changing their meanings in Shakespeare's England. This polyvalent, mutable island ideology connects *The Tempest* to a richer maritime historical context than conventional source study and New Historicist contextualization have allowed.

1593. The English sailor Henry May, traveling on a French ship, was wrecked on Bermuda on December 17. May noted that the pilots reported the ship to be twelve leagues south of the islands at noon and "demanded of [the Captain] their wine of height, the which they had." By the time the islands were in sight, the pilots were no help, "being as it were drunken, [and] through their negligence a number of good men were cast away."[40] May and the French sailors spent five months on Bermuda before their makeshift boats sailed for Newfoundland.

Waller's "Battle of the Summer Islands" (1645)

The seventeenth-century poetic history of Bermuda includes two substantial poems that extend the tantalizing reference to the islands in *The Tempest*: Edmund Waller's mock epic in three cantos "Battle of the Summer Islands" and Andrew Marvell's shorter lyric "Bermudas." These two poems, often read as companion pieces, with the parliamentarian Marvell rebutting the royalist Waller, demonstrate how these islands had infiltrated English consciousness by midcentury. After several decades of colonial presence, Bermuda had become, in D. K. Smith's phrase, a "domestic" Atlantic island.[41] Both poems trade on Bermuda's mild climate and supposed fruitfulness, as also propagandized by John Smith's *General History of Virginia* (1624). Glossing over the relative lack of productivity that had begun to hamper the colony by the 1620s, Smith insisted that the island was rich in "red and yellow coloured Potatoes, Tobacco, Sugarcanes, Indicos, Parsnips, exceeding large Radishes."[42] For Waller and Marvell, however, neither of whom seems especially interested in colonial economics, the riches of the island were essentially ideological. For Waller the "happy Island where huge Lemons grow" represents a perfectly Edenic site of cultivated leisure where courtiers struggle with oceanic beasts.[43] His mock-epic tale of a fruitless combat between "a Nation and two Whales" (1.2) laughs away the possible disasters of colonial living and presents the ocean as a site of poetic recreation.

The two whales against which Waller's Bermudans fight represent oceanic power on a less epic scale than would Melville's white whale. The "mighty Whales" (2.11) in shipwrecking themselves "in a poole among the Rocks" (2.15) create a visual symbol of rocky Bermuda amid the wide Atlantic. Like the Somers Island colony itself, the whales arrive on Bermuda via shipwreck, a point Waller makes explicit as he describes the colonists' viewing of the trapped creatures:

The man knew what they were, who heretofore
Had seen they like lye murdered on the shore,
By the wild fury of some tempest cast
The fates of ships and shipwrackt men to taste. (2.17–20)

Literalizing the fates of George Somers and the *Sea-Venture,* these whales display the full force of the "raging Ocean" (2.23). Waller emphasizes the cruelty of the sea in thus exposing its creatures in a striking metaphor: "As carelesse dames whom wine and sleep betray / To frantick dreams their Infants overlay" (2.21–22). Imagining the stranded whales as smothered babies emphasizes the inhospitable nature of the sea, in direct contrast to the fruitfulness and maternal care that Bermuda displays toward the colonists. Waller's poem, as part of the ideological domesticating of this island space, also terrestrializes Bermuda by exporting its oceanic nature onto the two stranded whales, which the "Nation" (2.31) views as "a certain prey" (2.34). The Bermudan whale killers become a landed nation in the act of dispatching oceanic monsters.

The combat between colonists and whales, rather than expanding upon this quasi-imperial message, appears fraught with ambivalence. The crucial classical allusion comes in the third canto, in which the child whale, who because of his small size has been able to escape into the open sea unlike his larger mother, returns to defend her against Bermudan arms. In returning for his mother, the whale exceeds Aeneas's piety at the fall of Troy:

He (though a league escaped the foe)
Hasts to her aid, the pious Trojan so
Neglecting for Creusas life his own,
Repeats the danger of the burning Town,
The men amazed blush to see the seed
Of monsters, human pietie exceed. (3.61–66)

The young whale's more-than-Aenean loyalty to his mother exceeds Aeneas's own failure to rescue his wife, Creusa, from the flames of Troy. If "pietie" is the essential virtue of the *Aeneid* and its classical tradition, here the "seed / Of monsters" occupies the pious position more than the predatory colonists. The ambivalence the poet feels toward his nonhuman antagonists includes fear of their massive strength and also greed for the riches of their bodies, including valuable "bones" and "oyle" (2.37). In the thick of the fight, the whales together raise a storm like Prospero's: "Their surges joyn'd, the Seas with billows fill, / And makes a tempest, though the winds be still" (3.27–30). As creatures of oceanic power, the whales are both admired and feared, representing both the mysteries of the deep and the resources the colonists seek.

Unlike Melville's epic of man against whale, however, Waller's poem does not champion the human urge to dominate oceanic life.[44] Instead, Waller's poem develops the oceanic meanings attributed to the Bermudas by ceding initiative to the sea itself. When provoked, the whales resemble the ocean, roaring "Loud as the Seas which noursh'd him" (3.4) after being pricked by a "harping Iron" (3.2). The "raging Ocean" (2.23) that lies outside the tidal pool in which the whales are trapped represents the source of the beasts' power as well as a threatening blankness. As Waller narrates the conclusion of his mock epic, the whales' enmeshment with watery force becomes complete. The connection between Venus, mother of Aeneas, and the sea underwrites the nobility of the young whale who defends his mother: "Well proves the kindnesse what the Grecians sung, / That loves bright mother from the Ocean sprung" (3.67–68). Contrary to the expectations of human readers, including those who might be familiar with whales taken in inshore waters in seventeenth-century Europe, these trapped creatures return, wounded but alive, to the vast deeps. The decisive force emerges not from human valor nor technology but from "Great Neptune . . . who finds / A tyde so high that it relieves his friends" (3.85–86). The power of this great tide, which reconnects the rocky lagoon briefly into open ocean, displaces mortal combat from the center of this tale. In the end, Waller narrates a story in which the ocean reclaims its own.

At the crucial ambivalent crux of Waller's poem, in which the whales have been wounded and cannot escape, the Bermudans vacillate in their desire to plunder the riches of the sea. Having come to admire the young whale's piety, the men wish for alliance rather than combat: "Their courage droops, and hopelesse now they wish / For composition with th' unconquer'd fish" (3.69–70). This fantasy of "composition," with its intriguing echo of the term Bruno Latour has recently introduced to ecophilosophy, gestures toward an intermingling of human and cetacean in Bermudan context.[45] Only after failing in this effort to sympathize do the Bermudans seek heavier arms, "pieces fram'd to batter walls" (3.83), the effects of which get forestalled by Neptune's liberating tide. At the heart of this mock conflict, then, appears Waller's not-quite-articulated fantasy of enmeshment and sympathetic embrace between humans and sea monsters. In Bermuda royalist poets seek utopias. They find salt water.

Marvell's "Bermudas" (1653?)

Andrew Marvell's lyric "Bermudas" is probably the best-known early modern poem in English about the islands, but it has been read mostly in terms of religious politics in mid-seventeenth century England. In 1653, when he was a tutor for Oliver Cromwell's ward William Dutton, Marvell visited the home of John Oxenbridge, a Puritan who had been to Bermuda twice, in 1635 and 1641.[46] The contrast between the factional strife on pre–civil war Bermuda that Oxenbridge experienced and the utopian rhythms of Marvell's verse has long been a staple of critical responses to the poem.[47] The interpretive solution, for most critics, has been to think of the poem "Bermudas" as an effort to fashion an ideal contrast with war-torn seventeenth-century England.[48] In the terms of my analysis, Marvell's poem fashions an antishipwreck, in which oceanic engagement, or watery "composition," facilitates a new and beneficent human and aesthetic order. Whereas Waller's tale imagined combat between shipwrecked sea creatures and island-dwelling humans, Marvell's poem mentions these creatures only to victimize them, emphasizing that God "the huge sea-monsters wracks / That lift the deep upon their backs."[49] These lines clearly gesture back to Waller's "Battle of the Summer Islands" and indicate that Marvell will replace the royalist poet's story of struggle with a vision of harmony. There are no shipwrecks, no conflicts, not even any living fish in Marvell's poem. Nonetheless, it too draws some of its meaning from oceanic entanglement.

1603. Captain Diego Ramirez, sailing as part of the fleet of Don Luis Fernandez de Cordova, wrecked on Bermuda after the fleet lost four galleons in a storm. Ramirez produced the first rough map of the island during his stay there. He also described the devilish voices of the many birds of the island and examined the local oysters, which convinced him that no pearl fishery could be developed. He left with his repaired ship after a twenty-two-day stay.

My oceanic reading of Marvell's "Bermudas" returns to that supreme oceanic experience, disorientation. As Smith cogently observes, the poem is not so much "static as disoriented [through] Marvell's poetic manipulation of space and perspective."[50] For Smith this disorientation enables Marvell's poem to undomesticate these now familiar isles, thus working against Norwood's map, with its regular border and names of English landholders. To extend Smith's insight, I submit that "a poem that highlights the instability of the physical organization of the world" (169) is not only an anticartographic poem but an oceanic one. The "wat'ry maze" (5) in which the passengers on a "small boat" (3) chant out the words of Marvell's lyric does not conform to English standards in part because it is water, not land. The poem describes the maze as something to be "led . . . through" (5) by divine aid, but given that the singers are in the boat, not on the island, they seem deeply entangled in oceanic space at the moment of their song. The familiar objects of fruitful Bermuda—"eternal spring" (13), oranges, lemons, pomegranates, cedar, ambergris—are to some extent simply held over from Waller's description, or John Smith's, but the movement of Marvell's list from fruit (17) to ambergris (28) shifts the reader's attention from fertile land to sandy beach. The greatest treasure, of course, is the "gospel's pearl" (30), which possibly refers to unsuccessful efforts to institute pearl diving on the island and, more directly, recalls the shipwreck of George Somers and the *Sea-Venture.* Landing English Christians on the beach represents the greatest triumph of these isolated islands.

Framing the thirty-two lines of the rowers' song, Marvell's poem contains eight lines of introductory and concluding verse that emphasize the more-than-human nature of this oceanic space. The opening couplet observes not simply that the Bermudas are "remote" but that they "ride / Upon the ocean's bosom unespied" (1–2). As Shakespeare's Ariel and memoirists including Strachey and Jourdain recognized, these islands are maximally oceanic. As Marvell's English believers sing and row, they create, particularly in the framing verses, a sympathetic engagement between sea and humanity. This process works less through drying out the watery space than by engaging sympathetically with it. The winds of Bermuda, long demonized for their shipwrecking storms, are "listening" (4) to the English singers; the oceanic waters "received this song" (4). The penultimate couplet, which rhymes "English boat" with "holy and cheerful note" (36–37), emphasizes the intermingling of human and nonhuman structures. The ocean in this poem remains the face of God's power, but it has, mysteriously and disorientingly, become beneficent. The point of access for poet and singers is both a global geography, ranging from Ormus (20) to Lebanon (26) to "the Mexique Bay" (35), and aesthetic continuity. The poem's final image emphasizes the productive entanglement of oars entering water: "And all the way, to guide their chime, / With falling oars they kept the time" (39–40). The believers do not become marine creatures, but the "falling" rhythm of their physical engagement with the sea maps their progress across the ocean and through spiritual space. Marvell's imaginary Eden, unlike that of his friend John Milton, seems deeply oceanic, at least in this poem. To row in the warm waters surrounding Bermuda represents a deeply sympathetic enmeshment in the space of salt water. This utopia contrasts not only with an English of civil war and conflict but also with the terrestrial imagery of private gardens that feature so heavily in Marvell's pastoral verse. In "Bermudas" the poet briefly appears in a blue, rather than green, shade. Like the islands themselves, this poem anticipates the global oceanic reach of English culture.

Interchapter

Pearls That Were His Eyes

I WANT TO DIVE FOR PEARLS off Margarita Island in the 1530s!

Because undersea divers work inside the shipwreck of human immersion.

Because after 1526, Spanish colonists began to import African slaves to expand their New World pearl fishery, making Margarita and Cubanga Islands off the coast of present-day Venezuela a leading edge of the expanding American/African/European hybrid protoindustrial culture, in which slave and free labor extracted New World resources for global dissemination.[1] The global ecology was born in the warm salt of these Caribbean waters.

Because things happen to your body when you work underwater.

Because the pearl fishing canoes contained mixed crews of Americans and Europeans and Africans. They did not work equally; they did not work without violence; but they worked together.[2] Sometimes the vessels sailed without Europeans.

Because underwater labor marks the edge, the limit, the place at which biology and environment impinge directly on human bodies.

Because I might be a Native American pressed into service, and the warm water would feel familiar.

Because I might be an enslaved African, violently transported across the ocean. When I dive under the water, I escape, for a little while.

Because even though I would prefer not to, I might be a Spanish colonizer, standing on deck and refusing immersion.

Because of coral.

Because of salt.

Because of pearls.

Because the fish who live on every particular fragment of reef would come to know me.

Because gravity does not pull as hard underwater.

Because by the end of the sixteenth century, the pearl-diving industry devastated the biotic wealth of Margarita Island's oyster beds, sending their pearls around the world into a global economy and ecology.

· CHAPTER 4 ·

Metis

Jeremy Roch

SEEN FROM THE WATER, the ocean is neither history nor slavery. Shipwrecks happen, but the sea is not always disastrous, except in potential. To a sailor's eye, the sea is work: skilled, technical, and dangerous. Maritime labor defines the human experience of the deep oceans in the Age of Sail.[1]

To put it more directly, the influential abstraction of Hugo Grotius's "freedom of the seas" (*mare liberum*) falsifies maritime experience by overlooking labor. The sea is not a free space but a laboring one. The ocean's essential human term is *metis*: skilled, tool-driven work. Not liberty but labor: the premodern ocean comprises a space in which human actors modify and engage with a threatening and dynamic environment. The liberty that Grotius celebrates was built by the laboring hands of sailors.

The precise technicalities of maritime labor assume center stage in representations of crisis, which is why episodes of shipwreck overflow with jargon. The Boatswain in *The Tempest* provides familiar examples. His language interposes a host of sea terms—"yare," "topsail," "room," "topmast," "bring her to try," and "main-course," among others—alongside the scene's resonant political and philosophic claims.[2] While Shakespeare's command of sea terms was imperfect, he recognized the dramatic power of opaque, technical language in moments of crisis.[3] I use the Greek term *metis* to describe the expert labor of the mariner in these extreme situations. This ancient term, which I adapt from *The Odyssey,* combines "cunning intelligence" and skill with technology.[4] Metis captures both physical and intellectual practices; it represents seaman-like labor and defines an imaginatively charged engagement with physical reality. The Greek word also names a Titan; Hesiod relates that Metis was Zeus's first wife, a daughter of Tethys and Ocean who, after being swallowed by the King of the Gods, was the secret mother of Athena.[5] (Zeus swallowed Metis to prevent her from bearing sons wiser than their father, and through this tactic the Thunderer kept Metis's wisdom in his own belly before passing it into the world in Athena.) This mythological figure glosses the skilled labor and rapid judgments that impose form on chaos. As ships founder and rigging snaps, sailors struggle to maintain orderly forms of action and thought. Like the shipwreck writer, the laboring sailor salvages order from disorder. Laboring metis provides a physical way to dry out wet experiences. Seaman-like practice also parallels the formal efforts of literary writers to represent maritime scenes. Reproducing the *jeitzteit* crisis of shipwreck in poetic or descriptive language requires matching the physical labors of the mariner with the formal shaping of the writer. Performing metis involves hands, tools, judgment, and language.

This chapter and the next turn to historical first-person narratives to explore maritime labor as a counterdiscourse to Grotian liberty. The labor of the sailor, often overlooked in studies of Atlantic or global history, positions human bodies and maritime tools in wet contact with oceanic forces. I begin first by defining several key features of maritime metis, including its social character, its technical nature, and its partial overlap with theological languages of salvation and redemption. Metis, as I explore it, represents both an essential human response to shipwreck and a tool for creating partial connections between human actions and the extrahuman forces, such as God, Providence, storms, or the ocean. Specialized labor represents a tactic of accommodation by accumulation, through which mariners and writers unite diverse strands of physical and symbolic experience. A form of intellectual and physical composture as well as anthropotechnic practice, seaman-like metis folds expertise into disorder. In this way, practitioners of metis, from Shakespeare's Boatswain to the historical mariners whose memoirs are my primary texts in this chapter and the next, enact on a local and human scale the mixing and overlap of forces that typify early modern cultural change. Sailors navigating stormy seas become figures for humans in the destabilizing grip of cultural transformation.

The most suggestive recent critical approach to metis appears in Margaret Cohen's long chapter "The Mariner's Craft" in her 2010 study *The Novel and the Sea.*[6] Borrowing the term "craft" from Joseph Conrad, Cohen draws on a wide assortment of sixteenth- to twentieth-century seamanship manuals to outline the essential features that comprise maritime skill.[7] She extracts fourteen common elements: Prudence, Sea-Legs, Protocol, Remarkable Occurrences, Endeavor, Resolution, Jury-Rigging, Collectivity, Compleat Knowledge, Plain Style, Providence, The Edge, Reckoning, and Practical Reason. Together, these elements articulate a cumulative narrative of wandering and survival, which Cohen calls, borrowing the phrase from Thomas Carlyle, "a Romance of Fact" (16). In some ways, Cohen's fourteen-point analysis of craft parallels my previous thirteen-point reading of the wreck of the *S. João*; in both models multiple unlike causes overlap and coexist.[8] The simplest elements of craft for Cohen consist of physical skills—Sea-Legs, Endeavor, Jury-Rigging—but most of her elements combine intellectual qualities with physical skills: Prudence, Resolution, Compleat Knowledge, Plain Style, Reckoning, and Practical Reason. In a painstaking analysis of Captain James Cook's efforts to bring his ship off a reef in Australia in 1770, Cohen delineates how her analysis of maritime craft strongly rebukes Horkheimer and Adorno's famous reading, in *The Dialectic of Enlightenment,* of Odysseus the mariner as a "harbinger of bourgeois *ratio*" (57). After showing how deeply physical and material maritime labor is, Cohen notes that Horkheimer and Adorno "take [Odysseus] to task for an abstraction that in fact marks the limits of their own perspective" (57). Performing craft or metis requires exactly the opposite of abstraction. Seamanship accumulates the physical in dialogue with the rational.

The dynamic physical-and-intellectual efforts of the sailor distinguish maritime labor from Frankfurt School critiques of Enlightenment reason, but another important feature of seamanship is its social nature. Two more of Cohen's categories—Protocol and Collectivity—emphasize that laboring sea knowledge gets produced and employed through carefully ordered social groups, as well as through relations between human bodies and their tools. In Bruno Latour's sense, a working ship is an assemblage of human and nonhuman actants, all working together—or failing to work together, as sometimes happens in moments of crisis.[9] Sailors laboring in mobile human and nonhuman groups perform embodied and material work through a shared process one modern scientist has termed "cognition in the wild."[10] Working in this way requires a hybrid physical and intellectual understanding of one's body, one's tools, and one's fellow sailors. Metis in this composite sense serves as a model for social and political organizations, as in the familiar metaphor of the "ship of state."

When Hugo Grotius published a portion of his legal argument in favor of the Dutch East India Company's expansion into the Portuguese-dominated East Indies under the title *Mare Liberum* in 1609, his argument pivoted off the vastness of the oceans. Seeking to displace Portuguese claims for exclusivity in the East Indies trade, which were based on both papal decrees and nearly a century of mercantile practice, Grotius argued that the sea, unlike the land, was by its nature resistant to human control. "Now," he wrote, "in the legal phraseology of the Law of Nations, the sea is called indifferently the property of no one (*res nullius*), or a common property (*res communis*), or public property (*res publica*)."[11] Glossing over the meaningful differences among these three notions, Grotius insists that there can be no ownership of the sea, because there can be no lasting occupation of oceanic space: "That which cannot be occupied, or which never has been occupied, cannot be the property of any one, because all property has arisen from occupation" (27). This model of ownership implies that human labor is the essential component in converting space into property, but it also ignores the mobile labor of mariners. In the Grotian model, which would for centuries provide a baseline for international maritime law, the labor of sailors was invisible.[12]

It is important to recall that metis combines the technological with the social. A Latourian perspective suggests the fundamental continuity among the contributions of disparate actors that include social networks, human laborers, and inanimate tools.[13] Maritime labor provides an exemplary case of collaboration between human and nonhuman actants.[14] In forming this sort of network, the essential thing is to have reliable collaborators, human and not. Thus, as Cohen quotes from Samuel Champlain's *Treatise on Seamanship*, "experience is better than knowledge" (35). It is more valuable to learn seamanship from observation and experience than to generate theoretical knowledge through intellectual abstraction. Seaman-like metis is a social and historical product. As Cohen notes, large bodies of maritime knowledge appeared in print in the early modern period, and a great deal of this information "also passed down in an oral culture" (35). The human experience of technological labor was not new, though the English word "technological" does make its first appearance in a prefatory poem to John Smith's *Sea-*

Grammar (1627), the first published dictionary of maritime knowledge in English.[15] The interaction between human hands and precise tools assumed paramount importance during crises at sea. To rebuild a fracturing anthropotechnological assemblage (i.e., a ship and her crew) during a storm required a special combination of skill, tools, social organization, and the ability to manage all these things under chaotic conditions.

In the context of craft and shipwreck, the most stimulating features of Cohen's analysis are the ones that characterize the imagined relationship between human labor and supernatural order. Shipwreck was often retrospectively interpreted as evidence of divine control or anger, but in moments of crisis Cohen identifies three strands of more-than-natural understanding: Remarkable Occurrences (i.e., observing that certain events are out of the ordinary), Providence, and The Edge, which is the geographic and conceptual site of maritime exploration, "at the edge of dynamic knowledge" (52). In categorizing the remarkable, speculating about Providence, and reaching for an ever-receding edge, maritime craft connects human actions to inhuman forces. For shipwrecked sailors, including many who were not as skilled or fortunate as Captain Cook, tenuous connections to an unseen divinity could be precious, even if they were seldom as instructive as moralizers such as Edmund Pet or Jonathan Dickinson hoped they would be. Diverse examples of physical, intellectual, social, and supernatural forces coexisting in Cohen's analysis suggest how narrative representation reproduces an accumulative experience: multiple categories assemble themselves at once. As sailors struggle on what Cohen calls, in her reading of the *S. João* wreck, the "jerky seesaw between survival and salvation" (47), they register the force of cultural change on their bodies. Metis comprises an intellectual and practical response to disorder and uncertainty. Representations of metis in turn become symbolic attempts to unify an increasingly diverse set of physical and cultural referents. For many writers, even nonliterary ones, the technical efforts of seamanlike metis parallel the technical making that goes into creating poetic forms. Metis itself becomes an embodied technopoetics, a specialized dialect inside Sloterdijk's general anthropotechnics.

Grotius's argument about free seas did not emerge directly from the *res nullius* he imagined as defining the ocean. In fact, the ideological parameters of his claim for the sea as international space emerge from two strains of medieval canon law. As the historian James Muldoon has observed, Grotius's argument attacked "the claim of Pope Alexander VI (1492–1503) to restrict access to the New World to the Portuguese and the Castillians," but his argument also built upon earlier papal pronouncements that made the oceans free for sea travel in order to facilitate the conversion of non-Christian peoples.[16] As Muldoon notes, the key factor for Grotius was the need for viable "communication" (18) to enable the spread of the Gospel. Against Grotius's plea for freedom, Muldoon identifies two responses: a *microargument* put forward by the Scottish jurist William Welwood and the English scholar John Seldon in favor of sovereignty by states over the waters adjacent to their shores (21–22) and a *macroargument* articulated by the Portuguese writer Serafim de Freitas, who insisted that the papal donation of exclusive trade rights to Portugal in the East Indies was justified in order to spread Christianity globally (22–24). Muldoon emphasizes that, despite their disagreements, Grotius and his adversaries "were working within the same intellectual framework" (24). In fact, Muldoon continues, "the debate over the sea was an extension of the medieval debate about the relationship between Church and State" (24). Neither Grotius nor his micro- and macroantagonists found the labor of sailors essential in understanding human claims on maritime space.

This chapter and the next take as their primary texts for analysis the manuscript journals of two seventeenth-century English mariners: in this chapter, Jeremy Roch, a naval officer from Plymouth who served intermittently from 1659 to 1690 before being expelled from the service, and in the next, Edward Barlow, who began his career as a runaway seaman apprentice in 1660 and served in various capacities for the Royal Navy and the East India Company before being lost at sea in 1706.[17] I have selected these journals because of their hybrid recourse to historical facts and literary forms. Roch and Barlow, like a pair of salty Don Quixotes, shaped their lives and their narratives according to recognizable literary models, though at times with results comparable to Cervantes's knight. In presenting themselves as maritime heroes, these men reveal the changing understanding of the human–ocean relationship in the seventeenth century. The two were very different kinds of seamen; Barlow ran away from home as a boy and learned his craft the hard way, whereas Roch, in his egotistical telling, was born to the sea. They appear among the handful of other seventeenth- and early eighteenth-century seaman-diarists, an assortment of naval officers, privateers like Woodes Rogers, William Dampier, and Bartholomew Sharpe, the chaplain Henry Teonge, and the slaver Nathanial Uring.[18] Like some but not all of these writers, Barlow and Roch were amateur poets as well as sailors. They versified at dramatic moments like embarkation and homecoming and, most valuably for my purposes, when recounting crises at sea. These two figures' efforts as sea poets reveal suggestive parallels between the technical labors that (sometimes) saved ships and the formal labor that shapes poems. Both kinds of making attempt to impose a human order onto an oceanic form that often refuses such ordering.

Expanding upon Homer's pun between the metis that navigates a ship and the poetic ambiguity that tricks the Cyclops, I use the poems and journals of these sailors to highlight parallels between salty labor and poetic making.[19] Both forms of craft are fundamentally technical; the mariner's work and specialized language counteract crises at sea in ways that match the differently technical labors of poets who represent such events. Sailors like Barlow and Roch directly encountered the inhuman maritime world that poets from Shakespeare to Dryden represented in texts from *The Tempest* to *Annus Mirabilis.* Sometimes, these amateurs used classical or biblical topoi or alluded to well-known poems. They often used the mythic-and-physical ocean to represent the limits of their own nautical and poetic praxis.[20] In poems and storms, a crisis pits human efforts to create order against the insurmountable vastness and unintelligibility of the ocean. Sailors, like poets, struggle to respond.

Jeremy Roch, Mariner of Plymouth

Jeremy Roch of Plymouth began the part of his career that his manuscript journals record as a naval lieutenant and experienced seaman who would serve on various vessels for several decades. He was dismissed from the service in 1690 in somewhat unclear circumstances and then undertook a final recorded voyage on a merchant ship in 1692 before retiring to Plymouth. A fairly obscure figure who does not merit an entry in the *Dictionary of National Biography,* Roch (or Roach, according to naval records) served with several more prominent figures, including Sir Frescheville Holles, who was knighted for valor after the Battle of Four Days, in which he served with Roch.[21] In his own account, Roch began his career already possessing the metis that his voyages required. For some historians, Roch has been taken to exemplify the "tarpaulin lieutenants" that represent the saltier side of Macaulay's well-known cliché about the Restoration navy, which was comprised of gentlemen and sailors, but the gentlemen were not sailors and the sailors were not gentlemen.[22] The most recent historical study of aristocrats and seamen in this period suggests that the old phrase exaggerates the rivalry between these groups.[23] Roch's career, as I explore it, epitomizes maritime labor, but not simply the technical sort. His work bears out Cohen's definition of maritime craft in that it is social and experiential and relies on his special knowledge of supernatural forces. Despite being expelled from the Royal Navy, Roch defines the hybrid and polytechnical nature of maritime metis.

Roch's manuscript, currently preserved in the Caird Library at the National Maritime Museum in Greenwich, is divided into five "journals," each recounting a single voyage between 1665 and 1691.[24] The volume's framing title page announces Roch's ambition and egotism. Using a faux-Greek form of his first name and writing in red ink, Roch proclaims his book "Hieron Roch his Journal of some Remarkable Voyages and Adventures at Sea" (unpaginated leaf 2).[25] This title page describes him in epic and heroic contexts, as it emphasizes the "grand Engagements" in which he took part, including the Battle of the Four Days in the second Anglo–Dutch war. In addition to descriptions full of technical seamanship, however, Roch's journal includes many pages devoted to supernatural knowledge, including a lengthy "Astrological Appendix" (75–87) to four of his five voyages that explains his fortunes through the influence of the stars.[26] In his journals Roch's maritime heroism emerges through physical and intellectual labor; he celebrates his skills as practical sailor and also his knowledge of the secrets of astrology. The tension between maritime skills and celestial knowledge makes Roch a compelling image of the multiple discourses of shipwreck modernity.

When his attention turns from legal principles to the direct experience of sailors such as Jeremy Roch, Grotius's language emphasizes the ephemerality of ships on the sea: "A ship sailing through the sea leaves behind it no more legal right than it does a track" (40). This poetic phrase works counter to a long-established tradition in which powerful states projected political control beyond the shore. The Roman treatment of the Mediterranean as *mare nostrum,* for example, provided ancient authority for a powerful state's efforts to regulate commerce and tamp down piracy. Medieval and early modern states followed suit in claiming power over local waters: Venice asserted control over the Adriatic Sea, Genoa over the Ligurian Sea, Denmark over the Baltic, and James VI and I over the herring fisheries around Britain in a long-running dispute with Dutch fishermen.[27] Grotius's counterargument insists that the vast basins of the Atlantic, Indian, and Pacific oceans broke the Mediterranean and Baltic molds. Grotius claims these newly explored waters represented a different kind of space:

> The OUTER SEA, the OCEAN, that expanse of water which antiquity describes as the immense, the infinite, bounded only by the heavens, parent of all things, the ocean which the ancients believed was perpetually supplied with water not only by fountains, rivers, and seas, but by the clouds, and by the very stars themselves; the ocean, which, although surrounding this earth, the home of the human race, with the ebb and flow of its tides, can neither be seized nor inclosed; nay, which rather possesses earth than is by it possessed (37).

The language here anticipates Byron's or Coleridge's Romantic oceans. Grotius advances a legal argument buttressed by a fully supernatural conception of the sea. To this grand vision, the voice of a practical sailor adds intimacy and laboring detail. Human skill cannot mark or control the sea, but it can build temporary alliances with it.

Brought up a sailor in Plymouth and proud of his seaman-like skills, Roch reveals little anxiety or melancholy in his seafaring journal. In direct contrast with Edward Barlow, he never presents himself as disturbed by oceanic life.[28] Even his trial and expulsion from the navy pass quickly, after which his career at sea continues for another voyage on a merchant vessel. The unpaginated flyleaf that opens the manuscript contains a brief summary of his first voyage, in the man-of-war *Preston.* These two pages simply provide a list of place-names, followed by "but having lost my journal, of that voyage, I forbear to say any more, not daring to trust my memory with particulars after so long a time" (27). His manuscript really begins with his second tour of duty, on the *Antelope* in 1666. (The *Antelope,* as Roch fails to note, is the *Preston* renamed, with a new commanding officer.) Roch includes a short embarkation poem on the flyleaf facing the manuscript's title page. This poem clarifies the literary ambition undergirding the journal. Roch strains awkwardly toward epic form in heroic couplets that ape Dryden's. Roch attributes his voyages, like those of Odysseus or Aeneas, to fate: "My stars to Travel, did incline me strong, / Which made me seek for an Occasion Long" (28). As elsewhere, Roch in this poem maximizes his own power and control over his seaborne life. War against Holland provides him with an opportunity to travel as a martial hero: "Farewell England, now for ye Coast of Spain / Thro Hercules his Pillar we must pass / To drive poor Jack before us like an Ass / Up the Levant & Midland Seas to range / To purchase gold, or see Adventure strange" (28). Patriotism, apparently, plays a small part in Roch's motivations; in fact, it is not very clear whether "Jack" refers to the enemy, to the common "Jack Tar" British sailors over whom Roch exerts a lieutenant's control, or to the Union Jack on the masthead. In this poem he goes to sea as an adventurer and hero, seeking gold and glory.

The first episode in Roch's first journal narrates a scene that continues his self-aggrandizement through the visible possession of maritime metis. He celebrates his public reputation for seaman-like skill. He opens the narrative, "Walking on the New Key, or Change of Plymouth" (30), where he receives word that "some Gentlemen" wished to speak with him. The gentleman turns out to be "one Frescheville Holles" (30), a captain who offers him a lieutenancy on the *Antelope*.[29] Roch reports their dialogue in self-flattering terms. Holles says, "Now Mr Roch . . . to satisfy you wherefore I made bold to send for you, was to offer you the command of the *Antylope* as Lieutenant under me" (31). The phrasing emphasizes a possible split on board; Roch will "command" the ship while Holles rules over Roch. Holles apparently takes Roch for his seamanship and maritime reputation, asking him to accept the post "by the Character I have of you from several persons here as well as from some of my own men that were in that Ship with you formerly, and by the little skill I have, that you are a person capable and fit" (31–32). To be "capable and fit" matches the "diverse [and] heterogonous skills" that Cohen calls Compleat Knowledge.[30] Roch's maritime reputation comes from three different social sources: "several persons" in Plymouth, the sailors on board the *Antelope,* and Holles's own "skill" and judgment. This triple combination emphasizes the social and communal nature of metis. The sailor was happy to accept the offer, especially when Holles offered to share his provisions on board, thereby saving Roch the trouble and expense of supplying his own. But there seem to be two versions of Roch's embarkation. The first, narrated in verse, describes the heroic sailor seeking adventure. The second, presented in the narrative, shows the social inferior taken aboard for his technical skills. This distinction emphasizes the tension between practical metis as the essential quality for success at sea and the larger social contexts of the Restoration navy. Roch, notably, always seems more comfortable with sailors than with officers.

Metis or Poetry: War on the *Antelope* (1666)

After his encounter with Holles in late 1665, the main narrative of Roch's first journal begins with a storm at sea. The implied contrast between seaman-like labor and social connections, as represented by the lieutenant and the captain respectively, soon elaborates itself into a veiled protest against decorative artistry. In an episode that epitomizes Roch's self-conception and his relationship with Holles, he describes a storm in the Bay of Biscay on February 5, 1666 as follows:

> Being horrid dark and stormy weather our main mast gave way in the partners, and (was) like to carry all by the board, so yet all were at their wits' end, for, being embayed, if we escaped drowning we must fall into the hands of our enemy, the French; which to prevent we had but one way & that was to get down our Topmast yards, but ye danger was so eminent that nobody would undertake it. At length I cried "Who follows me," and presently stepped into the shrouds. Then was I soon followed by a couple of daring fellows, which did the work, and having got down the topmast we soon mended the mast by fishing it with anchor stocks and other things, so we got up our topmast and yards again and made sail. (32–33)

Roch's metis displays itself conspicuously and technically. His labor and leadership save the ship; in Cohen's terms he displays Jury-Rigging, Resolution, and Endeavor. His key initiative appears during a short pause, in which "the danger was so eminent that nobody would undertake it."

Into this breach he enters with his commanding voice—"Who follows me?"—and his physical presence in the shrouds.[31] He undertakes dangerous work when no one else has the heart for it. Once-fearful men follow his lead into the rigging, and together they repair the damage, avoiding both the weather and the French. When Roch makes his cry and climbs aloft, he embodies a leadership based on metis rather than legal or aristocratic authority. He follows his verbal appeal by stepping "into the shrouds," and the narrative implies that it is Roch's demonstrated seamanship—his ability to perform dangerous work under pressure in the technical environment of the rigging—that carries the crew along with him. Roch represents himself as making a sailor's claim for the value of specialized maritime labor.

For Grotius maritime freedom has two ultimate sources: God's will and natural law. He opens his treatise with a celebration of God's omnicommunicative power, which makes divine laws legible to all of humanity: "He [God] had drawn up certain laws not graven on tablets of bronze or stone but written in the minds and on the hearts of every individual, where even the unwilling or refractory must read them" (2). These divine commands are easily translatable, according to Grotius, into a "Law of Nations" that establishes "navigation . . . free to all persons whatsoever" (7). The ocean, like God's will, flows to everyone in common, "navigable in every direction with which God has encompassed the earth" (8). These twin principles, God and natural law, operate from a global perspective, gazing from on high and pronouncing freedom on the mutable sea. For a mariner like Roch, however, dealing with the technical questions and split-second judgments of ships in crisis, such abstract freedom holds limited value. When Roch leapt into the shrouds, carrying the crew with him by force of personality, he is free in Grotius's sense but also entangled in the human and nonhuman networks of craft.

Against Roch's seamanship, the journal juxtaposes Holles's poetry. In this struggle of form against form, physical prowess carries the day. Immediately following his description of leading the crew into the rigging, Roch recalls his captain:

> In the midst of this dismal accident Holles flashed out this distich—
> Blow Windes beat Seas in vain you spend your breath
> My Fate's too great by you to Suffer Death! (33)

Roch makes no direct comment on Holles's poem, but the contrast between inventing a couplet and cutting away the topmast in a storm seems pointed (Figure 5). Holles's miniature poem echoes, or parodies, Lear's rage against the storm: "Blow, winds, and crack your cheeks!" (3.2.1). In this context the passage emphasizes the sharp contrast between poetic play and practical labor. Holles focuses on Fate; Roch, on work. By placing this episode at the start of the journal, Roch distinguishes between sailor and poet, practitioner of metis and "flasher" of distichs.

The contrast between Roch and Holles need not suggest that the two were rivals for the loyalties of the crew or that they understood themselves to be in competition with each other. Elsewhere in the journal, the relationship seems cordial. In fact, the naval historian J. D. Davies holds up Roch's relationship with Holles as an example of mutual support.[32] But the split between metis and poetry seems meaningful, especially when contrasted with Roch's efforts elsewhere in his journal to make his poetry, his seamanship, and his astrological insights work in concert with each other. Roch's first journal initially suggests that technical skill conflicts with humanist rhetoric and that, in a moment of crisis, seamanship trumps poetry. In this episode Roch's essential skill is practical seamanship. As his journal continues, however, he invents maritime hybrids that include poetry and supernatural knowledge.

As Roch's journal of the *Antelope* voyage continues, he expands upon the heroic, seaman-like, laboring self he first presents in juxtaposition with his captain and also includes more of his own poems. His lines, unlike Holles's, do not compete with maritime labor but supplement it. They also, along with his elaborate astrological tables, emphasize that Roch's heroic destiny, like Holles's, is guided by Fate. A key episode here for Roch as poet-hero is his description of the Battle of the Four Days (48–50). Roch introduces the battle with a typically oblique reference to his own heroic self-sufficiency. Before the battle a colleague on the *Antelope* notices that Roch has "but an ordinary or ammunition blade" (48) and offers to exchange it for a "brave scymetar" (48). In refusing, Roch states, "That which I had was fine enough to kill Dutchmen" (48–49), at which point suddenly "comes a crossbar shot from the enemy and cuts him off by the middle" (49). The sudden death of Roch's shipmate accents the danger of the battle and Roch's own heroic disdain for personal peril.

To describe the close fighting during the battle, Roch resorts to

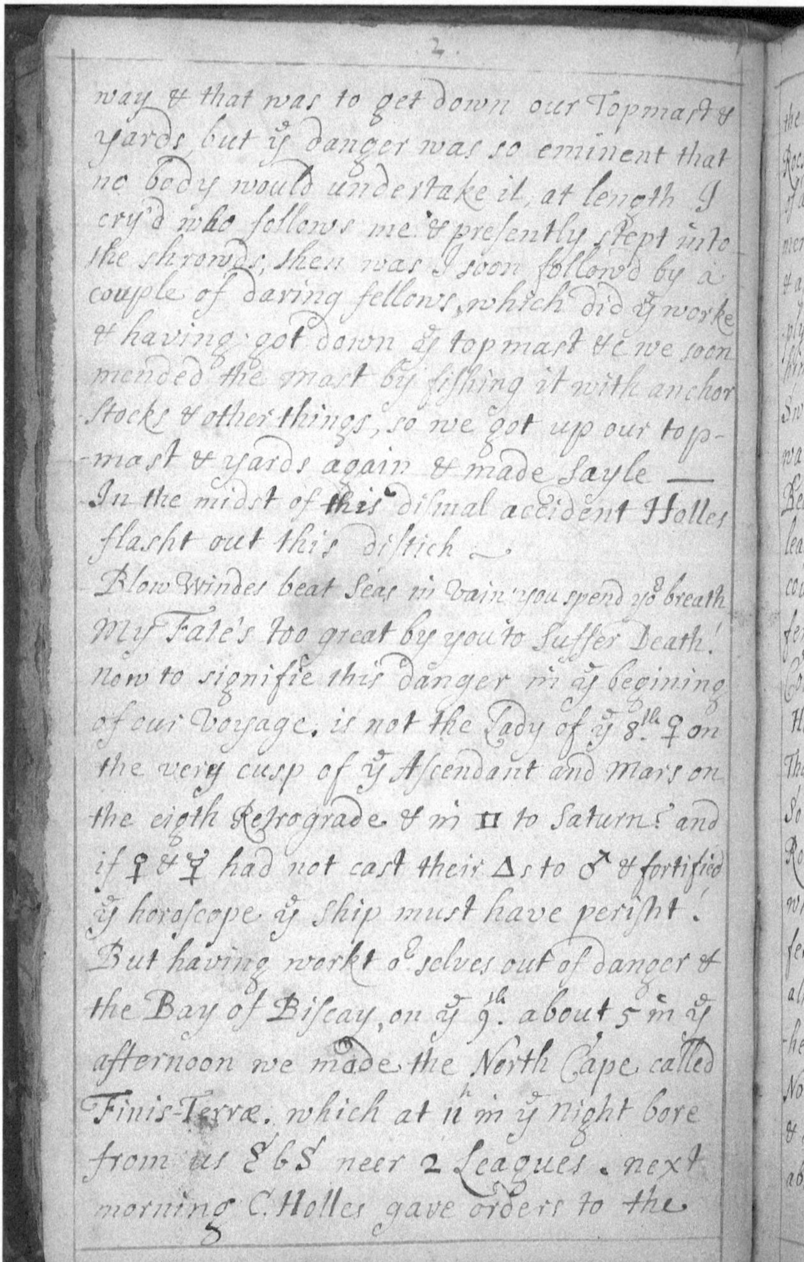

2.

way & that was to get down our Topmast & yards but ye danger was so eminent that no body would undertake it, at length I cry'd who follows me & presently stept into the shrowds; then was I soon follow'd by a couple of daring fellows, which did ye worke & having got down ye topmast &c we soon mended the mast by fishing it with anchor stocks & other things, so we got up our top-mast & yards again & made Sayle —

In the midst of this dismal accident Holles flasht out this distich —

Blow Windes beat Seas in vain you spend yor breath
My Fate's too great by you to Suffer Death!

now to signifie this danger in ye begining of our Voyage, is not the Lady of ye 8th ♀ on the very cusp of ye Ascendant and Mars on the eigth Retrograde & in II to Saturn! and if ♀ & ♃ had not cast their △s to ♂ & fortified ye horoscope ye Ship must have perisht! But having workt or selves out of danger & the Bay of Biscay, on ye 9th about 5 in ye afternoon we made the North Cape called Finis-Terræ, which at 11 in ye night bore from us E b S neer 2 Leagues. next morning C. Holles gave orders to the

FIGURE 5. A two-line poem by Captain Frescheville Holles in response to a storm. Jeremy Roch's Journal. Copyright the National Maritime Museum, Greenwich, London.

poetry: "The Noise, the Smoke, the Fire, the Blood, / Was not to be expressed, nor understood" (49). This couplet displays the stoic understatement that characterizes Roch's martial persona. It contrasts significantly with Holles's couplet; where his captain is flashy, clever, and allusive, Roch is staid and mystified. As his description of the battle continues, Roch resorts to a pair of slightly garbled quotations from Dryden's *Annus Mirabilis.* He quotes the concluding two lines of stanza 80, "Where not to be o'ercome was to do more / Than all the conquests former kings did gain," and also Dryden's celebration of Roch's own captain, "Young Holles on a Muse by Mars begot / Born Cesar-like to act and write great deeds" (54–55).[33] The long battle scene in Dryden's historical epic provides a model for Roch's public, poetic self. The battle would lead to Holles being knighted for valor and also, perhaps, to Roch becoming more respectful of his commander's poetic and martial capabilities.

At the end of the *Antelope* voyage, Roch seems to have imagined a new place for himself as sea poet, if not exactly maritime warrior-poet like Holles. Having engaged two different forms of seaborne poetry—Holles's witty couplet and Dryden's historical epic—Roch celebrates his own poetic style in explicitly supernatural terms that distinguish him from both Holles and Dryden. In the first of several journal-closing poems, he describes himself as one who has escaped "proud Neptune, and thou fiery Mars" and their contests "for Honor's Empty Name" (74). Refusing the epic deities of sea and war allows Roch to embrace more emphatically his own supernatural ordering principle: astrology.[34] His journal teems with careful astrological tables and notations for each departure and fleet action. In a pair of poems given in an appendix (75), Roch explains his loyalty to "Fair Urania" and her principles of higher order. He asks to "Observe her [Urania's] Motions, & thy Aspects Ken, / That I may show to the dull sons of Men / How happiness, how woes come, or commence / From well or ill dispos'd Stars Influence" (75). This summatory poem replaces the seamanship-against-poetry system presented during the storm with a hierarchical structure in which astrological patterns control both verse and labor. Roch even insists that biblical truths are compatible with astrological systems. In the appendix he paraphrases Proverbs, "To every Thing there is a Season . . ." (82), in such a way as to make these lines support astrological claims: "The election of which Tyme or Season, must be of exceeding great Consequence, for on it dependeth all the good or evil Success of the thing"(82). These lines lead him to produce a series of detailed astrological illustrations for different moments in his career (Figure 6). The stars control even the Bible.

The last of Roch's astrological "schemes" for the *Antelope* voyage concerns an episode in which the ship wants to engage a Dutch fleet but is hindered by a storm. Holles, ever deferential, asks Roch's opinion on what the ship should do. Roch's advice exploits astrological more than maritime expertise: "I then opening before all our officers and Gentlemen, declared by Judgment, that we should not fight or engage the Dutch for that bout, nor till our return, if we kept the Sea never so long" (82). The other officers laugh as Roch proffers the stars as his reason: "First, Jupiter Lord of the seven fortunating that house by his presence there. Secondly, the Moon transferring the benevolent beams of Jupiter to Mercury . . ." (82). The point of Roch's story is that he and Urania predicted the storm that eventually prevented the fleet action. In the end the officers view him as a kind of star-infused Prospero: "I laughed at them, who knew not what to say but that I had raised the storm by Magick Art, to make good my Judgment" (82). Roch's seamanship gets underwritten by the "stars influence, & that by Jove" (83), as another red-inked poem in the "Astrological Appendix" relates. His special knowledge of the seas reflects, supports, and is supported by his intimate understanding of the stars. Almost explicitly, he recalls classical heroes singled out by fate to survive shipwreck.

Grotius's argument for maritime freedom excludes the Mediterranean. Taking up Portugal's argument for controlling seas through "title of prescription or custom," he admits examples of unfree seas in classical and more recent history. He argues, however, that these examples have no bearing on the East Indies trade, "for they are talking about the Mediterranean, we are talking about the Ocean; they speak of a gulf, we of the boundless sea; and from the point of view of occupation these are wholly different things" (58). From the point of view of a shipwrecked sailor, however, the monsoon that wrecked the *S. João* off southeast Africa would have looked quite similar to the storm that drove Aeneas or Odysseus to rocky shores in northern Africa or Phaeacia.

The *Mare Liberum* was part of a larger project of legal argument, the *De Jure Praedae* ("On the Law of Capture"), which was intended to build an international framework for maritime law on the high seas.

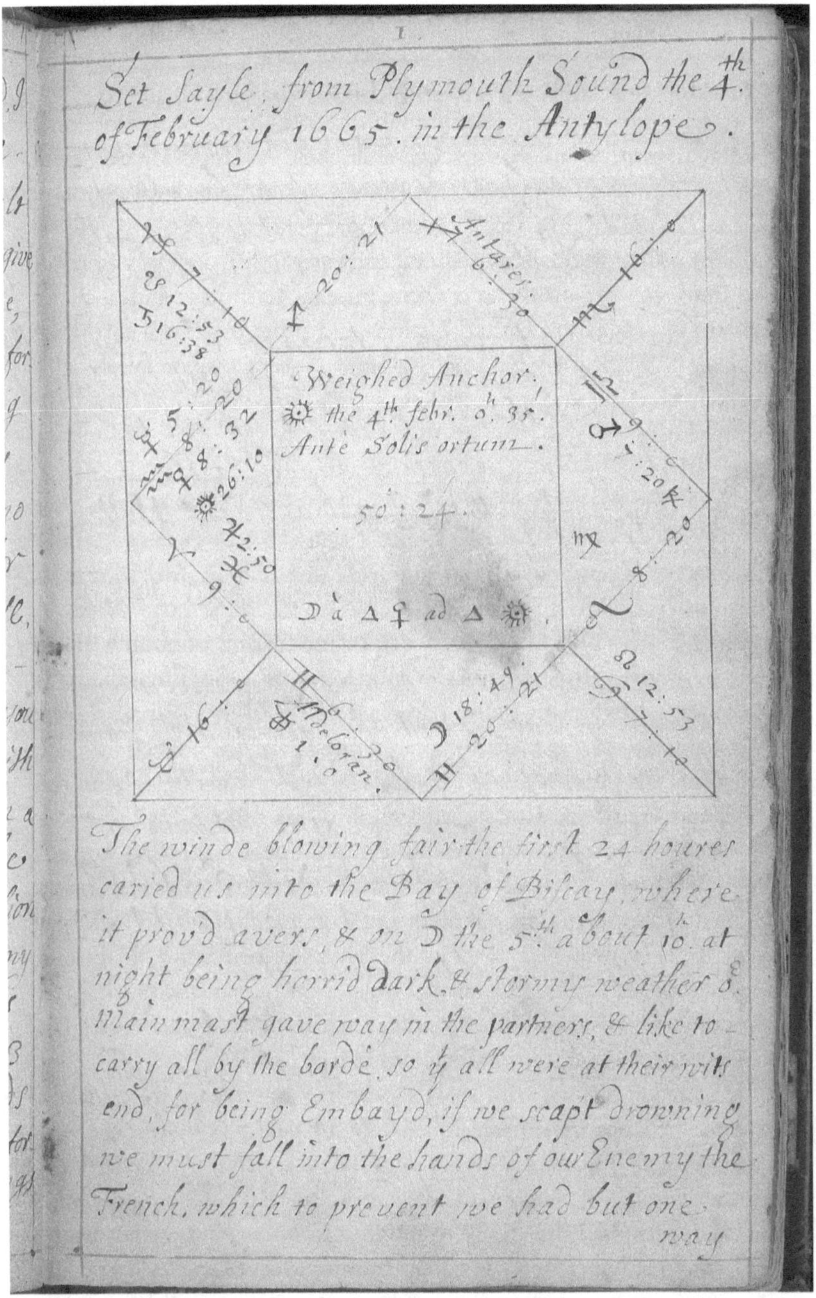

FIGURE 6. An astrological chart plotted by Jeremy Roch for his voyage on the *Antelope*. Jeremy Roch's Journal. Copyright the National Maritime Museum, Greenwich, London.

The bulk of this manuscript, with the exception of the chapter that became *Mare Liberum,* remained unpublished in Grotius's lifetime, only coming to print after it was discovered in 1864. As James Muldoon observes, Grotius's attempt to devise a universal and global legal structure that would undergird a true "international political order" (25) recalls both the efforts of the late-medieval and early modern papacy to regulate European expansion into non-Christian territories and also the modern efforts of the United Nations and other bodies to formalize the Law of the Sea. Global legal systems intersect only obliquely with the daily practices and order-making systems of sailors from Ulysses to Jeremy Roch.

Roch on the *Neptune*: Metis at Play

The most self-conscious display of pure seamanship in Roch's journals does not take place on a naval vessel but on the "little boat" *Neptune,* in which Roch sailed in 1677 between Plymouth and London with no crew but "on[e] Robert Curtis & my Dog, one as good company as the other to me for any help I had need of" (89). As Figure 7 shows, the voyage celebrates maritime craft within a narrow collectivity; the primary actants on the voyage comprise just Roch, his small boat, the wind, and the ocean. Roch's celebration of his seamanship, however, consistently contradicts his purported isolation by showing a maritime community laboring around him. Metis in this voyage consists of creating and rebuilding a human and technological assemblage over time. This voyage, which alone of the five described in Roch's journal does not merit astrological analysis, isolates the human and mechanical components that contribute to skilled maritime labor and shows the social prestige associated with successful navigation.[35]

After tagging along with Holles's war heroism aboard the *Antelope* in 1666–67, Roch disappears from view for a decade before his next journal, which describes a voyage undertaken in private.[36] The *Neptune* journal also occasions a generic shift, from martial epic to comic play. He vaguely explains his desire to travel to London as "some occasion" (89), for which he "proposed going by water to save charges" (89). His planned companions, however, perhaps seeing the small boat Roch has prepared, will not embark with him. The journey, for which Roch

FIGURE 7. Jeremy Roch on board the little boat *Neptune*, with one passenger and a dog. Jeremy Roch's Journal. Copyright the National Maritime Museum, Greenwich, London.

recruits only "a young lad that had never been in salt water" (89), appears to have grown out of Roch's stubbornness and pride. It becomes an occasion to celebrate metis in near solitude, as a sailor alone on the ocean—but even so, maritime collectivity asserts itself.

The description of the voyage combines technical details about anchorages and wind conditions with Roch's desire to show off his skills. The "compleat" sailor chafes at solitude; he wants to show off his achievement of sailing in a small open boat.[37] At the Isle of Wight, he takes on "un povre Frenchman dat want de passage to Londra" (91). He also shows off his profound awareness of his nonhuman environment. In an emblematic moment, he sails all night under a cloudy sky, keeping his course offshore by gauging the sound of the surf striking the rocky shore.[38] There is relatively little real drama in the voyage, though at one point a great ship almost swamps the *Neptune* near the entrance to the Channel (92) and both Roch's passengers are seasick during a rough night (92). This episode enables Roch to mock the French passenger's Catholic devotion "to his beads" and also his disheveled appearance:

"My poor Frenchman . . . now looked but shittenly" (92). Roch, hero of metis, remains unperturbed.

The reward for this navigational feat is notoriety. He is particularly gratified when he speaks to an East India ship in the Thames estuary between Gravesend and London Bridge and the captain does not believe he has sailed all the way from Plymouth in that "yacht" (93). When he ties up at Wapping, he notes with pleasure that "people daily come from all parts thereabout to see the wonder of a boat that was from Plymouth" (93). The city and his business there remains opaque; he loses his dog and visits with his father in London, but the journal passes quickly over these events to focus on the return trip. The voyage is again relatively uneventful, despite some trouble when villagers mistake him for a pirate (95). He recruits a more maritime crew, including an able seaman who needs transport back to Plymouth and helps Roch manage the boat (97). He also edges closer to the supernatural knowledge that elsewhere defines his maritime practice. A storm on the return voyage "wet us to the skin, put out our light, and filled us half full, so that we were forced to bail all hands and throw our Ballast overboard, and some other things, a Sacrifice to proud Neptune" (98–99). This "sacrifice," however, does not require the astrological analysis of his other voyages. Throughout, as he insists when talking with the mayor of Lyme, he claims to be simply "a gentlemen on my frolick" (100). The arrival of his boat disturbs the people of Lyme and other towns, but Roch insists that his navigation is a purely private matter.

The deeper motives behind this casual voyage emerge in the red-ink poem that ends the episode. Once again, Roch trumpets seamanship, but poetry also connects him to maritime heroes of an earlier age:

> Thus Ends a voyage none ere performed before
> In such a Boat, to Coast Albion's shore!
> From Plymouth to London, and back again
> Is a great wonder to the Sons of Men,
> And may in future times be deem'd as Strange
> As those with Ships ye Round ye World did range. (100)

Roch's self-aggrandizement is comical but consistent: he distinguishes himself from his fellow Restoration sailors by superior seamanship and epic stature. The final couplet of this poem joins Roch with English circumnavigators like Drake and Cavendish. He enters, at least in his own verse, England's maritime gallery of heroes.

Shipwrecked: The *Mercury Yacht*

The next two journals in Roch's manuscript describe, with his usual egotism and lightness of touch, disastrous voyages. First, on a private voyage in 1678, he wrecks the *Mercury Yacht* off Holland and has to make his way back from the Netherlands without a ship. The crucial episode occurs when a storm drives the *Mercury* toward shoals off the Dutch coast. To survive, Roch must nearly lash himself to the tiller, since, as he writes, "[I was] forced for my own security to trust the helm in no other hand but my own so that I was continually wet from head to foot, and what was worse than that the want of Sleep, for I durst not close mine eyes except I intended to shut them forever!" (103). By refusing to give up control of his ship, Roch isolates himself among his crew, obviating temporarily the collective nature of maritime work. His nightlong trick at the helm, however, does not prevent shipwreck and the loss of the *Mercury.*

Making sense of this wet loss requires intellectual labor, and Roch employs his talents as poet and astrologer to the task. He prefaces the storm with a distich that contrasts with Holles's on board the *Antelope*: "But in the Way Cross windes and Tempests toss't / Our Yacht, until on Hellends Coast 'twas Lost" (102). While Holles focuses on himself alone—"My Fate's too great"—Roch versifies collectively about "Our Yacht." The "Cross windes and Tempests" appear to be impersonal forces, but in the "Astrological Appendix" Roch reveals his prior knowledge of the storm: "Whoever set sail when Saturn and Mars are in the Ninth house, as here, it must be only a Miracle that can prevent their shipwreck" (83).[39] In fact, he further suggests that only the stars preserved him and the crew: "If Venus had not helped a little, though she be weak enough, the Company had all perished" (83–84). The contrast between Roch's triumphant voyage on the *Neptune,* in which the stars do not interfere with practical seamanship, and the subjection of the *Mercury* to celestial powers suggests that while small boats can sail unmolested, larger vessels implicate supernatural forces as well as human ones.

Arguing that Roch's career amounts to a small-scale rebuttal of Grotius's brief for a free sea need not suggest that the mariner supports the

Mare Clausum arguments of John Seldon or the religious sectarianism of Serafim de Freitas. The sea as Jeremy Roch worked on it was a site of technical labor, supernatural control, and heroic pattern making, none of which principles need be subject to Seldon's landed temporal control or Serafim's global religious order. Roch pushes back on Grotian juridical arguments in part through scale: his narrative remains singular, speaking of himself and his succession of ships with little apparent interest in larger geopolitical or mercantile strategies. The Anglo–Dutch wars provide him with occasion to display his maritime talents but are not otherwise meaningful to him; his voyage on the *Neptune* with dog and boy shows off his skills as clearly as do his exploits with Holles on the *Antelope.* From the point of view of the skilled sailor, maritime space is disorderly and contingent, "free" in the sense of being not subject to landed authorities. That radical contingency, however, also subjects sailors to the mercy of time and tide.

As Roch describes the crucial maneuver he undertakes while he struggles to save the *Mercury Yacht,* the crew and vessel have to "obey the laws of the storm and spoone before it without the least sail" (103). To "spoone afore," as Ingram notes by way of Mainwaring's *Seaman's Dictionary,* means to head the ship directly into the wind with little or no sail (103n). In this naked position, subjected to wind and waves, the *Mercury* faces the ocean directly. After the vessel strikes ground about a half mile from shore, Roch looks carefully for a break in the surf. As in Ulysses's landfall and, later, Robinson Crusoe's, timing the ocean's surge becomes critical: "At length the sea drove us a little nearer, so the boy and I, watching our opportunity, escaped to shore safe, but the other two that ventured before us took their habitation among the haddocks" (104). Roch's term "opportunity" represents a complex balancing of human agency, the forces of wind and water, and the competing powers of Venus, Mars, and Saturn.

After his landfall this journal never returns to this pitch of drama and intensity. Seaman-like metis delivers him to land, where Roch bargains and negotiates his way home with the help of Englishmen living in Amsterdam. The closing lines of this journal explore work at sea and leisure at home. Near this journal's end, the lure of land becomes palpable. In the red-ink poem at the end of the voyage, Roch imagines himself retelling his story in a pub: "Thus after Dangers past, now safe & well / The story to our friends we often tell; / And they to Recompense us for our Tale, / Do strive to Drown us in a cup of Ale!" (109). Beyond the joke, what seems meaningful here is that Roch's attitude toward poetry and storytelling has changed: he no longer contrasts his own labor, or even his astrological insights, to the professional work of other officers. Rather, he now imagines himself as part of a group of landed "friends" rather than exclusively as a hero. The end of the voyage, for this heroic sailor, becomes a homecoming on land. The only drowning he fears comes in ale.

Cashiered: The *Charles Galley*

Roch's misfortunes continue in the next episode of his journal, when after commanding the naval vessel the *Charles Galley* in 1688, he is expelled from the navy.[40] This voyage follows Roch's familiar template, with perhaps even more emphasis on his extraordinary seamanship. He is recruited to the ship by an aristocratic patron, "my every honoured and good friend Sir John Carew of Anthony" (111). After nearly losing two members of his carpenter's crew to poisonous air in the bilge, Roch demonstrates his supreme knowledge of craft by diagnosing the problem—"The occasion of these damps is the tightness of a ship and, lying still a long time, the bilge water corrupts and stinks, so that it is enough to poison the Devil"—and also his ability with machines and men alike in fixing it: "Upon which I made the carpenter bore a plughole to let in water and then to cleanse it, and so pump it out again which in little time did the business" (115–16). He joins the English fleet, in which he cannot forebear to notice that his ship was "the best sailor in the fleet" (116). For a time Roch seems perfectly integrated into the navy, professionally and socially.

As on the *Neptune,* Roch both needs and disdains social collectivity. His expulsion from the service comes, he explains, from personal betrayal: "My Boatswain and Carpenter, 2 rogues that I had saved from the gallows, made false information against me, and swore to it" (131). One aspect of maritime metis—human sociability—betrays him. Notably, he cannot confront his accusers because he, "being taken sick soon after, was forced to keep my chamber" (131).[41] Sick and isolated, Roch "cared not which end went forward" and was summarily cashiered. His betrayal by his junior officers, however, gets contrasted with Roch's warm relations with his superiors, including Sir Cloudsely

Shovell, commander of his fleet.[42] Shovell loans Roch's ship a pinnace, and the two form an implicit alliance of skilled mariners.

Neither sociability with commanders nor skill in navigation preserves Roch from baleful influences. The stars break his career but save his life. "Certainly," he writes, "some invisible hand steered our ship, for 'twas impossible for the best pilot on the coast to lay her in the same place again, for just under her was pretty smooth ground, but ahead and on both sides the sharp rocks lay very thick" (85). This fourth journal is the only one of the five that does not close with poetry, perhaps because Roch may be bitter about his dismissal. The final line, however, suggests the sort of philosophical response that he elsewhere produces through verse: "But who durst be angry with Providence?" (132). A good sailor, as Cohen observes, always maintains a philosophical attitude toward Providential mysteries and future events.

Captured: The *Tamer*

While manuscript journals are not always fully formed narratives, in Roch's case the author's final voyage provides a formal resolution to his maritime career. His fifth and last journal sees Roch a private mariner in the service, again, of his friend Sir John Carew. Having failed to recruit a master for Carew's ship, he captains her himself, only to be captured by the French and returned home a prisoner. As usual the astrological scheme knows it all along; his chart, Roch claims, provides "a clear convincing argument of the force of the Stars over all beginnings of elections, or Journeys or Voyages" (87). In a short poem that concludes the "Astrological Appendix," he further claims that this celestial knowledge can be acquired only retrospectively: "Thus Dear bought Knowledge by Experience got / Some Satisfaction doth afford to all / That Love it" (87). "Experience," as Roch and Samuel Champlain know, comes prior to knowledge. Through maritime experience and astrological knowledge, the sailor, even without his ship, can arrive home at last.

Roch's final moment of maritime crisis, when he is a prisoner aboard a French vessel in a storm, captures the essence of his jury-rigged metis. Despite lacking his own human or technological resources, the hero manages to save the ship. He first observes that the (semicompetent) French captain is "obliged to scud before [the storm] without a Knot of sail and yards down, the sea now raking us fore and aft" (137). Roch tries to tell the captain that they were running upon the "Seven Stones" (137), but his experience-derived knowledge is ignored. In an episode that expands upon Roch's tense relationship with authority, which was already visible during his first storm with Holles, Roch takes matters into his own hands: "I, being loath to be drowned with such company, stepped forward upon the foreyard and, it clearing a little, I saw a great Breach a head. Upon which I ran to the helm and thrust the fellow away that had it, and put it up hard a port. So we just touched a little and rubbed over, or else we must all have inevitably perished" (137). As so often in Roch's career, he combines knowledge with timing and audacity and assumes control of the vessel. He notes that after this episode the French crew were so disordered that he might have taken the ship with "but 3 or 4 lusty fellows" (137). The key point seems to be that even as a prisoner Roch is the best seaman aboard. This supersailor is always "stepping forward" to the shrouds or the helm. Even his enemies recognize his prowess, and the grateful French captain afterward puts Roch ashore, where he works as a pilot for a Dutch boat before returning home to England. Being captured and returning home here seem to be basic facts of maritime life, not a tragic fate. Roch finds more hospitality from the French and the hostile ocean than he does from the Royal Navy.

The journal concludes with one last poem on his maritime career, written in brown ink on the final page of the manuscript. The poem reiterates that maritime labor is the author's defining characteristic, and the analogy with Ulysses, implicit throughout Roch's journal, now becomes explicit. He defines himself as a wandering sailor: "By Sea and Land, o're Waves and Mountains high / We Toyle and Moyle; when what we seek is Nigh" (139). Working his way toward a landed life, however, Roch now rejects "Wealth and Honor . . . ye Worldling's Gods" (139) in favor of a new understanding of Fate. He has always assumed that his technical knowledge, of the sea and the stars, singled him out from his peers. But now, preparing to resign his watery ways, he treats Fate as a force outside his ken: "therefore no more I'le strive / Against ye Stream to Swim, or cross my Fate / I'le Stop, and be Resign'd, 'Tis not too Late!" (139). The image of Roch as a swimmer resonates at this still point in the journal: the consummate sailor imagines himself submerged in hostile waters. During most of the previous adventures, his images of himself assuming power usually involved ascending: climbing the rigging, reaching up to the helm, or reading the stars. This last image of him down in the waters, however, strikes a cautionary note. This sailor, like Homer's but unlike Dante's Ulysses, wants never to go to sea again—or at least, his poetry wants us to believe that he will rest on land. Whether his stillness seems believable—whether metis can really be followed by stasis—remains an open question.

· CHAPTER 5 ·

Metis

Edward Barlow

This world to me is as a lasting storm.

Pericles (4.1.18)

Banka Strait, 1672

Over the course of a frantically mobile life at sea, Edward Barlow spent nearly a year floating perfectly still. During this imposed immobility, his metis turned from nautical to literary tasks, and he began writing his massive journal, the manuscript of which now resides in the National Maritime Museum in Greenwich. The best literary study of Barlow's journal classifies him as an outstanding example of the mobile consciousness of early modern England's working poor. Patricia Fumerton's *Unsettled: The Culture of Mobility and the Working Poor in Early Modern England* (2006) opens its reading of Barlow's career with the striking event of his running away from home in Lancashire as a teenager. Fumerton emphasizes the shocking speed and "odd casualness" (63) with which Barlow leaves home and family.[1] My analysis instead begins with his moment of stasis, in Banka Strait between Sumatra and Java, on the East Indiaman *Experiment* homeward bound from Japan in the autumn of 1672. Barlow's company of three merchantmen were blockaded in the narrow strait between Banka Island and Sumatra by a fleet of eight Dutch ships. Having left England in 1671, before the start of the Third Anglo–Dutch War (1672–74), Barlow and his companions were surprised by the aggressive attitude of the Dutch, "not in the least knowing or thinking that there were any wars betwixt them and us."[2]

An illustration in the journal shows eight powerful Dutch men-of-war bottlenecking three English merchantmen in a narrow strait.

This encounter would lead to the English sailors spending over a year in the heat and miasma of various ships and prisons, in the waters around Banka Island and in the colonial capital Batavia (now Jakarta). Barlow laments in his journal that this turn of events unravels his relative prosperity, "seeing that in an instant all our goods, chests, and clothes, and ship and all, were made prize of, and we ourselves prisoners, and for how long we could not tell" (226). Barlow managed to hide most of his gold and distributed some of it to his fellow sailors for safekeeping (227), but the main consequence of his capture was to create a year-shaped hole of immobility in his peripatetic maritime career. His months in captivity forced Barlow into temporary stasis, during which he would retrace the events and adventures that had taken him from a Lancashire boyhood to the Pacific Ocean. Stuck at anchor, the sailor took up the pen:

> And keeping us in the Straits two months, and I having a great deal of spare time, which I thought might be worse spent than in declaring of what I have here in this book, and thus I thought good to describe to my friends and acquaintance and to any which might take the pains to read it over, and here they may understand in part what dangers and troubles poor seamen pass through, and also of the manner and situation of most places which I have been at since I first went to sea. (228)

Barlow's two declared motives in writing, bearing witness to the misery of sailors and presenting his view of the watery globe, underlie the documentary heft of the 138 folio leaves of the journal. He describes early modern maritime life from the point of view of a sailor always anxious about the possible disruption of his barely achieved stability. A recurring trope in Barlow's journal is complaint: he is poorly treated by his superiors, often goes without food or pay, and, while his demonstrated expertise enables him to climb in rank, encounters recalcitrant captains who refuse his good advice. The result is misery, as Barlow gets betrayed by his captains, the weather, and his master and mistress, not to mention global affairs like the Anglo–Dutch wars. The writer presents his maritime self as essentially disoriented but also able, sometimes, to reorient itself. The journal, as well as the acts of writing and drawing that it contains, provides literary and visual evidence of one sailor's efforts to resist the disorientation of a wet maritime globe. Writing operates as a talisman against shipwreck.

The copy of the journal that survives in the National Maritime Museum in Greenwich is very unlikely to be the same pages that the seaman began during his imprisonment in Banka Strait. The clear, even handwriting of the surviving manuscript seems likely to be a fair copy written out sometime later.[3] The two frontispiece pages that open the manuscript, however, have some claim to be framing Barlow's experience of captivity in Dutch Asia (Figure 8).[4] As an imaginative response to that year of enforced immobility, the two images and long poem with which Barlow opens his journal provide a literary self-portrait of Barlow as mobile mariner. His life, as he represents it, is thoroughly immersed in the ocean's global ecology. Barlow himself, like Jeremy Roch, shipwrecked only once, in Barlow's case on Goodwin Sands in 1675. But Barlow's career even more than Roch's seems unremittingly disoriented by encounters with the ocean.

The opening pages of the journal create a formal prefatory structure, with images on front and back. The top page contains a single-column poem with a color drawing of Father Time in the top-right corner and a hand with a quill pointing to the first letter of the first line. The allegorical struggle between Time the destroyer and the poet as preserver appears clear and conventional. The verso of this leaf contains one of Barlow's relatively few full-page illustrations—most of Barlow's drawings share space on the page with some text—a large compass rose. I take these two framing devices, the poem and the compass, as formal representations of what Barlow wanted his journal to represent, as he fashioned it textually from 1672 until 1703. The journal uses the resources of writing, including poetic form, and illustration in a struggle against time and the ocean. It offers its own labors, poetic, visual, and nautical, as orienting devices and salvaging tools.

The poem, like all of Barlow's verse, is conventional, written in four-beat couplets and indicating the fairly doctrinaire attitude toward divine control that has led J. D. Davies, in his *DNB* entry, to attribute to the mariner "more than a hint of puritan self-righteousness" (3:916). The contrasting images above the poem, Time with his scythe facing off against the writer's pen, suggest that Barlow asks his poem and, perhaps, the journal that it begins, to salvage lost time, to order and

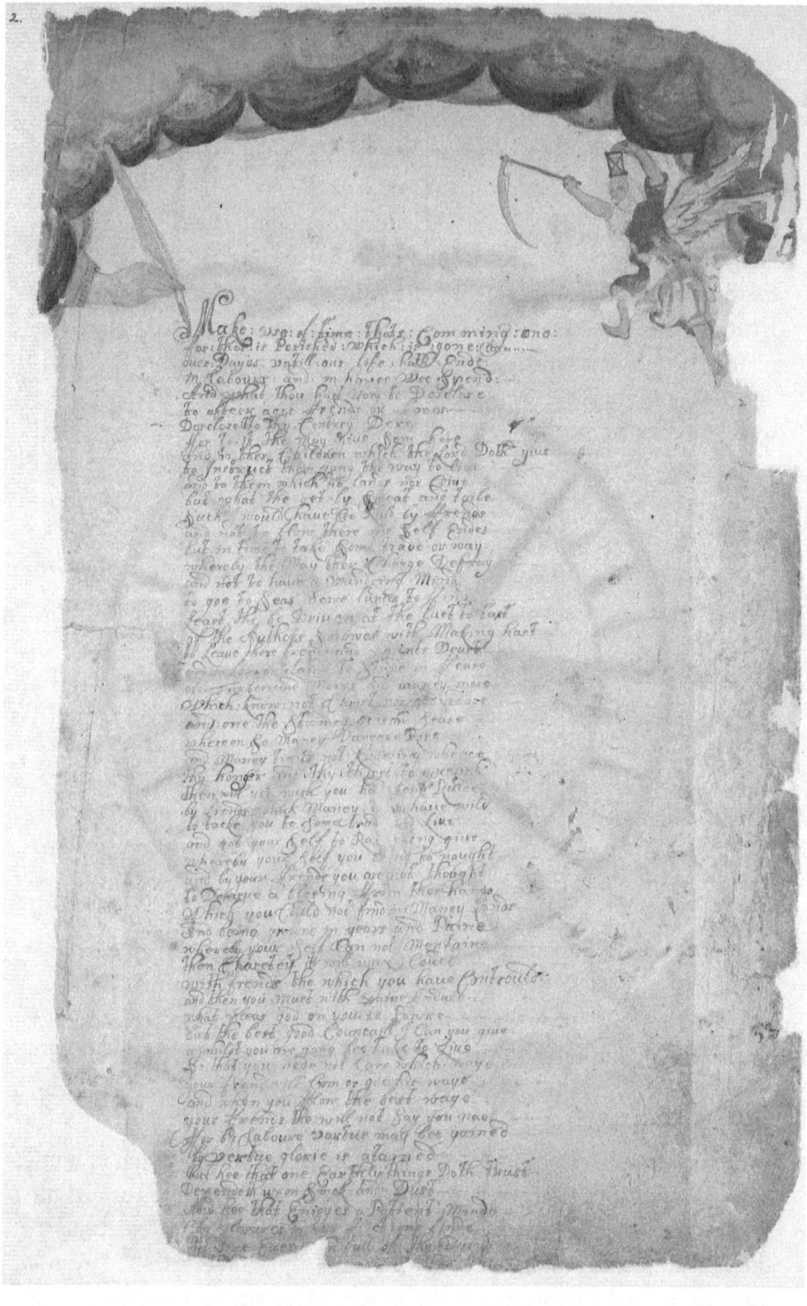

FIGURE 8. The opening poem of Edward Barlow's Journal. Edward Barlow's Journal. Copyright the National Maritime Museum, Greenwich, London.

codify what his poem calls his "Wandering Mind." The verse opens with straightforward advice: "Make use of time that's coming on[e] / for that is perished which is gone" (sig. 2).[5] What Barlow means by "make use" becomes clear as the poem reads his oceangoing "wandering" as a failed example. The poem insists that the task of the journal is to "disclose" the author's mind, which his wandering has hidden from his family's view. The problem with disclosure, however, is that it comes too late.[6] Barlow advises his readers not to follow his own practice of after-the-fact poetic disclosure, but instead "what thou has now to Disclose / To after Ages friends or foes" should be offered directly to one's family. "Desclose it to thy Country Dere," he continues, "For to it she may give some here / And to her Children which the Lord doth give / To instruck them young the way to live" (sig. 2). Barlow himself never seems to have taken that advice; the journal may have been designed to reveal his life to posterity, but he seldom mentions his wife or children in its pages.[7] His opening poem evinces regret for a roving life: "Then will you wish you had be[en] Ruld / By friends which maney you have wild / To take you to some trade and live / And not your self to Rambling give" (sig. 2). Faced with disorderly "rambling" and what Fumerton calls the sailor's "unsettled" nature, Barlow's journal announces itself as a retrospective orienting device, a way of coming to terms with the subjective experience of disorder. The poem's last line is illegible, but its later verses include praise of patience: "And hee that enioy a Patient Minde / Past pleasures and afflictions finde / Sure even till the end of Dayes . . ." (sig. 2). Poetic structure provides an order in which Barlow can redeem his own unstructured life.

The verso image of the compass rose provides a visual representation of the order that Barlow's poem and journal seek. As Fumerton observes, Barlow was influenced by practical developments in marine cartography, but his employment of the compass rose suggests that he views the emblem as a symbol for the order his life never really finds, except perhaps in his journal.[8] The drawing illustrates order in several ways. It traces a complete circle, with thirty-two directional points penciled in and identified numerically. Each ten-degree arc of the circle also contains ten individual marks for each degree. North is shown by a red-and-green fleur-de-lis, and the eight cardinal directions by red-and-gold arrows. At the center is a (slightly blurred) ship, tilted northeast as if sailing before a strong southwesterly breeze. As in so many of Barlow's drawings, the ship itself, rather than humans or even coastlines, takes center stage. Presenting the ship under sail surrounded by the orderly compass, Barlow represents his hope that the mariner's life can assume, by means of maritime technology and labor, a kind of order. The numerical structure of the compass and the orderly rigging of the ship create a vision of clarity within disorderly oceans. Here, more than in the semi-Puritanical poem, is Barlow's image of the stable, or stabilized, self at sea. The massive body of the 138 folio leaves of the journal provides narrative and occasionally poetic shape to the ideological fantasy of the compass rose.

As much as any figures except perhaps Shakespeare and the queen herself, Elizabeth's naval captains, the Elizabethan sea dogs, epitomize her reign in the historical imagination. The piratical exploits of these mariners drove England's ships out into the wide oceans of early modern globalization. Despite their triumphs, these men suffered at sea. This chapter's historical interruptions describe their catastrophic final voyages. Like Barlow, many of these figures died at sea. Brief biographic interjections accent the human cost of saltwater globalization.

A longer interruption in this chapter explores the shipwreck of Ulysses, the hero of this book.

On June 22, 1611, mutineers placed Henry Hudson, his son John, and six others into a small shallop, towed them to open water, and set them adrift. No trace of them was ever seen again.[9]

London, 1659

Barlow's first voyage to sea, in 1659, came two years after he left his mother's home. This voyage occasioned the largest spread of illustrations in the journal (twenty-five consecutive pages, from sig. 7v to 19v) and also Barlow's second inset poem. After the long run of illustrations brings him to the mouth of the Thames, he writes, "I thought it good to insert the follow[ing] lines concerning my longing desire to go to sea" (sig. 20). What follows is a carefully constructed poetic insert and counterpoint to the moralizing prefatory pages. On the page Barlow rules out in red ink a two-column text box of twelve lines each that fills the folio leaf to the right-hand margin (the left-hand margin has been trimmed by binding). Within the box his poem appears neatly written (as all of the journal is, especially in these early years) with a colon between each word and an ellipsis at the end of each line. Like the mass of illustrations, which provide views of Barlow's journey from London Bridge to the Suffolk coast, this poem memorializes Barlow's transformation from landsman to a seaman. The transformation is supernatural in character and not entirely trustworthy.

Barlow opens his poem by attributing his maritime "longing" to supernatural forces: "I know not by what Deity I incited / To see the oshan [ocean] sease [sic] I was delighted" (sig. 20).[10] Like many sentimental sailors before and after him, Barlow enjoys emphasizing his own courage in venturing onto "such a Dangerous and Watery Element, / Where many times both ships and men are sent / Unto the bottom of those gulfey waves" (sig. 20). Like sea poets before and after him, Barlow emphasizes the fundamental alterity of the waters. In fact, as the poem continues into its second column (the two columns may function as distinct stanzas), Barlow's sense of his own danger grows: "And many times I after did sustain / A hungry belly and a thirsty brain / and also of great Stormes are blo[w]ne / unto such places as are not knowne" (sig. 20). As in his introductory poem, here Barlow's reflections on his life at sea figure himself as disorderly and unrepresentable. As seaman he becomes opaque to himself. His conclusion in this second poem, however, is not a lament for the landed life he did not follow but praise of his own maritime faith: "Yet I always put my trust in god and will / Whatsoever to my fortune will come still" (sig. 20). Barlow's "god" (which he writes in the lowercase, though it is not clear that his choice of case is always meaningful) provides him with a sense of order, or at least it serves as a principle of order that Barlow can trust even if he cannot see it. God replaces the compass rose. The sea and seafaring appear destructive, particularly of Barlow's always fragile sense of an orderly self. Against oceanic chaos, he places one final couplet (*will/ still*) and a fairly generic deity.

After his successful circumnavigation of 1586–88, Thomas Cavendish attempted a catastrophic second voyage in 1591. His fleet scattered in the Atlantic; he quarreled with cocommander John Davis; and no vessels made it through the Strait of Magellan. Cavendish died in spring 1592, perhaps two months after his ship *Leicester* arrived back in Plymouth. Legend says he died of a broken heart.[11]

The Atlantic, 1662

Perhaps the most striking image Barlow provides of the destructive sea comes in his description of catching sharks in the mid-Atlantic from on board the *Queen Katherine* in 1663 (Figure 9). Like many other seventeenth-century maritime diarists, including Henry Teonge, Woodes Rogers, and William Dampier, Barlow was an amateur naturalist, and he drew many pictures of exotic marine life. His description of the shark, like other contemporary descriptions, emphasizes its ferocity: "Sharks . . . will keep company with a ship and take anything that is heaved overboard, they are so hungry and ravenous, and will seize upon a man if he should be swimming in the water, so that in some places men, if they have been swimming for recreation, have had their legs bitten off and also have been carried quite away and never seen more" (sig. 38).[12] Barlow is interested in sharks' teeth, "three sets of teeth, one within the other" (sig. 38), but he is even more animated by the things found in their bellies, including a slain sheep's feet, a dead rat, and "a whole ox-hide, being newly flayed from the ox" (sig. 38). Sharks figure what Shakespeare's sonnet calls the "hungry ocean" (Sonnet 64), a place of insatiable desire, consuming anything in its path.

Barlow's illustration literalizes the threat of the ocean to human bodies. Beneath a descriptive caption that mentions the shark, "the Most Ravenous fish that Swimms in the Sea," and the two pilot fish, "his fish that goe along with him," Barlow sketches a huge beast with a man's leg in his jaws. The human figure is stiff but recognizable, even anatomically correct, and Barlow has used red pencil to show blood on the shark's teeth. It is a brutal image, and by not mentioning the man being bitten in his caption or his narrative, Barlow suggests either that he is not concerned with his fellow humans, which the relative lack of human interest in the journal might also imply, or that he provides a picture not of an individual human but of the shark's emblematic relationship to humankind in general. Here, Shakespeare's poetic description of the "hungry ocean" seems painfully apt: the shark-as-sea consumes human bodies. This illustration represents what Barlow understood to exist beneath the waves. As a symbol of oceanic meaning in the early modern period, it shows how empirical observation—seeing what the sea does to human bodies—was supplementing theological and classical topoi. Barlow's ocean, like Shakespeare's, is hungry—but

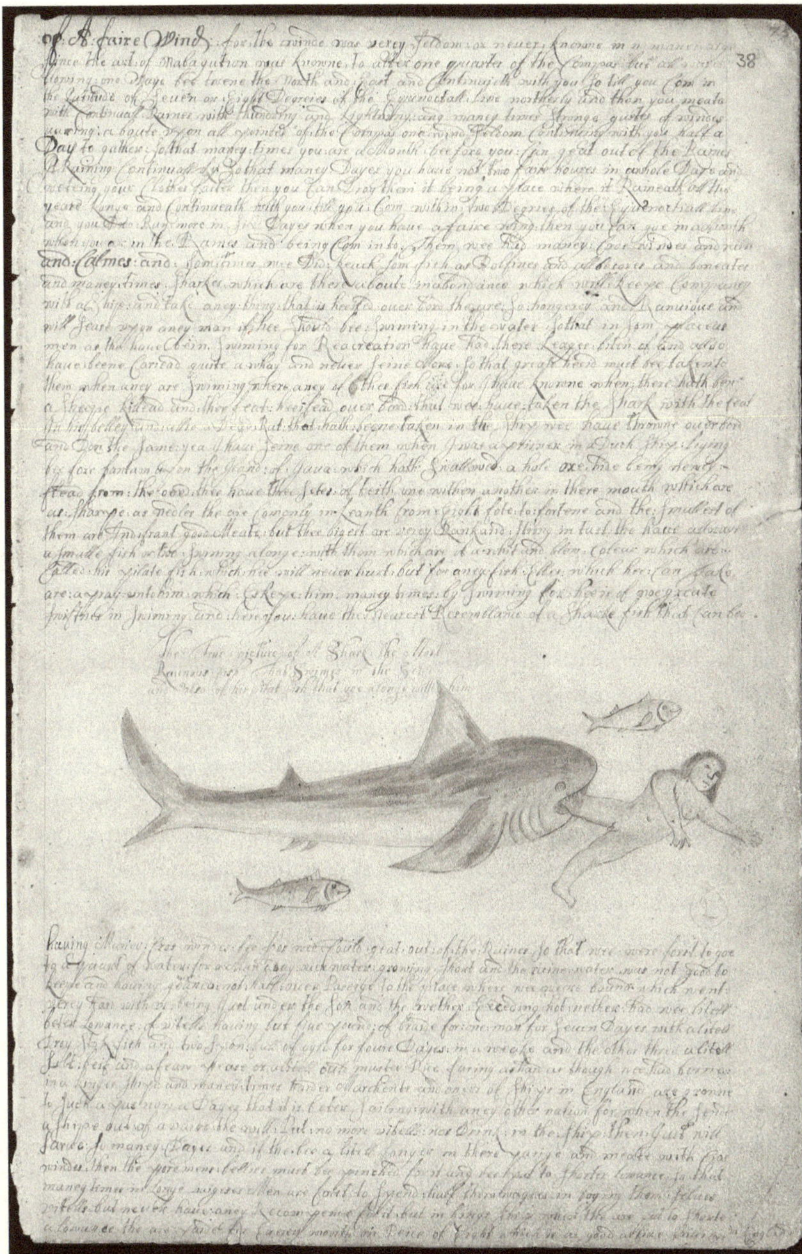

FIGURE 9. Barlow's image of a shark biting a sailor. Edward Barlow's Journal. Copyright the National Maritime Museum, Greenwich, London.

that seems true in a more literal sense for the sailor than the poet and playwright.

After quarrelling with Cavendish on their failed circumnavigation of 1591–92, the Arctic explorer John Davis took service in the East Indies as a pilot. He was slain defending the *Tiger* from pirates off the coast of Borneo in December 1605. The ship's planned voyage to China was never completed, and the *Tiger* returned home in July 1606.

The *Experiment,* 1671

Of the more than two-dozen ships on which Barlow sailed, the *Experiment,* an East India ship on which he made two voyages between 1670 and 1674, stands out for two reasons. On his second voyage, as previously discussed, the ship was captured by the Dutch in Banka Strait, during which captivity he started his journal. The first voyage, however, shows Barlow's particular affinity for this vessel at least as clearly. In describing a near shipwreck that he experienced on the earlier voyage, while homeward bound from India in January 1671, Barlow provides one of his clearest and most detailed pictures of his sea-self. To depict himself and his fellow sailors' struggles against the threat of shipwreck, he uses in full the triplicate resources of his journal. In presenting this adventure on the *Experiment,* Barlow is narrator, illustrator, and poet. The episode spans two folio leaves of the manuscript (sig. 74v–75). A dense, technical description of maritime labor frames both pages: twenty-seven lines in the upper of sig. 74v, twelve in the upper of sig. 75, and nine in the lower of sig. 75. At the bottom of sig. 74v, another of Barlow's red-lined text boxes appears in two columns, each containing thirty lines of poetry. The centerpiece in the middle of sig. 75 is a color drawing of the ship in distress, with the mizzenmast overboard and men aloft cutting away the tops of the main and foremasts. The two pages, when viewed side by side, as they would have been when the journal was bound, though we do not know if Barlow planned to have it bound, present in triplicate Barlow's formal resources in representing maritime crisis: exacting prose, resonant verse, and visual depiction. What we see in these pages, I propose, is metis itself: the exacting labor necessary for maritime survival (Figures 10 and 11).[13] Barlow unfolds this episode in full not only because the episode would have been relatively recent

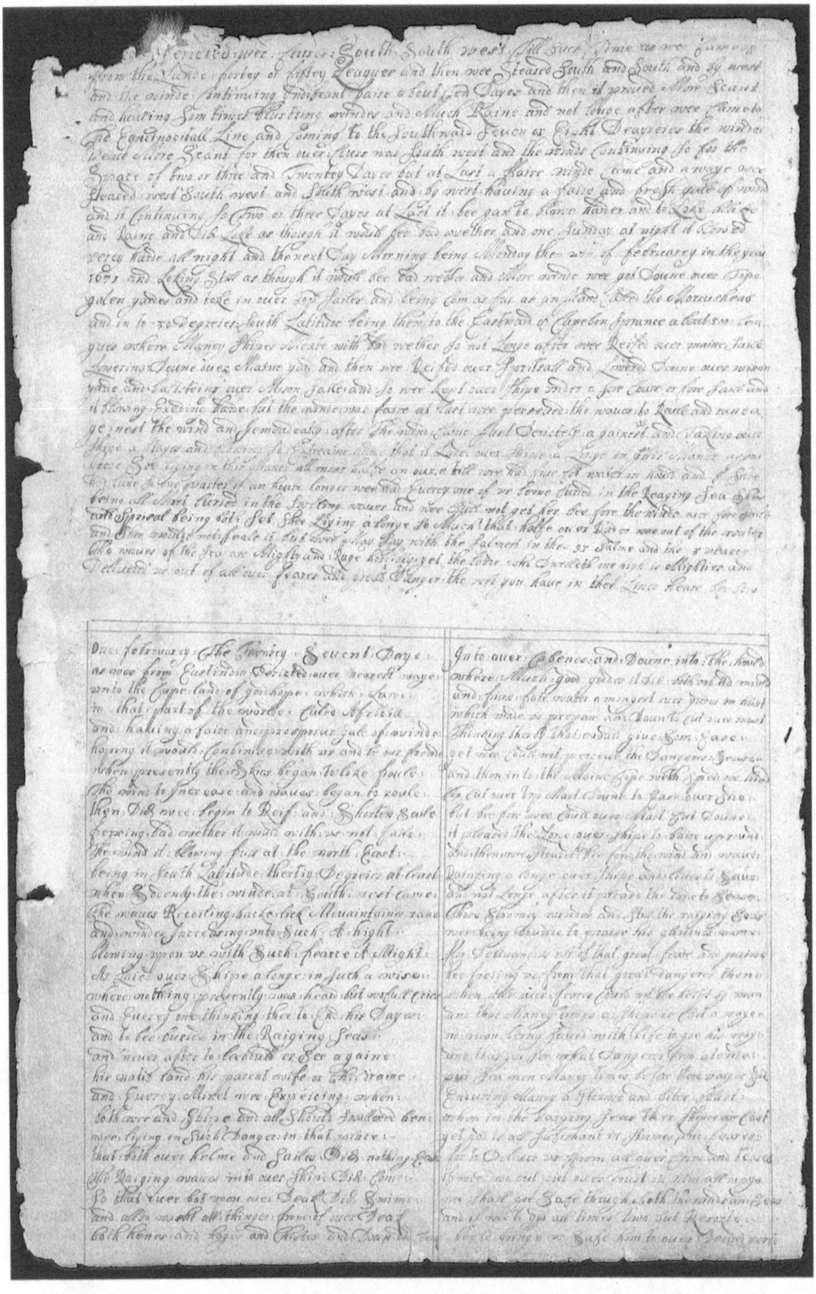

FIGURE 10. Barlow's poem describing the struggle of the ship *Experiment* in a storm. Edward Barlow's Journal. Copyright the National Maritime Museum, Greenwich, London.

FIGURE 11. Barlow's image and prose description of the *Experiment* in a storm. Edward Barlow's Journal. Copyright the National Maritime Museum, Greenwich, London.

when he began his journal on the same ship in 1672 but because this three-headed presentation allows him to show, intimately and exactly, how he managed life at sea.

The narrative follows the familiar template, which Barlow, whose literacy seems to have been largely self-acquired, may not have known, from Virgil or Ovid. A calm descends upon the ship as it crosses the line, and then the storm hits. Barlow, using the communal "we" throughout, describes careful preemptive labor: "We got down our top-gallant yards and took in our topsails, being come as far as an island calle Morrusheus . . . where many ships meet with bad weather" (sig. 74v).[14] The weather for homeward-bound East India ships in late February was reliably bad, and Barlow carefully enumerates all the preparations the ship employed: "So not long after, we reefed our mainsail, lowering down our main yard; and then we reefed our spritsail and lowered down our mizzen yard and balistering our mizzen sail, so we kept our ship under a fore course or foresail, it blowing extreme hard" (sig. 74v.) The precise technical language measures human metis against the storm. As in the case of Odysseus, who despite his skill is repeatedly wrecked, the *Experiment* cannot match the ocean: "The wind came just directly against us, taking our ship a-stayes and blowing so extreme hard that it laid our ship along, in the manner you here see, lying in this manner almost half an hour, till we had five foot water in the hold; and if she had lain so one quarter of an hour longer, we had, every one of us, been buried in the raging sea" (sig. 74v). Being in stays—facing directly into the wind so that the sails provide no headway—is a position of maximum weakness for a sailing ship, and Barlow focuses on exactly this moment. It leads him to write a poem, produce a detailed illustration, and quote a textual authority: "Yet we may say with the psalmist in the 93 salme and the 5 vearce The waves of the sea are mighty and rage horribly, yet the Lord who dwelleth on high is mightier and delivered us out of all our feares and great danger. The rest you have in these lines here below—" (sig. 74v). The relationship between Barlow's three representations of metis in three distinct media seem progressive: his technical description leads to nautical impasse, being caught in stays, and from that still point biblical inspiration generates poetic creation. These phases represent Barlow's sea-self forming through seamanship, illustration, and poetry.

The poem that follows, while not quite as neatly presented as the embarkation poem, serves in a similar fashion to order this page. In a red-ruled text box of two columns, Barlow presents another conventional description of the storm and the need to trust in God's good will. The language of the poem embroiders typical metaphors into the language of Barlow's own description: "When suddenly the wind at south-west came / The waves recoiling back like mountains ran, / And winds increasing unto such a height, / Blowing on us with such fierce a might / As laid our ship along in such a wise / Where nothing presently was heard but woeful cries" (sig. 74v). Barlow treats the storm not just as an opportunity for technical labor but as an emblem of the seaman's pitiful lot: "And every minute we expecting when / Both we and the ship and all should swallowed been" (sig. 74v). But while the poem eventually emphasizes submission to God, who is "all sufficient in storms and fears," the second column/stanza shifts from describing the misery of being in stays to presenting a close description of the maritime labor that Barlow's main narrative has not yet detailed: "Which [i.e., the water in the hold] made us prepare and cut down our mast / Thinking thereby we would get some ease / . . . And then into the maintop with speed we hied / To cut our topmast down to ease our side" (sig. 74v). This dangerous labor, which Barlow also sketches in his drawing, in notable ways counteracts the pious submission with which the poem finishes. Barlow may well have believed that only God could guide his ship to port; he would hardly have been the only sailor aboard to believe that. But he also saw the storm as an opportunity for skilled labor. The poem's divided authority—its appeals to divine Providence and to maritime praxis—captures Barlow's own divided self.

On the facing recto leaf, Barlow provides a detailed image of what human metis does during a maritime crisis. His illustration of the *Experiment* shows the mizzenmast down in the sea (the first narrative lines after the poem explains, "having cut down our mizzenmast" [sig. 75]). Even more dramatic, he shows the tiny figures of two men in the main top with axes cutting away the main-topmast; two more on the foretop, presumably for the same purpose, though no axes are visible; two more climbing the main rigging; and one on the bow, perhaps furling the spiritsail. The illustration presents nine men aloft and another ten to twelve on deck. (Barlow's ship illustrations often show men working aloft, though few of these portraits show as much concentrated labor as this one.)[15] The sailors aloft practice the most technical and dangerous elements of their craft. They do not save the ship, exactly; Barlow is quite clear that "the ship [is] by God's great mercy bearing up, and the winds and waves something abating" (sig. 75) when they regain control of the ship. But seaman-like metis seems a necessary, if not sufficient, aspect of surviving a near shipwreck like this one. The multimedia message of these two pages appears to be that it requires multiple actors—God, men, the sea—and multiple genres—narrative, poetry, visual art—to capture seamanship in crisis.

Ulysses in the Surf

All Western shipwrecks begin with *The Odyssey,* and the metis of Ulysses provides a master code for all sailors. The example of Ulysses helps reveal the larger cultural patterns behind Roch's and Barlow's efforts to unify their star-driven fates with skilled labor. By exploring Homer's depiction of the social, intellectual, and technological hybrids that create metis by reading Arthur Golding's Elizabethan translation of the *Odyssey,* I also analyze the composite form in which classical models arrived to early modern readers, in this case combining a Greek original, the hero's Latin name (Ulysses), and Elizabethan iambic couplets.[16] Metis, for Homer as for Barlow, requires the careful, painstaking unification of human skill and divine aid. This interface appears in the most detail in the culminating shipwreck episode in Homer's poem, Ulysses's landfall on Phaeacia (book 5). Homer's narrative replies to an ancient fear of the ocean best represented by his near-contemporary Hesiod, who in *Works and Days* includes among a list of features of the good life "hav[ing] no need to go on ships" (ll.236–37).[17] Hesiod emphasizes the contrast between settled farmers, whose lives are rich and productive, and wandering mariners, who are constantly at risk. The same land–sea distinction underlines Tiresias's prophecy of Ulysses's death, in which he travels so far inland that the local people "know no sea, nor ships, nor oars" (11.155–56).[18] The hero of craft and manipulation distinguishes himself by being able to survive at sea.

To reach the "shady hills of the Phaeacian shore" (5.351), Ulysses faces Roch's and Barlow's task of uniting physical skill, social context, and supernatural insight. The killing storm Neptune raises parallels the whirlpool that drowns Dante's Ulysses, in that human maritime success gets figured as transgression. Homer's Neptune describes the hero's safe landfall as a crime against divinity: "O impiety . . . now the Gods' inconstancy / Is most apparent, altering their designs / Since I the Aethiops saw . . . But I hope he shall / Feel woe at height, ere that dead calm befall" (5.362–65, 368–69). The sea-god, speaking for the tempest that he raises, insists that a successful, trouble-free journey violates the proper relationship between divine power and human ingenuity. Ulysses may survive, but not easily. The "dead calm" that Neptune describes as the hero's eventual fate refers to his happy homecoming, but it also resembles the more complete death that ends Ulysses's story in Dante. Storms represent divine anger, but winds create oceanic possibility. Heroes and sailors alike need wind.

In the shipwrecking storm, Ulysses responds like Roch and Barlow by mixing things human and divine. Accepting his own belatedness, Ulysses terms himself "man of misery" (5.381) and predicts that he will die at sea: "Fear tells me now, that, all the Goddess said, / Truth's self will author, that Fate would he paid / Grief's whole sum due from me, at sea, before / I reach'd the dear touch of my country's shore" (382–85).[19] Like Barlow's, Ulysses's seaborne exploits teach intimacy with Fate. Looking at a newly wrought storm, the classical mariner pronounces the lament that Dante's Ulysses never speaks: "Thus dreadful is the presence of our death" (5.390). Homer's hero recognizes he is not foremost a warrior; Ulysses contrasts his solitary fate to the honored deaths of his companions at Troy, who were "Thrice four times blest" and "By all the Greeks with funerals glorified" (391, 399). The contrast is not simply political—like Aeneas, Ulysses wishes he had died in battle—but also social: he does not want to die alone. He fears death less than being forgotten, "by no man mourn'd nor known" (401). The opposite of single-minded Achilles, Ulysses embodies the sociability and integrating practices necessary for success at sea. The loss of the shipmates who followed him from Troy makes this storm the nadir of Ulysses's exclusion from civilization.

Immersion entails confronting the salty immensity of the ocean with one's body. This sudden shock, which neither Barlow nor Roch describes, challenges Ulysses's heroic resources in book 5. Ulysses resists complete individualization and instead creates plural human–tool assemblages even when he is alone in the ocean. Ulysses clings to the last mechanical vestiges of his craft, but his route to safety will be not sailing but swimming. Swimming, on the face of it, is an unnatural task, one to which humans, even heroes, are ill suited.[20] Unwilling to abandon the trappings of landed life, Ulysses clings to the robes Calypso has given him, though they are "Hind'ring his swimming" (414). Later, he returns to his "drenched vessel" and "gat at length again, / Wrestling with Neptune, hold of her" (415–17). He is a hero who loves his tools.

Tools preserve Ulysses's life for a time, but to rescue himself he requires a human–divine hybrid. Even on a sinking ship amid a tempest, the hero of maritime practice is never fully alone. The nymph Leucothea gives him an enchanted amulet and advises him to swim. Following her advice means trusting supernatural community—Leucothea recalls Athena, of course—rather than solitary ingenuity or even nautical skills. The nymph makes the choice explicit when she advises the hero to "leave thy weeds and ship to the commands / Of these rude winds, and work out with thy hands / Pass to Phaeacia" (446–48). Relying on "hands" rather than tools, however, does not come naturally to Ulysses. He resists her advice: "As long as I perceive / My ship not quite dissolv'd, I will not leave / The help she may afford me, but abide, / And suffer all woes till the worst be tried. / When she is split, I'll swim" (468–72). Always practical, Ulysses will not put his faith in supernatural rescue before he has exhausted mechanical tactics. His Latourian composition of human and nonhuman alliances models the behavior of historical sailors such as Barlow and Roch.

After losing his boat to the "huge . . . high, and horrid sea" (475), Ulysses embraces metis as human–divine mixture. Swimming to shore requires putting himself naked into the elements, but Ulysses makes the most out of the last tools left, first "mount[ing] on a rib . . . Like to a rider of a running horse, / To stay himself a time" (480–82), and then remembering the nymph's amulet before he "all his forces set / To swim, and cast him prostrate to the seas" (485–86). Ulysses's version of delivering himself into the sea includes getting as much use as possible out of his tools and maximizing his chances for supernatural rescue. The solitary swim to Phaeacia remains a feat of superhuman endurance—"Two nights, yet, and days / He spend in wrestling with the sable seas" (504–5)—but his tactics remain resolutely hybrid: both tools and his body, both his strength and the nymph's aid. This moment of perfect solitude—of oceanic immersion—becomes a fulcrum around which turns the hero's reintegration into a social but not only human world. His landfall gets introduced by an extended simile that emphasizes filial piety and human connection: "look how to good sons that esteem / Their father's life dear, (after pains extreme, / Felt in some sickness, that hath held him long / Down to his bed, and with affections strong / Wasted his body . . .) / When on their prayers they see descend at length / Health from the heavens" (513–19). The hero's deliverance from sea to land reintegrates him into a metaphoric family, even if his own father remains one more island away.

The landfall itself, the result of Ulysses's physical endurance and heroic skills, gets presented as the product of supernatural agency, "health from the heavens." Just as Dante's Ulysses finally gets destroyed by the overwhelming force of God as "Another," so Homer's hero, despite his shrewd sailing, resourceful use of technology, and numerous allies, finally depends on supernatural power. In his final speech before making land, Ulysses emphasizes his dependence on the gods:

> O . . . now Jupiter
> Hath given me a sighte of an unhoped for shore,
> Though I have wrought these seas so long, so sore.
> Of rest yet no place shows the slend'rest prints.
> The rugged shore so bristled is with flints . . .
> And should I swim to seek a haven elsewhere,
> Or land less way-beat, I may justly fear
> I shall be taken with a gale again,
> And case a huge way off into the main . . .
> I well have prov'd, with what malignity
> [Neptune] treads my steps. (537–50)

Fearing Neptune and appealing to Jupiter at the same time emphasizes the complexity of the divine powers with which Ulysses interacts; his world includes hostile and beneficent forces in constant conflict. His articulated anguish forces the hand of his benefactor, Athena, who urges him to swim forward: "But She prompted him, / That never fail'd, and bade him no more swim / Still off and on, but boldly force the shore" (564–66). Athena's cunning balances angry Neptune and distant Jupiter. To early modern Christian humanists, God's Providence combined the powers of all three of these classical figures, making divine power at once fearful, distant, and comforting.

The hero's landfall performs hybridity. It does not emerge simply from Athena's rescue; Ulysses's last efforts combine his own "wisdom" with the goddess's powers. Following Athena's command to "force to shore," he gets sucked back by the surf. Homer's description of the interaction between natural labor and supernatural control is exact: Ulysses first triumphs by grasping a rock in the surf—"And hug the rock that him so rudely tore; / Which he with both hands sigh'd and clasp'd, till past / The billows rage it was" (567–69)—but then gets wrenched from it by the force of the sea—"when 'scap'd, back so fast / The rock repuls'd it, that it reft his hold, / Sucking him from it, and far back he rolled" (569–71). At the end of his endurance, having exhausted companions, ship, and even the advice of Leucothea and Athena, Ulysses sinks "Quite under water . . . and, past fate" (584). His rescue comes at last from both Athena and his own internal mental prowess: "there had lost the state / He held in life, if, still the grey-eyed Maid / His wisdom prompting, he had not assay'd / Another course" (585–88). Rather than swimming again to the rocks, he locates the mouth of a stream and makes a last appeal to the river's god: "King of this river, hear! . . . / Reverend is / To all the ever-living Deities / What erring man soever seeks their aid. / . . . Yield then some rest / To him that is thy suppliant profess'd" (596–603). Invoking the law of hospitality that binds even the gods, Ulysses's wisdom, prompted by and in concert with Athena's advice, convinces the river god to welcome him to his shore. "Dead weary" (614) upon the sand, the hero of social craft's first action is to repay a social debt by returning Leucothea's amulet to the sea. Slinking off into the woods to sleep, the mariner briefly resembles one of Hesiod's farmers avoiding the sea. For the rest of *The Odyssey,* his labors take place mostly on land. Seafaring, in the Homeric model, always points toward landfall.

Barlow's Wrecks, 1673–1700

Several other illustrations in Barlow's journal after his voyage on the *Experiment* also show ships in distress: the *Florentine* wrecked on Goodwin Sands in August 1673 (sig. 93), the *Rainbow* aground in Banka Strait in 1688 (sig. 115), the *Sampson* in a gale in 1695 (sig. 126), the *Wintworth* similarly beset in 1700 (sig. 136v). On none of these occasions, however, does Barlow again employ the triple resources of technical description, poetry, and illustration. The description of the wreck of the *Florentine,* the only ship of Barlow's to be lost prior to his final voyage on the *Liampo,* presents a simple error of navigation, and while the illustration is evocative—the masts of the wrecked ship are shown upside down, in what appears to be either an awkward attempt at perspective or an emblem of her loss—it does not present technical details. The *Rainbow* appears at the center of a compass, with indicators of depth scattered throughout the image of the strait, so that this illustration could be used to help future mariners avoid the Banka rock, but the only maritime labor it shows is sailors in longboats preparing to tow the boat off the rock at high tide.[21] The *Wintworth* has a half-dozen men in the rigging, perhaps having just furled the topsails, but the ship appears in no great danger.

The *Sampson's* plight is more desperate, and the episode seems particularly resonant when Barlow notes that the gale strikes the ship "much like the wind we had in the ship *Experiment* in my first voyage to East India, and near the same latitude" (sig. 125v). No men are shown aloft in the illustration, although all six of the set sails have been blown loose.[22] In fact, Barlow's description of the episode inverts the conventional praises of seaman-like labor and good materials: "Had it pleased God," he writes, "that our sails had been new and strong and our masts and rigging held, it had certainly caused the sea to swallow us up in the twinkling of an eye, the fierceness of it [i.e., the gale] being past description at that time" (sig. 126).[23] This episode presents the unusual case of poor workmanship saving the ship. Sailors crowd the deck, but none seems engaged in productive labor. As it happened, the splitting of the sails prevented a greater catastrophe: "For if the sails had been good, masts and all must have gone" (sig. 126). The event as a whole leads Barlow to speculate about "God's great mercy to us" and to resort to illustration rather than narrative description, as he writes that they were "in great fear of losing our passage about the Cape, being in such condition as you may see here below, being described as well as I can, being but an indifferent moralist" (sig. 126). The *Sampson* manages, by patching sails, to weather the Cape, but Barlow's self-description as "indifferent moralist" (which Lubbock accents in his marginal notes) suggests that he was aware of the difficulties in representing crisis moments like these. The *Sampson*'s plight did not lead him into verse as had the *Experiment*'s two decades earlier, but he recognizes that these brief, intense episodes require a more elaborate representation than many other episodes in his voyages. The near wreck of the *Sampson* provides one of the last images of maritime crisis in Barlow's journal; only the illustration of the *Wentworth* follows it. This image shows him painfully aware of the limits of human labor and artistry in such events. The tension within Barlow's journal between his ambition to represent metis in full, as in the case of the *Experiment,* and his awareness that sometimes the sea is beyond representation, as in the case of the *Sampson,* defines his two-faced sea. His ocean, like Shakespeare's, remains slightly beyond representation.

Following a career as a privateer, Arctic explorer, and admiral in the Armada Campaign, Martin Frobisher led a foray onto the continent in August 1594, attempting to forestall a French–Spanish Catholic alliance. In an assault on the Spanish fortress of El Léon, he received a pistol wound in the thigh. Nearly three months later, he died of a gangrenous infection of the lower body in Plymouth.[24]

The Thames, 1703, and the Indian Ocean, 1706

The endings of Barlow's life and of his journal seem particularly resonant because the historical record provides three different versions of closure. The first is the textual ending of the journal as we have it, which concludes with the description of riding out the Great Storm of 1703 at the mouth of the Thames. This ending, which has the sailor deciding in the end to return to his wife and children after a storm in which "more than a thousand good seamen lost their lives, making many poor widows and fatherless children" (sig. 140v), provides a resonant sense of completion, which appealed to both Barlow's editor, Basil Lubbock, and his biographer, A. G. Course.[25] East India Company records, however, provide a second possibility. Barlow made one more journey, as captain of the *Liampo,* bound for Mocha in 1705. That ship was lost off Mozambique on January 7, 1706. We cannot be certain that Barlow went down with the *Liampo,* but it seems probable that he did. The journal clearly did not, but the surviving copy appears to have been transcribed from initial manuscripts, though Barlow does describe, during the wreck of the *Florentine* on Goodwin Sands in 1675, taking pains to retrieve "this book" (260) from his chest. Death at sea, however, would provide a generically satisfying end to his adventures. Finally, a third ending text, Barlow's will, survives in the National Archives to provide another version of the sailor's final act. I will explore all three versions of Barlow's end—the retired sailor, the drowned captain, and the controlling father—to elucidate the competing subtexts of the final lines of the journal and the final pencil drawing of Cork Harbor, Ireland.

The great storm of November 1703, still believed to be the most powerful storm ever to strike England, found Barlow a passenger on the *Kingfisher* at the mouth of the Thames. He had left the *Fleet Frigate* in St. Helena after arguing with his captain over the handling of the sails. Despite not being a member of the *Kingfisher*'s crew, Barlow, as usual, describes the crew's labors aboard the ship with the pronoun "we": "We escaped very narrowly, losing one of our best anchors and drove with our sheet anchor and small bower ahead, and our best bower cable broke, and near to the Shew and Blacktail Sands in a dismal condition we cut all our masts by the board" (sig. 140v). The crew's seamanship, here depicted with neither poem nor image, saves the ship, but not before Barlow the "indifferent moralizer" reads this storm the same way Daniel Defoe would in *The Storm* (1704), as evidence of God's displeasure with England: "I pray God we may repent, for doubtless it was a warning of God's anger against us, for a worse generation scarce can be in all wickedness" (sig. 140v). Barlow focuses on maritime England, perhaps thinking of the captain of his last ship who had put him off in St. Helena: "All commanders and masters are grown up with pride and oppression and tyranny. I want words to lay out the business and unworthy dealings of many men I have met with, not acting like Christians" (sig. 140v). Barlow reads the storm in allegorical terms, and his prescription for the nation matches that of Defoe, who placed on the cover of *The Storm* a quotation from the book of Nathanial: "The Lord hath his way in the Whirlwind, and in the Storm, and the Clouds are the dust of his Feet."[26] Against this theological anger, seaman-like metis keeps the ship afloat, enabling sailors to bear witness of God's displeasure.

On the final page of his journal, Barlow applies the corrective maxim of the great storm to his own life. He leaves the *Kingfisher* at Gravesend and heads into London "to see my wife and children; and [I] ou[gh]t never to forget the goodness of God in preserving me from such imminent danger in the late storm, where more than one thousand seamen lost their lives, making many poor widows and fatherless children" (sig. 140v). He then extends this conventional moral to include not only the just-passed storm but his entire maritime life: "And I must thank God in his goodness in preserving me in all my voyages through many and great dangers, having used the sea employment so many years" (sig. 140v). These are the last words in Barlow's journal, and the awkward phrasing of his final reference to his labor—"used the sea employment so many years"—underlines the ambiguity of his relationship with the maritime world. He is, in the phrase Conrad would later popularize, "one of us," a member of the brotherhood of the sea, but he also feels estranged from his own labors.

The final illustration in the journal is a pencil sketch of Cork Harbor in Ireland, which complements the description of the *Kingfisher* limping into Gravesend (Figure 12). The drawing fills about two-thirds of the last folio leaf, showing twenty-two ships in various places along the river. It is tempting and, probably, reasonable enough to see it as a final image of the sailor's homecoming. If so, Barlow's world has changed considerably from the Lancashire farmhouse from which he said goodbye to his mother in 1657. His new world is wider and more watery, but also much less personable: no human figures are visible in this illustration. Coming home to port has special resonance for any sailor, and Barlow includes more illustrations of ports than any other subject. It is hard not to see special resonance in this final image of ships coming safely to road before the Great Storm. To read Barlow's journal as having a literary shape may be a category mistake, although I certainly agree with Fumerton that the journal is an "aesthetic artifact" (127) as well as a historical record. The journal as a whole creates the sense of an ending by repeating on its last page the theological maxims with which it opens. Returned home to God and family, Barlow's wanderings parallel those of these ships he draws heading up to Cork.

But the historical Barlow's journey, as we know, did not end in 1703. If we take the loss of the *Liampo* off Mozambique as the true "end" of Barlow's voyages, the generic shape of the journal becomes tragic, a cautionary tale about "a Wandering Mind" and "Rambling" life, as Barlow suggests in the journal's prefatory poem (sig. 3). In this reading, Barlow's reunion with his wife and child after the Great Storm cannot hold him at shore for long. Like Ulysses in Dante's *Inferno,* he returns for a last fatal voyage.

In addition to the textual ending, in which Barlow returns to his family, and the historical ending, in which he goes down with the *Liampo,*

FIGURE 12. The final image in Barlow's journal shows ships at rest in Cork Harbor, Ireland. Edward Barlow's Journal. Copyright the National Maritime Museum, Greenwich, London.

the archives reveal a third possible structure for Barlow's end: his will, which he made in November 1705 before embarking on the *Liampo* and which survives in the National Archives.[27] In this reading, neither the theologically minded writer of the journal nor the tragically destined captain of the *Liampo* takes top billing. Instead, we see a Barlow determined to order his family in ways that his own family had failed to order him. He makes his "lawful and loving wife Mary Barlow my true and lawful Attorney for the term of her life" (175), gives to her all his "goods and furniture," and then splits the financial estate three ways, among his wife, his son Edward, and his daughter Anne. (Edward also gets one-half of the silver plate.) The bequest to his daughter, however, comes with a condition: "with proviso to my daughter that if she is not obedient, obliging and willing to take her mother's advice in all things for her good and show herself loving and in all things dutiful as a child ought to be to her parent, then I give her no more than one quarter of what estate I may appear to be worth at my decease" (175). The disciplinary structure of Barlow's will—his desire that his daughter, at least, should live a more structured life than his own—suggests that he to some extent struggled against his own wandering life. It also provides a third governing genre for the journal, a parable of education, in which Barlow finally learns the error of his ways.

Barlow's journal thus appears a creature of three genres. It can be read as a prodigal's journey home, following the last entry in the journal; a tragic failure to control his waywardness, following his death at sea; or, alternatively, as an educational process, in which Barlow's disreputable life, like Magwitch's in *Great Expectations,* makes possible a more settled existence for his heirs. We do not, unfortunately, have much information about his family after the will, except that when his wife made her own will in 1713 (proved 1715), the family silver had been reduced to a single tankard, suggesting that Mary had needed to sell the other items to support the family.[28]

We have little evidence to help us choose among these three models, but I emphasize that the interpretive choices here are fundamentally generic: the journal is either a prodigal's tale, a tragic history, an educational saga, or some hybrid combination of these three. With those genres in mind, I will return briefly to the final image in the journal, of ships in the Cork estuary. Mostly in gray pencil with small touches of red for ships' pennants, the image of twenty-odd ships returning to port can serve as an emblem of Barlow's imaginative homecoming. It is a deeply abstracted, even nonhuman, scene: the bird's-eye view and large scale make it nearly impossible to pick out any human forms, except, possibly, on deck on the two central ships. The distance makes it hard to ascertain the details of rigging and sails, about which Barlow is usually so careful. The *Kingfisher* had visited Cork Harbor just before returning to the mouth of the Thames, and there is something compellingly estranging in having the final image of the journal be not Barlow's last but his second-to-last port of call. Unlike so many of Barlow's portraits, which depict particular ships, harbors, or moments during his voyage, this final image abstracts itself from local knowledge to present a representation of Barlow's homecoming that is somewhat at odds with the events he has narrated. It is a picture of ships that are almost, but not quite, home from the sea. I suggest that Barlow the artist—the maker of his extraordinary book—would have found this image more resonant than any of the three purely textual options the record makes available to us. It is less the sailor's home that matters to him than the last safe port to which he came before the storm. As poet, sailor, and artist, he presents a world in which skilled labor can provide stability, albeit only of a temporary kind.

The most celebrated of the Elizabethan sea dogs, hero of the armada, and the first English circumnavigator (1577–80), Sir Francis Drake died during his final voyage, a failed attempt to assail the Spanish Caribbean with John Hawkins in 1595–96. The cause of his death was "bloody flux," probably dysentery.

Interchapter

Philosopher at the Masthead

IN THE MIDDLE OF A LONG PASSAGE, sometimes, we are not just in the water but also—suddenly—high above it, at the masthead, seeing the planet's curvature spread out across vast blue horizons. We look out into emptiness where sea becomes sky. All of a sudden, we speak in Ishmael's voice:

> In the serene weather of the tropics it is exceedingly pleasant—the mast-head; nay, to a dreamy meditative man, it is delightful. There you stand, a hundred feet above the silent decks, striding along the deep, as if the masts were gigantic stilts, while beneath you and between your legs, as it were, swim the hugest monsters of the sea, even as ships once sailed between the boots of the famous Colossus at old Rhodes.[1]

To be a ship! Walking across silent seas, salt darkness tickling your immense and unseen toes. In calm latitudes, half-hidden moments of sublime uneventfulness. It is as distant from the now-time of shipwreck as you can imagine.

> There you stand, lost in the infinite series of the sea, with nothing ruffled but the waves. The tranced ship indolently rolls; the drowsy trade winds blow; everything resolves you into languor.[2]

We bury corpses at sea.

> He takes the mystic ocean at his feet for the visible image of that deep, blue, bottomless soul, pervading mankind and nature; and

> every strange, half-seen, gliding beautiful thing that eludes him; every dimly-discovered, uprising fin of some undiscernable form, seems to him the embodiment of those elusive thoughts that only people the soul by continually flitting through it. In this enchanted mood, thy spirit ebbs away to whence it came; becomes diffused through time and space; like Wickliff's sprinkled Pantheistic ashes, forming at last a part of every shore the round globe over.[3]

Sea burial does not send corpses away but speeds up the organic processes of decomposition, diffusion, and reintegration into a circulating biosphere. I remember when the U.S. Navy buried Osama bin Laden at sea. The Arabian Sea is far from my home swimming waters of Long Island Sound, but it is all one salt body. We swim together, me and that dead man. We share a planetary commons, a wet wonderworld of trash and plastic and global networks. Does his sea burial mean that those of us who swim in and think about the sea need to embrace the desert dweller, too?

> But while this sleep, this dream is on ye, move your foot or hand an inch, slip your hold at all; and your identity comes back in horror. Over Descartian vortices you hover. And perhaps, at mid-day, in the fairest weather, with one half-throttled shriek you drop through that transparent air into the summer sea, no more to rise for ever. Heed it well, ye Pantheists![4]

Shipwreck waits, in empty air.

· CHAPTER 6 ·

"We Split"

Sea Poetry and Maritime Crisis

Life is storm—let storm!

Herman Melville, "John Marr"

THE CURSE OF SHIPWRECK is fractured orientation. Its cure is—may be—poetry. Or if not a full cure, poetry at least provides a navigable route inside shipwreck's chaos. This chapter on how sea poetry responds to maritime crisis foregrounds chronological dislocation by beginning and ending outside the early modern period. I start with one of Melville's less well-known figures, the land-locked sailor John Marr. The chapter ends with Thomas Hardy's famous lyric about the sinking of the *Titanic,* "The Convergence of the Twain." I use both poems, as well as the early modern material in between, as formal models for the ways poetic form counters maritime dislocation.

The hybrid prose and poetic work "John Marr" comprises the title piece of *John Marr and Other Sailors* (1888), a privately published book that initially appeared in only twenty-five copies. The piece begins with a third-person prose narrative that follows the sailor from his career "under divers flags" (263) to a "crippling wound received at close quarters with pirates of the Keys" (263). After the wound Marr strands himself on the Great Plains through marriage, landed settlement, and the cruel loss of wife and baby to "fever, the bane of new settlements on teeming loam" (263). The "kinless man" (263), isolated midcontinent on "the bed of a dried-up sea" (265), craves the community of maritime comrades, since he cannot speak to landsmen. The saltwater "checkered globe" (263) that has been denied him represents a wider point of view and expanse of vision. Marr's isolation admits no narrative solution, but the poem reframes his dilemma artistically by shifting from prose to verse. Halfway through "John Marr," the narrative changes from third to first person, and Melville's grandiloquent prose re-creates itself as verse. The moment of that transformation pinpoints poetry's powers to liberate experience through oceanic resonance. The last lines of the prose section assert the absence of Marr's maritime comrades:

> He invokes these visionary ones,—striving, as it were, to get into verbal communion with them, or, under yet stronger illusion, reproaching them for their silence:—

The abrupt shift into verse that follows brings the absent into view:

> Since as in night's deck watch ye show,
> Why, lads, so silent here to me,
> Your watchman of times long ago? (267)

While the prose strains toward lost maritime "visionary ones" by way of imagined "communion" or "reproach," the poetry re-creates absence as presence, assembling "lads" into a "night's deck-watch" that merges "times long ago" with Marr's present isolation. Melville's poem, written in and through late-life despair, models the sought-for connection between shipwreck's dislocation and poetry's consolation that this chapter explores. As the poem demonstrates, poetic form enables sailors and writers to respond to the saltwater now-time of shipwreck.

This chapter's exploratory voyage into the massive corpus of English sea poetry ranges idiosyncratically through early modern and modern maritime works. From Melville's Marr, I move to a little-read subset of seventeenth- and early eighteenth-century verse, "piscatorial" poems that adapt traditional pastoral language to a watery setting. From the piscatorialists I turn to a famous early modern diptych, "The Storm" and "The Calm" by John Donne. My reading of Donne's lyrics engages the mythological giant of Camões's *Lusiads* and modernist poetry by Wallace Stevens and Thomas Hardy.[1] In all these poems, basic poetic techniques such as rhymed couplets and triplets index the power of saltwater communities to endure oceanic disorder. End rhymes for poets are what ropes and sails are to Roch and Barlow: tools of metis. Sailor-poets, accustomed to the rhythmic catches of work songs, craft sea poetry through rhyme.[2] By starting with the tragically dry fate of John Marr, I emphasize that sea poetry, particularly its shipwrecked strain, sings a harsh ecological love story. Marr's ringing phrase "*Life is storm—let storm!*"(267), italicized in Melville's first edition, pinpoints the fluid desires the ocean calls up in sailor and poet. The longed-for sea is a place of more-than-human disorder and also human communities. Recalling this vastness incites Melville into verse, and the sailor's oceanic longing hails the sea as divine, gorgeous, and intractable. This chapter begins with John Marr's eruption into verse to show how poetry facilitates the human engagement with maritime disaster. Poetry engages the ocean's destructive force and aesthetic pleasures.

The opening poetic stanza of "John Marr" measures the poem's artistic structure against the narrator's impossible desire to be reunited with his seafaring comrades. The end rhymes "show" and "ago" in the first and third lines emphasize the literal impossibility of recapturing the past, together with the deeply felt desire to return. The prose section of the work also tries to "recur to the past . . . with the mass of men, where the past is in any personal way a common inheritance" (264). Drawn back into his maritime past, John Marr at first appears cut off from it, as the unrhymed second line, ending with "me," isolates the speaker. The desolate "me" of this line, however, gets reintegrated into a larger poetic whole when the second stanza (lines 4–14) sounds out a series of rhymes, repeating and enclosing the narrator's "me" with "the darkling sea" (4) and a series of positive phrases ending with ringing rhymed adverbs: "clearly" (5), "cheerily" (7), "as fated merely" (9), and "too dearly" (11). The repetition across five rhymed lines of the sound of "me" emphasizes the poem's attempt to build a literary structure for the maritime self. Seafaring community comprises both subject and form of "John Marr"; the poem asks for community on the narrative level and fashions it through poetic form. Assembling human bonds while under the shared threat of oceanic dislocation becomes a model for assembling literary meaning out of disparate linguistic tools.

Melville's poem builds a fantasy communion of sailors in verse if not reality. The poetic imagination sets its task as reaching or perhaps inventing the corporate identity that human history and, in Marr's case, landed settlement have dispersed. At the center of its vision, the poem cannot clearly be distinguished from a dream:

Ye come, ye visit me, or seem
Swimming out from seas of faces,
Alien myriads memory traces,
To enfold me in a dream! (267)

Melville's rhyme scheme, which varies from stanza to stanza, contains the fragments the narrator wishes to connect—seas, faces, myriads, and traces—inside the couplet envelope of "seem" and "dream." Repeatedly in the center of the poem, the narrator asserts a heroic connection that rhymes cannot quite close. "Twined we were, entwined, then riven, / Ever to new entanglements driven" (268), writes the narrator, placing the speaking self and his comrades in deep connections. The following line refuses to extend the rhyme and instead describes the sailors as unconnected fragments: "Shifting gulf-weed of the main!" (268). As in the opening three-line stanza, these lines build connections through repeated end rhymes but stop before the solidifying triplet. "Main," in this line, like "me" in the opening stanza, does have a rhyming match, in this case a double match: the stanza begins with a couplet—"I yearn as ye. But rafts that strain, / Parted shall they lock again?" (267). This couplet is then displaced by a second couplet about ecstatic joining—the *riven/driven* couplet quoted above—and then at last the first rhyme returns with "main." In neither stanza does a complete triplet, in which a single end rhyme repeats itself in three consecutive lines, appear, though both stanzas court this form's solid, full repetition.

While John Marr never finds his shipmates, the poem finally arrives at a triple rhyme in its last stanza. After the poem has lamented deaths at sea on whalers and men-of-war, it employs a symbol of unity and emotional connection in the human heart, "A beat, a heart-beat musters all" (268). Recalling both the dying body of the landlocked sailor and the created unity of a ship's crew, the poem gestures from the mustering heartbeat to a last glimpse of sea comrades at work that is physical, aural, and visual:

It musters. But to clasp, retain;
To see you at the halyards main—
To hear your chorus once again! (268).

The triplet *retain/main/again* accomplishes on a formal level the unity that the narrative has failed to provide. Poetry, via English's dominant poetic trope of the end rhyme, replaces lived reality as guarantee of shared experience. There on unseen halyards, holding with imagined fingers and hearing unsung words, the dying sailor recaptures the human continuity that emerges from the encounter with stormy oceans. "John Marr" may not technically be a shipwreck poem—the sailor's death on the prairie may be the driest death of any mariner in this book—but by employing the resources of poetry to represent the untenable yet desired community of metis in the storm, this poem captures the fundamental affinity between poems and shipwreck.[3] In the Naufragocene, John Marr should join Ishmael and Queequeg in Melville's pantheon.[4] Far from comrades and the music of the sea, his song plunges into the poetic heart of shipwreck ecology: storm, dislocation, and partly dashed hopes for redemption.

Melville's unseen but audible echo of communal redemption flavors John Marr's solitary death with the salt tang of utopia. That ecstatic, exhilarating maritime vision, what Emily Dickinson calls the "exaltation of the going / Of an inland soul to sea," represents the positive achievement of maritime poetry, whether written by an old salt like Melville or an Amherst landlubber.[5] The phrase from *The Tempest* that titles this chapter, by contrast, registers pure disorder. Against the death-fueled reunion of John Marr, I juxtapose the underlying fear of all who entrust their bodies to wooden boats, with an inch of oak between their selves and eternity. "We split, we split," cry unnamed mariners near the end of the first scene of *The Tempest*: "Farewell my wife and children!—Farewell brother!—we split, we split, we split!" (1.1.60–62). To split means to separate, to plunge individually into the sea. Splitting inverts the consoling connections of rhyme. Amid the political and nautical chaos of this scene, the mariners plumb despair. Rather than "sink[in] wi'th' King" (1.1.63) with the royalists Antonio and Sebastian or lamenting the absence of "long heath, brown furze, anything" (1.1.66–67) with humanist Gonzalo, these nameless men voice pure loss, the wetness of the encounter. Like Pericles at the center of his shipwreck play, they arrive with water on their bodies: "Enter Mariners, wet"(1.1.49SD).[6] Like Edward Barlow and Jeremy Roch, as well as John Marr, Shakespeare's mariners live entangled with ocean. After their seamanship has proved insufficient in the storm but before Prospero's supernatural control, they pronounce their watery deaths in protest. "We split" represents the limit case of shipwreck poetry, the last gasp of human voices before immersion.

In the storm scene that opens *The Tempest,* the rhythmic repetition of the mariners' lament stands out from the larger dramatic arc of the play. The strong iambic beats of "we split!" echo amid the crowded stage. No modern texts set these lines as verse, though the mariners' first lines upon entering the stage, "All lost! To prayers, to prayers! All lost!" (1.1.50), would fit into a regular iambic tetrameter four-beat line. This almost inaudible fragment of poetic phrasing, which never quite assembles itself into a recognizable line of verse, represents a temporary failure of poetry's unifying perspective. Prospero and Miranda will soon arrive, speak hundreds of lines of gorgeous blank verse, and replace the mariners' poetic failure with dramatic triumph.[7] While the attention of most audiences and critics follows the island plot, the mariners' cry of protest lingers, marking the physical and emotional costs of immersion. The crisis in orientation produced by the opening shipwreck requires a countermovement to reclaim order from chaos. G. Wilson Knight's famous reading of Shakespeare's career as divided between the principles of music and tempest takes its core examples from this play and, in particular, from the contrast between its first and second scenes.[8] Purely aesthetic readings like Knight's, however, ignore the extent to which the challenge of the storm is also ecological. Facing the storm requires human bodies to engage nonhuman environmental forces. Poetry, both in its dramatic form after the second scene and in the mariners' repeated laments of "we split!," replies to an ecological challenge with artistic form. Its meaning making operates in the interstices of disorder and reorientation.

The poetic consolations created by aesthetic objects like "John Marr" or *The Tempest* seem human centered, existing largely in the minds or ears of their audiences. This chapter argues that these poetic solutions comprise potent visions of ecological entanglement. In close readings of individual poems from the piscatorial tradition, John Donne's maritime verse letters, Wallace Stevens's "Sea Surface Covered with Clouds," and Thomas Hardy's "Convergence of the Twain," I assemble a poetic recipe for ecological awareness. These poems represent the mismatch between human bodies and the ocean. Poetry of the maritime encounter reveals the literary craft not always visible in the amateur lines of Roch and Barlow. The poems of this chapter present fleeting, dangerous, discontinuous instants in which human bodies engage the world ocean. Like John Marr and the sailors in the opening scene of *The Tempest,* we cannot hope, finally, to survive that encounter. Sea poetry sings a self-aware music of destruction, a vocal drown song that recognizes—that cannot help but recognize—the untenable situation of the human in the nonhuman ocean. Poetic forms extract pleasure from terror. But an ecology of the sea poem has at least as much to do with pleasure as with death. It is worth remembering that the deathly sea change promised by Ariel's song in *The Tempest* turns out to be something of a ruse: there is no dead king under those waters.[9] The song describes salt water, endlessly and globally flowing corrosive to human flesh, ideals, and forms. That is the ecology in which we live, in which we must learn to stay afloat, for as long as we have.

A Brief History of Piscatorial Poetry, 1633–1729

From Homer forward, the sea occupies a special place in Western poetry. Increased cultural attention directed toward the sea would lead in the seventeenth and eighteenth centuries to the short-lived phenomenon of "piscatorial poetry," a revised strain of pastoral that shifts from the landscape of sheep, shepherds, and meadows to fish, anglers, and lagoons. Drawing on classical models, including portraits of undersea gods in Lucian, Homer, Theocritus and others, and responding to the example of Sannazaro in the 1490s, a series of English poets attempted to adapt the fisherman-poet to changing poetic tastes.[10] Tracing the brief flourishing of fishing poems from the mid-seventeenth into the early eighteenth centuries shows that this trend, while clearly an attempt by lesser-known poets to gain visibility in a crowded literary marketplace, gestures toward the interpenetration of human experience with maritime alterity. While these poems do not explore shipwreck as such—the pastoral mode prefers contemplative fishing to violent catastrophe—the water-infused projects of these poets display a deep fascination with the overlapping boundaries of bodies and water. These are not shipwreck poems but aqueous ecofantasies. To write piscatorial poetry entails a utopian vision of humanity as partly and potentially marine, a vision I have elsewhere described as "the Aquaman fantasy."[11]

As in the opening scene of *The Tempest* and Donne's verse letters, the tools of poetic making refashions human bodies to endure alien ocean. These poems posit an aesthetic and aqueous interchange, an idealized vision of human bodies in water.

These poems' lack of public success suggests that this piscatorial vision was not widely shared or fully amenable to changing tastes and understandings. Early attacks on the piscatorial mode appeared in the writings of French critics René Rapin and Bernard le Bouvier de Fontenelle in the late seventeenth century. Further attacks on piscatorialism appeared in a series of articles in the *Guardian* by Thomas Tickell in the early eighteenth century.[12] Dr. Johnson, summarizing and extending this critical tradition in *The Rambler* (July 21, 1750), emphasizes that piscatorial poems cannot please, because of human "ignorance of maritime pleasures" and because the sea has "less variety" than the land.[13] Johnson may not have been conscious of his precise inversion of Pliny's claim, repeated by Spenser among others, that the kinds of fish outnumber the species of land animals, but in any case he describes the sea as a blank space, ignored and unknown.[14] Johnson wants landed poetry because he sees humans as landed creatures:

> To all the island inhabitants of every region, the sea is only known as an immense diffusion of waters, over which men pass from one country to another, and in which life is frequently lost. They have, therefore, no opportunity of tracing in their own thoughts the descriptions of winding shores and calm bays, nor can look on the poem in which they are mentioned with other sensation than on a sea chart, or the metrical geometry of Dionysius. (24–25)

Johnson alludes here to shipwreck and loss of life, seldom a subject in piscatorial poetry, but the mismatch between the readers' "own thoughts" and a maritime landscape appears not to require elaboration. Notably, the watery spaces that Johnson thinks are inaccessible to the poetic imagination, shores and bays, are more terraqueous than strictly aquatic. Johnson's reader ventures no farther than the edge of the shore. The actual piscatorialists, as I will show, venture somewhat deeper.

The piscatorial genre in postclassical poetry appeared first in the lyrics of Jacopo Sannazaro in the 1490s in Naples and then arrived in

England in Phineas Fletcher's *Piscatory Eclogues* (1633).[15] When first published, these poems were overshadowed by Fletcher's Spenserian allegorical poem *The Purple Island,* published in the same volume.[16] An introduction to a second edition of the *Eclogues* written by Alexander Tytler, published in Edinburgh in 1771, defends piscatorialism by arguing that "the life of a fisherman admits often of scenes as delightful as those which the shepherd enjoys, and those scenes are much more varied."[17] Tytler imagines fisher poems as secondhand pastorals, valuable because the "Piscatory Eclogue has the advantage over Pastoral in displaying a field less beaten and less frequented" (sig. a4). Tytler's choice of metaphor—the field—speaks to his fundamentally terrestrial perspective. Fletcher's poems largely adapt existing pastoral tropes to a piscatorial scene, but they also hint at a fuller engagement with oceanic meanings. There are no shipwrecks to be found, but the poems display careful attention to the beauties of the underwater world:

> Here, with sweet bays, the lovely myrtils grown,
> Where the ocean's fair-chek'd maides oft repair;
> Here to my pipe they dancen in a row
> No other swain may come to note their fair,
> *Proteus* himself pipes to his flock hereby. (eclogue 1, 13–14)

The poet distinguishes his own saltwater view, including the changeable sea god, from that of familiar pastorals. The "fair-chek'd maids" of ocean represent an opportunity for poets crowded out of busy fields and literary circles. "Here," in and beneath the ocean, Fletcher's distinctive version of pastoral seeks independence.

This pleasing harmony would seem very far from the harsher face the ocean presents to shipwrecked sailors, but one important fantasy that Fletcher shares with shipwreck writers from Shakespeare to Edward Barlow is the fear, which is also a desire, that the speaking self may dissolve in the ocean. At the close of the first eclogue, which like so many of these poems laments unobtainable love, the narrator entangles his loneliness with the ocean's hostility: "Naught feared he fierce ocean's wat'ry ire, / Who in his heart of grief and love felt equal fire" (eclogue 1, 15). The dissonance between ocean's "ire" and the erotic "fire," which could perhaps be quenched by immersion, suggests that Fletcher cannot quite get out of the way of his own metaphors. The image of the lover's ocean heart, however, gestures toward a deeper entanglement. Later, in eclogue 3, another lover imagines himself intimately connected to the ocean: "Love stirs the desire, like stormy winde, / Blows up high-swelling waves of hope and fear" (eclogue 3, 42). This expansion of poetic selfhood into the natural world is typical of pastoral poetry, though the attempt to see oneself in nature would often prove frustrating.[18] Fletcher's easy embrace of the sea may seem somewhat facile compared to the darker struggles of Donne or Barlow. The piscatorialist does not register the same disorientation that earlier poets and memoirists do. But Fletcher shares the impulse to plunge in and the faith that the underwater world will reflect back himself.

Poets like Fletcher touch tangentially on the larger topos of the sublime, which in Joseph Addison's famous 1712 essay in the *Spectator* locates particularly in the sea:

> Of all the Objects that I have ever seen, there is none which affects my Imagination so much as the Sea or Ocean. I cannot see the Heavings of this prodigious Bulk of Waters, even in a Calm, without a very pleasing Astonishment; but when it is worked up in a Tempest, so that the Horison on every side is nothing but foaming Billows and floating Mountains, it is impossible to describe the agreeable Horrour that rises from such a Prospect.[19]

Addison's description points toward the Romantic sublime, which would come to dominate sea poetry in the works of Byron, Shelley, Cowper, and others.[20] Even before this sea change in oceanic meaning, however, contact with the sea generated a poetics of ecological intimacy and disjunction that distinguishes the piscatorial from traditional pastoral. If pastoralism embodies a deep fantasy of coliving, a green world that involves, to borrow William Empson's apt formulation, "putting the complex into the simple," piscatorialism's less-forgiving subject matter directs its authors to engage their environment differently.[21] The blue depths of the fisherman are less homelike than the green pastures of the shepherd.[22] Traces of proto-Romantic sublimity in piscatorial poems emerge from a struggle with oceanic estrangement. W. H. Auden's well-known claim that Romantic ideas of the sea epitomize one of the "revolutionary changes in sensibility or style" in Western cultural history describes an increased volume of cultural attention that would lead to popular sea fictions from Byron to Melville to Conrad.[23] Auden's very title, *The Enchafèd Shore,* however, quotes *Othello* (2.1.17), revealing that the critic's reading of the ocean was not really new to Romanticism. The Romantic sublime may be better understood to adapt to the sea as a whole, in calm and storm as Addison notes, the features and meanings associated with oceanic tempests in earlier eras. My ecological reading of shipwreck and the ocean in pre-Romantic poetry emphasizes the mismatch between pastoral simplicity and oceanic alterity. The piscatorial dead end, while arguably looking forward to poems such as Bryon's *Don Juan* or Keats's sonnet "On the Sea," represents a way of living with inhospitable environmental conditions. Fishermen know they cannot survive in the sea, but sea poets seek beauty there nonetheless.

A meaningful genealogy in English sea poetry might be traced from Milton's "Lycidas" forward to Moses Brown's *Piscatory Eclogues* (1729). Brown's eclogue 5, "Colin's Despair," announces itself as the first overt imitation of "Lycidas" yet written. "It has a long Time been Matter of wonder to me," Brown writes, "that among so many *Admirers* and *Imitators* of that *great Man* [i.e., Milton], none have taken Notice of this poem [i.e., "Lycidas"], which I can never read, for my own part, without the same Veneration and Partiality, which is paid to the most accomplish'd Words of *Antiquity.*"[24] Brown would go on to edit Walton's *Compleat Angler* in 1750, 1759, and 1772. Many of his footnotes to his own poems in the *Piscatory Eclogues* refer to Walton.[25] Brown's eclogue, subtitled "An Imitation of Milton's *Lycidas*" (74), shifts its setting from the Irish Sea to "the kind Stream of some cool River clear" (82) and replaces Milton's prophetic reach with a much more humble description of fishing practices and a hackneyed depiction of futile love.[26] The speaker at poem's end engages to a degree with his aqueous surroundings, rising "by the Moon-Beams pale, / While the horse Flood kept Moan, and echoing Night" (86), but Browne is never oceanic. His defense of piscatorialism and indeed of "Lycidas" is very much a freshwater pursuit.

The clearest example of an oceanic ecovision in English piscatorial poetry appears in the work of William Diaper. His *Nereides: or, Sea-Eclogues* (1712), together with his incomplete translation of *Oppian's Haleuticks* (1722), comprise the most oceanic works of early modern English poetry. The opening of the *Haleuticks* announces the poet's epic ambition: "I sing the Natives of the boundless Main, / And tell what Kinds the wat'ry Depths contain" (1.1–2).[27] Investigating "the liquid

Worlds below" (1.5), the poet produces what might be considered an antidote to shipwreck: his fishers embrace the water and eagerly look into its foreign world, rather than fearing it. Diaper, a part-time protégé of Jonathan Swift's who died poor and unknown, does not loom large in histories of English sea poetry. By examining arguably his best poem, eclogue 1 in *The Nereids,* I will argue that his art speaks compellingly in dialogue with the more famous maritime voices of Donne, Shakespeare, and Milton. Where Donne and Milton in particular provide evidence of thallasophobia in their verse, Diaper craves oceanic entanglement. Of all these poets, he is the most clearly animated by what I call "swimmer poetics."[28]

Diaper's affinity for the ocean defuses traditional fears of shipwreck by embracing the watery world. In his prefatory poem, which requests patronage from William Congreve, he analogizes his position to a merchant who has overinsured his cargo and thus sleeps soundly. Having no need to dread "the lurking Rocks," these merchants can ignore and even welcome shipwreck: "They hear of Wrecks, and fear no inward Pain, / But seeming Losses bring a real Gain."[29] Having inverted the shipwreck trope, Diaper's first poem begins with Glaucus, who, as his note informs, "was a Fisherman, who by eating a certain Herb is feign'd to have been chang'd into a Sea-God" (1.1). The Nymph Cymothoe, complaining that Glaucus has grown indifferent to her love, reminds him of how difficult it was at first to adapt to the aquatic environment: "I taught you how to plow the liquid way; / I show'd you all the Secrets of the Deep, / And vaulted Rocks where weary *Tritons* sleep" (1.2). Emphasizing the radical difference between aquatic and airy environments, Diaper has despairing Cymothoe threaten to invert Glaucus's journey "And yield my self to Fishermen a Prey. / I shall on shore be as a Monster shown" (1.3). Glaucus's defense of his love emphasizes the aquatic pleasures that life under the waves has brought him, "how you taught me artfully to swim, / To dive for Pearls, and steepy Rock to climb; / You taught me to hunt the Shark" (1.4). The great pleasure of this love appears hydrographic, as Glaucus receives secret oceanic vistas: "The Ocean has its Groves, and gloomy Shakes, / And chrystal Springs below, and cooling Glades" (1.5). Cymothoe contrasts these aquatic vistas against "Sunburnt, sapless Earth" (1.5). Their dialogue, which takes place near the shore, eschews land for the pleasures of the deep ocean.

The entire poem, to an extent rarely found even within the piscatorial genre, sings a love song to the underwater world. When Glaucus protests his constancy, he inverts the traditional image of the ocean as overly mutable and describes it instead as a model of stability. If his love should dissipate, he insists, "first the Waves shall lose their biting Salts, / The Winds shall cease to sound in hollow Vaults, / And wanton Fish shall leave their native Seas, / And bask on Earth, or browse in leavy Trees" (1.4).[30] In this poem, as in certain classical texts including Oppian and Lucian's *Dialogues of the Sea-Gods,* the ocean becomes normative, displacing the land. The movement of the concluding couplet of Diaper's opening eclogue, which gestures toward the bulk of his collection, is forward and into the water. Beneath the sea,

where neither Storms nor Rain
Molest the Trees, nor incommode the Swain;
Where unmixt Waters are as Churstal clear,
And warm as Summer glooms, and fine as Air.
A faintish Light shines thro' the watry Greene,
And lets us see enough, but–not be seen. (1.6)

The underwater fantasy, reimagining the depths to which wrecks and drowned men sink, occupies a place of privilege for Diaper and his loving sea nymph. "Dive, *Glaucus,* swift," she concludes the poem, "and let us sinking move / Down to the Center of the World, and—Love" (1.6). Sinking comprises moving into the water and moving closer to the "Center of the World," where the poem places Love. Recalling oceanic pleasure palaces such as Proteus's bower in *The Faerie Queene* and the Isle of Love in the *Lusiads,* Cymothoe's vision differs from these watery paradises in being a place of permanent rest, not a prison or a way station on the voyage home. To Diaper, almost uniquely of pre-Romantic English poets, the sea may be humanity's true home.

Diaper's harmonious vision of undersea life owes much to the landed pastoral tropes that he adapts, and his happy undersea love bower may not seem very much like a shipwreck, though Odysseus's time on Calypso's island seems in some ways comparable. Diaper's Glaucus, unlike Odysseus, never wishes to leave his new world. In the last of Diaper's eclogues, the eventual winner of the poetry contest, Chalcis, straightforwardly rejects terrestrial life: "I hate the Shore; for there the troubled Deep / Rowls all its Filth" (14.68). Against the strand of filth and "dying Dolphins," he juxtaposes the freedom of underwater mobility: "I choose to stay, where depthless Waters flow, / And sport with Fish above, or dive below" (14.68). Embodying the Aquaman fantasy in its purest form, having displaced even Dolphins at the center of aquatic life, Chalcis represents complete marine engagement. It is not a position that shipwrecked sailors want to embrace, but it may be one toward which their watery entanglements force them.

Donne at Sea

For sailors excluded from Diaper's underwater utopia, voyages trace human patterns across the formless ocean. These voyages do not always hold together, even when supplemented by poetry. The Islands Voyage of 1597 shattered to pieces not long after its ships left Plymouth. The voyage's military chaos, however, produced two short masterworks of poetic form, John Donne's verse letters "The Storm" and "The Calm." Donne's poetic diptych constructs a literary counterform that sutures up the catastrophically open structure of the Islands Voyage. Treating these poems as literary and formal responses to maritime crisis reveals in particular detail the mutual pressures of literary form and historical experience. Poetic counterforms cannot roll back historical disasters, but they can conceptually resist the felt experience of disorder. The Islands Voyage as modern scholars reconstruct it emerges from the deep mutual entanglement of historical records, nonliterary narratives, and other historical artifacts, including Donne's poems, which themselves form a historical-and-poetic composite. The meaning-making tropes and techniques of poetic composition enable Donne's verse to give structure to chaotic experience. In broad terms, poetry responds to maritime disaster through human-centered acts of reframing, in which national and political failures give way to personal survival and imaginative response.

The relation between poetic form and errant voyaging that the Donne section of this chapter explores is not quite as simple as the claim that broken voyages generate whole poems. My analysis takes Donne's two-verse letters as a single artistic unit, arguing that the poet's real and imagined relationship with Christopher Brooke, the courtier to whom both poems are addressed, creates an alternative sociopersonal space alongside which to judge the Islands Voyage. The first poem, "The Storm," highlights this friendship at its opening only to push it away in conclusion, while the second poem, "The Calm," elliptically returns to Brooke in its closing moments. In a formal sense, the most prominent poetic technique in both poems is the fundamental building block of English poetry since Chaucer, the rhymed couplet. The nature of rhyme, in which one word calls orally to another, serves as microstructure and macrostructure in these two poems; individual lines rhyme with each other, and in a larger sense, "The Calm" rhymes with "The Storm." This couplet-structured vision of poetry's response to voyaging has implications for scholarship of sea literature, especially in terms of how literary forms respond to ecological disruptions.

The essential structural feature of the Islands Voyage is oceanic disorder, which repeatedly interrupts progress. As in previous chapters, this pattern motivates repeated interruptions of my argument, in this case as alien poetic texts intrude upon Donne. Like storms or sudden calms, these texts interrupt this chapter's analytical journey. The interruptions represent literary temptations in writing about natural disasters. After my initial discussion of the facts of the voyage and Donne's first representation of it in "The Storm," the first interruption explores perhaps the most-striking representation of a sea storm in Renaissance literature. The giant Adamastor, from Luis vaz de Camões's Portuguese epic the *Lusiads,* allegorizes the Cape of Storms on the southern tip of Africa and transforms the hostile seascape into the symbolic machinery of classical myth.[31] After Adamastor my chapter resumes its appointed path into Donne's "The Calm," but then it encounters a second detour in a modernist literary becalming, Wallace Stevens's lyric fantasy "Sea Surface Covered with Clouds." While Adamastor represents the temptation to allegorize experience, Stevens's poem offers a purely fantastic, sensation-driven response to maritime experience. Donne's diptych, my twice-interrupted reading argues, produces a tenuous scaffold on which to hang poetic form and intimations of a semicoherent self. The poetics of uncertainty, which would become essential to the mature Donne's theological and erotic verse, emerges in dialogue with maritime catastrophe.

The Islands Voyage

In historical terms the failures of the Islands Voyage were personal, strategic, and navigational. Undertaken with two military objectives, it failed at both, neither defeating the Spanish fleet that was being assembled in the town of Ferrol nor intercepting the silver-bearing merchant flota returning from the New World by way of the Azores.[32] Historians blame tensions between the three self-interested commanders, the Earl of Essex, Sir Walter Raleigh, and Lord Thomas Howard, and their entanglements with their suspicious queen.[33] Donne himself accompanied the fleet as a "voluntary," a courtier who joined the expedition at his own expense to seek personal glory and, possibly, escape problems onshore.[34] In attaching himself to the popular commanders Essex and Raleigh, Donne may have anticipated a social benefit in going to war, especially after Essex's successful assault on Cadiz in 1596, in which Donne also participated. Like his fellow courtiers, Donne was presumably interested in the vast wealth of the Spanish plate fleet, as well as having the more patriotic motive of preventing Spain from launching another armada against England.[35] The Islands Voyage fractured twice, first scattered by a violent storm after leaving Plymouth in July and then becoming further disorganized later that summer when a part of the fleet was becalmed and missed their rendezvous at the Azores.[36] Taking as his titles two meteorological conditions that troubled voyages during the Age of Sail—storm and calm, too much wind or too little—Donne's poems engage the messy realities of life at sea. Reading the two poems as a single composite work in dialogue with the history of the voyage reveals a vexed interplay between stormy motion and calm stasis.

By claiming that Donne's poems represent in artistic terms the success that the military venture did not have, I do not mean only that the poems provided solace to failed warriors. It remains unclear how many readers may have encountered these poems in the late 1590s, beyond Christopher Brooke, Donne's friend to whom the verses were addressed. Rather than being simply metaphorical triumphs matched against historical failures, these poems reveal Donne's efforts as poet to reshape maritime experience. His private friendship with Brooke, a fellow student with Donne at Lincoln's Inn, serves via these poems to counterbalance the fractious community of sailors and soldiers.[37] The poet was not the only participant in the voyage to have written about it; Sir William Monson provided a detailed description in his *Naval Tracts,* and Sir Arthur Gorges wrote *A Larger Relation of the said Iland Voyage,* subsequently collected by Samuel Purchas in *Purchas his Pilgrimes* and published in 1625.[38] But Donne's poems emphasize form in a way that these historical narratives and other naval records do not. Poetic form treats the chaos and boredom of military life as challenges to the unity of literary work and speaking self. Expanding the traditional metaphor in which a voyage by sea corresponds to the journey of human life, Donne's poems, read in dialogue with the disastrous Islands Voyage, show poetic form counterbalancing historical events.[39] Without claiming that Donne's subsequent turn to landed pursuits, which led him eventually to become Dean of St. Paul's, was motivated by the catastrophe of this voyage, the interface between broken voyage and emerging poetics seems noteworthy.

Of the many failures in the Islands Voyage, three stand out: the voyage was divided between two incompatible military goals; the fleet was rife with social dissention and ambition; and the ships confronted the fundamental problems of oceanic navigation, especially the poorly known geography of the Spanish Azores and the broader sailing patterns of the north Atlantic. Oscillating between Ferrol and the Azores meant that the fleet was poised between countering a new Spanish armada readying itself to assail England from the mainland and intercepting the yearly plate fleet returning from the New World. It was almost certainly impossible to do both things at once. After being delayed by a storm and forced back to Plymouth, Essex arrived at Ferrol only to find that he was unable to entice the Spanish forces out of the harbor "upon indifferent terms to have fought with us" (23). The prospect of a long blockade did not appeal to the ambitious nobleman, at which point "it was thought fit no longer to linger about that coast lest we should lose greater opportunity upon the Indian fleet" (23). Soon after the fleet left for the Azores, Raleigh appears to have learned that the great armada, "which we supposed to be in Coruna and Ferrol, was gone to the Islands for the guard of the Indian fleet" (23).[40] This helpful news sent all the fleet quickly off toward the Azores, and little further thought seems to have been given to Ferrol. Later that season, a Spanish fleet from that harbor did sail against England, only to be destroyed, with the loss of eighteen ships, by a storm off the Scilly Islands southwest of Cornwall. According to Monson, "We must ascribe this loss of theirs to God only; for certainly the enemies' designs were dangerous, and not diverted by our force" (33). The strategies of Essex, Raleigh, and their fleet seem largely to have ignored this danger.

Donne's poems do not appear very interested in strategic questions.

"The Storm" focuses on chaotic experience at sea while reaching out to Christopher Brooke. "The Calm" replaces these physical details with a deep evacuation of self: "we are for nothing fit" (53).[41] As formal objects, neither poem is complete; instead the two form an aesthetic diptych, each reflecting the other and forming a complete structure only when considered as a duality. The epistolary form of these two poems implies that each must reach outside to a particular reader for completion. The complex artistic object of the two interlocked poems thus responds to the Islands Voyage by creating a complex, perhaps unstable, interpersonal order to supplement the historical experience of disorder.

"The Storm"

The first of the two poems imagines the sea storm as historical and symbolic interruption, shattering human experience. It fractures identity and the ability to perceive one's environment. After little more than eighteen couplets, the speaker is entirely lost:

> But when I waked, I saw, that I saw not.
> I, and the Sun, which should teach me, had forgot
> East, West, day, night, and I could only say
> If the world had lasted, now it had been day. (37–40)

Faced with an opaque world and a not-legible day, the poet grasps for literary structures, especially rhymed couplets, to make sense of disorder. The couplets and the poem they assemble represent partial conceptual stability, produced through an acknowledgment of inhuman pressures. The analogy between sun and self in this passage emphasizes the twinned failures of ego and visual world. Tension between poetic order and natural disorder run throughout the poem; the split at the poem's center recalls the fractured leadership of the Islands fleet. In his authoritative history of the voyage, Julian Corbett judges that the failure to intercept the Spanish flota was due to inconstancy; "to us at this unimpassioned distance," Corbett writes, "it is clear enough that the miscarriage was due to the oft-repeated error of not adopting one fairly intelligent system of cruising and doggedly sticking to it" (204). While Donne may not have recognized this strategic wisdom, his poem struggles with the excessive variability that, in Corbett's view, doomed the military campaign. For the poet the problem becomes less human error than human perception: "Pumping hath tired our men, and what's the gain? / Seas into seas thrown, we suck in again" (61–62). The couplet *gain/again* gestures ruefully at the financial gain that taking the Spanish fleet did not provide to either sailors or volunteers, but the larger point seems clear: inside the storm, boundaries vanish and nothing, including gain, can be located.

Further emphasizing the blurring of borders, the poem crosses the boundary between the poet and reader. "Sooner than you read this line," Donne writes, "did the gale, / Like shot, not fear'd, till felt, our sails assail" (29–30). In the second line of this couplet, the choppy rhythm and interrupted progress—"Like shot, not fear'd, till felt, our sails assail"—replicates on the level of sound the broken narrative of the sea voyage. The densely rhymed triplet of *gale/sails/assail* crams together reader, poet, and ship into one disorderly literary and historical space. Everything is together, or as the poem later says, "all things are one" (69). Donne's lyric refuses any sheltered isolation for the speaking subject; he remains always entangled with sea and storm and ship.

In formal terms the poem employs the human bond with Christopher Brooke to counterbalance the storm. The poem opens with this relationship through an elaborate pun on friendship and poetry as related aesthetic challenges: "Thou which art I, ('tis nothing to be so) / Thou which art still thyself, by these shall know / Part of our passage" (1–3). The basic claim that two friends share an identity, that neither is anything except in and through the other, was a cliché of humanist rhetoric.[42] Donne extends the familiar idea by repeating the word "art" and then repeating the sound of this word a third time in "part." The repetition of a word that means both "being"—*art* as "are"—and "literary creation"—*art* as "art"—emphasizes multiple attempts to represent disaster and also survive it.

The poem connects the storm to many things well-read courtiers including Brooke and Donne knew all about. The experience makes Donne pity Jonah.[43] He alludes to international politics; the waves are "like two mighty Kings, which dwelling far / Asunder, meet against a third to war" (25–26). The storm recalls "the last day," when "sin-burd'ned souls from grave will creep" (47); it makes Hell seem "somewhat lightsome," and even "the'Bermuda calm" (66). Politics, geography, theology, poetics, classical and biblical literary forms, these associations all help the poet fit disorderly reality inside poetic structure. They are tools to figure human and environmental trauma.

Representing disorder is not easy, and the poem never claims to complete what it attempts. The storm can be represented but not captured. The final lines analogize the experience to the unknowable Chaos from which matter was first created: "Since all forms uniform deformity / Doth cover, so that we, except God say / Another *Fiat,* shall have no more day" (70–72). The poem returns to the dayless day of immersion, now gesturing toward divine command, rather than human friendship, for rescue. In the final couplet, Donne temporarily rejects human connection: "So violent, yet long these furies be / That though thine absence starve me, I wish not thee." The poem at last pushes away the absent friend, and the dense triple rhyme of *be/me/thee* sandwiches the speaking poet—poor, starving me—between experience (*be*) and friendship (*thee*). The poem itself, "The Storm" as written, provides all that Donne can depend upon at sea. It ends in solitude.

Adamastor

Shipwreck, the iconic catastrophe of sea voyages, did not strike the Islands fleet. But especially in "The Storm," shipwreck functions as an insistent subtext, as allusions to Jonah (33) and wreck-filled Bermuda (66) emphasize. To surface the threat of maritime disaster in this poem, I interrupt my reading of Donne with Adamastor. An allegorical representation of the Cape of Storms in the *Lusiads,* Adamastor is, according to Josiah Blackmore, "shipwreck awesomely incarnate."[44] The giant literalizes the rocky coast of the southern cape that marks the division between the known waters of the Atlantic and the unknown seas that Vasco da Gama's voyage opens up for Portugal. Unlike Donne's lyrics, Camões's epic structures itself through narrative progress and the overcoming of successive challenges, with figures like Adamastor serving as obstacles to be overcome.

Adamastor represents the catastrophe that Donne's voyage fears but avoids. The Cape of Storms literalizes the human and financial cost of the imperial and mercantile voyage. "My cape will be implacably hostile," the giant says to Vasco da Gama. "Year by year your fleets will meet / Shipwreck" (5.43.3, 5.44.6–7). The disaster that da Gama's fleet, like Donne's, avoids gets visited on the imperial future of the

Portuguese India trade, as the examples of famous historical disasters recounted in the poem demonstrate.[45] Shipwreck in this formulation is the necessary but tragic cost of imperial expansion, as Blackmore observes: "In the Camonian understanding of epic, disaster exists conterminously with an espousal of imperialist ideologies, so there is no cause and effect between the two: empire exists alongside shipwreck, alongside its own undoing" (26). In the Portuguese epic, shipwreck serves as the visible countercurrent, the ever-threatening cost of imperial expansion. For David Quint, Adamastor represents the native African presence the Portuguese would encounter and then displace.[46] The eruption of Adamastor into the epic, his voice "Booming from the ocean's depths" (5.40.6), lays out Camões's tragic logic of sacrifice and achievement.

Donne's English lyrics follow a different path from this narrative of suffering repaid. Compared to the narrative thrust of the *Lusiads,* Donne's verse letters appear plotless, if not quite shapeless. The contrast between Donne and Camões recalls Richard Helgerson's influential reading of Portuguese epic's refashioning mercantile voyages as chivalric quests. In Helgerson's reading, Adamastor is a dragon, successfully defeated by the knight da Gama. By contrast, according to Helgerson, English narratives of maritime expansion represent the growing power of mercantile as opposed to aristocratic interests.[47] As a volunteer on a military expedition, however, Donne's position differs from that of a booster of trade like Richard Hakluyt, whose writings Helgerson takes to be normative for the Elizabethan maritime world. Donne as poet and courtier sails for gain, as he admits in "The Calm": "Whether a rotten state, and hope of gain, / Or, to disuse me from the queasy pain / Of being beloved, and loving, or the thirst / Of honour" (39–42). A privateer's gain, however, did not pose the same social risks as a merchant's; pirates like Sir Francis Drake were later knighted for their exploits. Donne's poems occupy a peculiar social position, neither fully part of the fleet's military mission nor fully separate from it. He writes from the margins of a fracturing voyage.

From this tenuous position, Donne's poems narrate a selfhood that strangely resembles that of Adamastor himself, speaking tragic history amid the wreckage of personal failure. In the giant's story, his love for the sea nymph Tethys causes him to embrace the rocky coastline into which his own body has been transformed. He mistakes the goddess for his changed body—"Convinced that my beloved was in my arms, / I found myself hugging a hillside" (5.56.3–4)—and finds himself imprisoned as a rocky cape, with the foaming waters of the goddess surrounding him: "And of all tortures, the most agonizing / Is that Tethys surrounds me, tantalizing" (5.59.7–8). The final position of Camões's shipwreck-making giant, surrounded by disorderly and desire-making surf, is precisely the position of Donne in "The Storm." Amid the chaotic motion of this poem, the English poet resembles the stony giant, instead of the always-advancing hero. Writing lyrics from storms, Donne seems closer to Adamastor's tragic stasis than to the full epic's vision of historical progress.

"The Calm"

The giant/cape's immobility within incessant motion gestures toward Donne's inverted companion poem, "The Calm," which turns to empty space and the unmovable ocean. "The sea is now" (9), says Donne's poem, and the formal work of its fifty-six lines fills that shapeless void with words. While "The Storm" seems on some level to be in dialogue with the fractured chain of command of the Islands Voyage, the second poem slides away from the clash of personalities to put its voice in direct contact with oceanic mystery. While "The Storm" faces on a local level the linguistic failures typical of humanist depictions of tempests, "The Calm" poses an ecological mismatch, in which humans enter an environment in which they cannot survive. The second poem recalls the pointed conclusion of William Cecil's letter to Queen Elizabeth about the Islands Voyage, which accurately predicted that Essex and Raleigh would fail in their stated objectives: "But the fleet at Ferrol will not be burnt, the carracks are come home, the Islands cannot be taken, so that their weak watery hopes do but faintly nourish that noble Earl's [Essex's] comfort."[48] The shrewd lord's biting comment about Essex parallels the structure of Donne's two poems: "The Storm" bobs on rough seas and maritime failures, whereas "The Calm" empties these events out and offers only "weak watery hopes." Out of such thin gruel, however, the second poem rebuilds a tenuous lyric selfhood.

The key trope in "The Calm" is inversion: everything that has happened in "The Storm" melts and inverts itself. After "that storm's tyrannous rage" (1) and that rage's political allegories, the calm is both "stupid"

(2), meaning that it lacks the specific actions of the previous poem, and literally "nothing" (2). The paradoxes of nothingness and liquefaction become Donne's subject. Pitch and lead lose shapes and become liquid, "As water did in storms" (11–12). The same dissolution strikes the social world, as the elongated period of stasis recalls other endings and leave takings: "Like courts removing, or like ended plays" (14). Extending beyond these political and dramatic spaces, the warlike nature of the ship vanishes: "The fighting place now seamen's rags supply; / And all the tackling is a frippery" (15–16). The poet seeks a suitably foreign analogy to capture their hopeless state, alienated from both "lost friends" and "sought foes," but the one he finds also fails: "But meteor-like, save that we move not, [we] hover" (21–22). The sailors are like meteors in their separation from the world but unlike these celestial bodies in immobility. "The Calm" narrates a situation that all poetry's varied metaphors, social, artistic, or meteorological, fail to capture.

Having inverted storm's chaos, the center of "The Calm" explores the rich metaphor of calenture, a particular fever that was thought to infect sailors in the tropics, because of which they would hurl themselves into the sea, thinking that it was a green field.[49] This image, which extends the inversion pattern of the opening of "The Calm," unites the dislocated crew: "Only the calenture together draws / Dear friends, which meet dead in great fishes' jaws" (23–24). Ironically rejecting the master trope of the verse letter, which asserts the power of poetry to unite absent friends, in this poem the crew meets only on the sea floor. For those, like Donne, who remain aboard, all is isolation: "Each one, his own priest, and own sacrifice" (26). To be in deathly togetherness below the surface or infernal separation on deck leads to an imagined middle space of swimming near the ship, but this "brimstone bath" (30) fails to ease "parboiled wretches" (32). As in "The Storm," Donne turns to classical and biblical allusions roughly two-thirds of the way through the poem, but in this case the cited figures, Bajazet "encaged" and Samson with "his hair off" (33), reemphasize the passivity of sailors in hostile nature.

As the poem nears its end, its representations of emptiness become starker. "What are we then?" (51), the poet asks. No longer struggling with the storm or feverishly leaping to their deaths, the crew dissolves into the humid air: "How little more alas / Is man now, than before he was! he was / Nothing; for us, we are for nothing fit" (51–53). In phrasing that anticipates the theological laments of later poems and sermons, Donne and his fellow crew members evaporate: "We have no power, no will, no sense" (55). Sitting motionless on a sea that is "Smooth as thy mistress' glass" (8), men become empty. The poem has room, however, for one last inversion. While "The Storm" ends with Donne pushing away his friend Christopher Brooke to spare him suffering, "The Calm" ends with the memory of Brooke awkwardly filling the poet's emptiness. "I lie," concludes the final iambic foot of the penultimate line, which is followed by "I should not then thus feel this misery." The half rhyme between *lie/misery,* especially when contrasted against the relentlessly strong couplets throughout both poems, implies that whatever survives the calm will be partial but also that some fragments of selfhood still "feel" inside voracious emptiness. The terms of this last appeal to friendship remain vague—"then thus . . . this"—as if friendship and selfhood have been nearly, but not entirely, lost. The misery that is the poem's subject calls upon, in its final line, the fellow feeling that Brooke, as imagined recipient of the verse letter, represents. Poetry as human transaction, written by one friend and read by another, provides a half-visible lifeline through which to escape the all-consuming calm of the poem.

Stevens in Florida

Storms produce shipwrecks, but what comes from catastrophic calms? This chapter's second interruption seeks a parallel for the stationary Donne in Wallace Stevens's modernist lyric "Sea Surface Full of Clouds." Though Donne's second poem crawls back to an interpersonal haven at its end, much of "The Calm" gestures toward a fully impersonal poetics of the sea, in which biography and human relations have no lasting place. Extending that conception of sea poetry brings Donne in touch with the twentieth-century poet Wallace Stevens and, in particular, his 1924 poem "Sea Surface Full of Clouds." Stevens's five-part poem is more formally complex than Donne's verse letter, and that structural complexity enables Stevens to write what Donne eschews: an almost person-less poem about the always-moving sea. Stevens shows what Donne cannot quite represent. The modern poem begins with an autobiographical fragment, "In that November off Tehuantepec," a line that gets repeated at the start of each of the five numbered sections of the poem without change or variation.[50] Spreading its five parts horizontally like so many outstretched fingers, the poem's lack of narrative progress replicates the stillness it finds in the sea. Like "The Calm," this poem traps itself within oceanic stasis. Unlike Donne's verse letter, however, Stevens's poem refuses the consolations of human bonds. The poem ends outside human emotions, with its closing focus on "the sea / And heaven" (5.16–17) rather than the narrator. It represents an extreme end point to the inversion that guides Donne from storm to calm.

Each of the five sections of "Sea Surface Full of Clouds" performs a two-stage interrogation of the sea. First, the poet celebrates the aesthetic value of the visible ocean. The first half of each section enjambs this meaning across the second and third of the six three-line stanzas. The first of these five parallel phrases reads, "Paradisal green / Gave suavity to the perplexed machine // Of ocean, which like limpid water lay" (1.5–7). Preceded each time by November in Tehuantepec and immediately prefaced by variations on chocolate and umbrellas, these versions of ocean present a massive externality, a "machine"—this word is repeated in all five sections of the poem—for aesthetic transcendence that remains alien to human feeling. The first repetition sets a pattern: the oceanic "machine" embodies such pleasing qualities as "suavity" and "paradisal green," but it remains static and out of reach, "like limpid water lay." Stevens's choice to make the ocean its own metaphor—it lies "like limpid water" when of course it is, itself, water—emphasizes the foreignness of marine space, its quality of being always beyond human comprehension. That pattern of excess and shifting meaning continues through all five variations on this phrase: "the tense machine // Of ocean, which in sinister flatness lay" (2.6–7); "the tranced machine // Of ocean, as a prelude holds and holds" (3.607); "the dry machine // Of ocean, pondering dark stratagem" (4.6–7); "the obese machine // Of ocean, perfected in indolence" (5.6–7). The movement through these variations rises to perfection in section 5 and, arguably, moves through a dramatic climax in section 3, in which the "tranced" ocean is held, temporarily, in place. Across this highly controlled pattern, the poem trains its reader to see changes within continuities. Slight movements, like ripples on still water, map the forward movement of the poem. The ocean spreads out in front of the poem after the manner of "The Calm," but for Stevens the sea's primary form is nonhuman opaque beauty.

In response to the repeated challenges of the oceanic machine, the five sections also contain questions that get answered in French. The first section sets the pattern: "Who, then, evolved the sea-blooms from the clouds / diffusing balm in the Pacific calm? / *C'était mon enfant, mon bijou, mon âme*" (1.10–12; italics in original). The poem's questions, like its depiction of the ocean, appeal to aesthetics. Stevens seeks the source of oceanic beauty and grandeur, and he assumes that the answer is not purely human. Shifting to French enables the poem to become more intimate and also more obscure in its portrayal of the sea and the sources of sea beauty. Notably, the only first-person words in the poem, *mon* and *ma,* are both in French, meaning "my," as if the poem can signal human possession only in a (semi)foreign language. The close intimacy of the first section's *enfant, bijou,* and *âme* varies over the remainder of the poem, reaching a climax of emotional intensity in section 3—"*mon extase et mon amour*" (3.12)—before retreating into nonpersonal phrases in section 4, "*la nonchalance divine*" (4.12), and section 5, "*mon spirit batard, l'ignominie*" (5.12). Stevens famously quipped that English and French together make up "one language," but in this poem the shift into French marks a concealing of the self through engagement with ocean.[51] Like "The Calm," "Sea Surface Full of Clouds" puts barriers between human figures and the oceanic environment. For Stevens the task of the poem is to invent complex ways to revivify that relationship. The sea represents that part of the natural world that most requires the impersonal poetic imagination, and the seascape becomes thoroughly nonhuman by the last section's "clearing opalescence" (5.16) and "fresh transfigurings of freshest blue" (5.18). At the end, a poem deeply committed to variation resigns itself, with perhaps an inaudible shrug, to repeating, in two different grammatical forms, the word "fresh." The still but moving ocean, in the end, cannot be captured by ingenious structures of poetic play of the sort that were pioneered by Donne and "perfected in indolence" (5.7) by Stevens. Finally, only simple words can gesture toward it. Stevens's "transfiguring" sea represents the space that Donne eschews in "The Calm" in order to return, haltingly, to human relationships. In that sense, "Sea Surface Full of Clouds," which even in its title gestures toward nonhuman things, represents a sea poetry beyond Donne's.

The irony of my account of poetic form as a response to maritime alterity is that the task of the poem can never fully complete itself. Poems are too insubstantial to change history, and poetic responses often acknowledge their own limits. Poems like these by Donne and Stevens provide order by formalizing—which is to say, falsifying—lived experience: expunging details, adding metaphors, rewriting, redirecting, turning the reader's attention away from those who were there (Essex, Raleigh, Howard) to those who were not (Brooke). Poems like these are in some basic sense escapist, in that they turn human attention away from physical experience and toward imaginative transformation. Reading Donne's lyrics in dialogue with naval histories and subject to literary interruptions by Camões's monster and Stevens's lyric replicates the strained relationship between poetic form and lived maritime journey. Insisting on the intermingling of historical facts and poetic language reminds twenty-first-century readers and voyagers that physical experience and poetic form respond mutually to each other, that the risks of experience are always entangled with the consolations of poetry. As we read poems and histories, we recall that no account ever reaches completion. Journeys end, but not conclusively.

Thomas Hardy and the Ends of Shipwreck

Nearly all shipwreck poems fall into the category of near misses in that the narrative of the drowned sailor seldom appears directly on the page. Before the high-Romantic melodrama of poems such as William Cowper's "The Castaway" (1799), most literary representations of shipwreck concluded with miraculous deliverance. Of the poems I explore in this chapter, with the exception, perhaps, of "John Marr," who might be assumed dead, if not at sea, by the end of his poem, all the central figures survive their ordeals at sea, even if deliverance comes after hope has been given up. The poetry of utter disaster, of sinking and drowning beneath cold waves, proved hard to write. One of the fullest elaborations of the "we split!" trope appears in Thomas Hardy's great modernist lyric about the *Titanic,* "The Convergence of the Twain" (1915). In its obsession with triple rhymes, careful expansion of an initial duality into a triplicate form, and final focus on more-than-human entanglements, Hardy's poem reads shipwreck from the bottom up, considering human tragedy from the ocean floor. Notorious for its lack of human interest or even named human characters, the poem begins where "John Marr" and *The Tempest* end: in an oceanic world where people cannot abide.

While "John Marr" arrives at the triple rhyme only in its final ecstatic stanza, Donne's two poems delight in doubled rhymes, and Stevens's ornate stanzas never quite arrive at full triples, Hardy's eleven short stanzas each consist of a triplet. The opening rhyme, *sea/vanity/she,* lays out the scene's players: nature, human folly, and the drowned ship. The repeated rhyme connects these elements to emphasize that none of these things can remain separate after the disaster. A poem about the "convergence" of two things, ship and iceberg, must also, the rhyme scheme insists, be a poem about connections between three things.[52] Across the first five stanzas, however, a basic split dominates the poem, between figures of human agency—"salamandrine fires" (2), "mirrors meant / To glass the opulent" (3), "Jewels in joy designed" (4)—and the countervailing power of brute oceanic nature—"the solitude of the sea" (1), "cold currents" (2), "The sea-worm" (3), and finally "Dim moon-eyed fishes" who swim through the wreck and say, "What does this vaingloriousness down here?" (5).[53] At that point, the moral seems simple, even crude: vainglory must, and should, be drowned. The insistent triplets, each rhymed sound repeated one more time than is common in English poetry, in the third line of each stanza that is elongated into an alexandrine, show the formal mechanisms of the poem straining against this clear binary.

The poem's *volta* comes almost halfway through, in the first line of stanza six, with the inconspicuous word "Well" (6). Like the asymmetrical turns of Renaissance sonnets, this near-blank word introduces a new perspective into Hardy's poem, a third force to match the triple rhymes. The "Immanent Will" (6) that writes the shipwreck microgenre adds organizing force to the story. From static visions of sunken opulence, the poem becomes fixated on motion. The "Iceberg" (8), introduced as the ship's "sinister mate" (7), is an improbable match for the great vessel, "far and dissociate" (7) as these two figures seem. The force of Immanent Will, historical fact, or necessity joins together these two mates, unlikely rhymed pair though they may be:

As the smart ship grew
In stature, grace, and hue,
In shadowy silent distance grew the Iceberg too. (8)

The poem's careful balance insists that these two creations are both joined and radical opposites, "stature, grace, and hue" opposed to "shadowy silent distance." Only the last rhyming word of this stanza, "too," recalls the future intimacy of ice and ship. Stripped of human emotions and narratives of chance, Hardy's shipwreck poem holds our eyes open as tragic halves collide.

The shockingly sexual word that describes the collision, "consummation" (11), while prepared for by the phrase "sinister mate," radically reimagines the disaster. The poem unfolds a dual language of causality and necessity: human folly and natural forces, unnamed pilots and Immanent Will, together become "twin halves of one august event" (10). Consummation and mating are not the only metaphors employed to describe that meeting; the poem also describes the "intimate welding" (9) of these two "alien" (9) forces. Shipwreck as Hardy writes it dispenses with the human anxieties that dominate the opening scene of *The Tempest* and most of Donne's diptych. Instead, opposed forces and hemispheres consummate into three parts, as the triple-rhymed stanzas drive the poem forward. The audience at the charity concert that commissioned the poem to help with the tragedy disaster fund must have been shocked by the utter absence of remorse or sentiment in Hardy's vision of the wreck.

Perhaps the strangest feature of "The Convergence of the Twain" is its inverted nature. It moves from undersea depths to the moment of the accident, from ruined wreck to still-moving ship. In subjecting the disaster to the "Spinner of the Years" (11), who stands ambiguously for God, History, and Necessity, Hardy reveals the hidden desire inside accounts of shipwreck. We, the audience, those who listen to the poem or watch the play, want the ship to go down. Shipwreck creates histories, events, morals. The "now!" of Hardy's poem brings together ship and iceberg. It names the "now" of dramatic performance and of Benjamin's now-time of catastrophe. Focusing on the moment, we covet intensity and power. Hardy the tragic novelist turned poet knew what shipwreck could mean. Only full disaster creates full emotional release.

· CHAPTER 7 ·

Castaways

Surviving Disaster

The sea will wash in
but the rocks . . .
are the stubborn man.

William Carlos Williams, "The Seafarer"

The First Wreck: North Haven, Connecticut, 1997

Shipwrecks are also, but not only, human stories. With my book-ship now nearly on the rocks, the time has come for a personal interjection. Some crucial piece of this project began almost two decades ago at the movies with Leo and Kate. During the summer of 1997, in the company of my wife's then-teenage cousins, we went to see James Cameron's blockbuster *Titanic* at the North Haven multiplex. The two cousins, self-named Titaniacs, had already seen it perhaps ten or more times, but I had until then resisted.

For the first hour or more, I twisted in my seat. The writing, the performances, the plot—all were too syrupy to bear. Leo won the ticket at cards, sketched the unhappy young wife, together they played "King of the World." It was pretty embarrassing stuff. When would the great ship wreck?

Then, at some point past halfway, they hit the iceberg. That was when shipwreck got its bait between my teeth. I bit, disaster set the hook, and I was on the line. Since then, I have struggled but have not gotten loose.

The drama of shipwreck, it turns out, has a narrative propulsion that can redeem almost anything. Images of the wounded ship, the icy water, the straining machinery, and flooding ballrooms made up for, or at least obscured, the overripe melodrama. I was then writing about Greek romance, so I had been thinking about shipwreck as, in Northrop Frye's phrase, "a standard means of transportation" in this long-lived narrative genre.[1] But something turned inside me that evening. What I had not realized until that ordinary evening in North Haven was how much work shipwreck could do by itself, even inside a mangled narrative.

I remember that evening at the movies often, though I have never again sat through the film. Shipwreck grabbed me that evening, reached out and claimed me through cinematic dreck. I have been living inside it ever since. As this book nears its end, I turn back to narrative as a tool of salvage. As the old woman almost says at the movie's end, story is what saves.

The Second Wreck: United States, September 11, 2012

Bob Dylan's waltz about the *Titanic,* the title track of his album *Tempest,* was released on September 11, 2012. The song hit me that fall with the weight of my musical hero laying down my own obsession. There in the cold water with the great ship on April 15, 1912, Dylan growled out his shipwreck parable. There was nothing about the 9/11 anniversary in the album launch and no explicit references to that catastrophe in the songs. The *Titanic* disaster, like 9/11, was taken by many as a hinge moment in history. The loss of the great ship in 1912 marked the end of European triumphalism and the start of the general disaster that would culminate in the Great War. The attacks of 9/11/01 initiated a new phase of American and global disorder, the disastrous "War on Terror." It seems typical of Dylan's obliquity that he might respond artistically to 9/11 by way of the *Titanic.* The song resonates inside a time knot of multiple historicities, gesturing at once toward 1912, 2001, and 2012. The careful balancing of the numerals in the album's release date, 9/11/12, reaches back in its day and month to the early twenty-first-century terror attack, while the calendar year emphasizes the century that had passed since the *Titanic*'s lone voyage. As a temporal hinge swinging both ways, Dylan's song captures the multiple temporalities of shipwreck modernity.

My reading of Dylan's song "Tempest" asks it to sing out a soundtrack for this book. When the album appeared, my project was already well under way. I heard the match the first time I listened to the long, rambling, beautiful song. The song traps its listeners just where I want to be, inside the revelatory chaos of shipwreck. Dylan snarled at a reporter who asked him if the title *Tempest* indicated that this would be his final album: "Shakespeare's last play was called *The Tempest.* It wasn't called just plain 'Tempest.' It's two different titles."[2] The angry denial seems unbelievable, but it also recalls that Dylan's song, which takes place almost entirely on a doomed ship, maps out an almost perfect inverse of Shakespeare's play, which contains only one scene on board a ship that does not, finally, sink. There is no tempestuous storm in Dylan and no real wreck in Shakespeare. The song's oblique gestures toward Shakespeare's not-quite-final play hint at how we should read Dylan's dark waltz.[3]

I bring Dylan's "Tempest" into my analysis by asking his song to rebut a resonant claim that I used to believe in from Michel Serres in *The Natural Contract.* "I live in shipwreck alert," Serres writes. "Always in dire straits, untied, lying to, ready to founder" (124). I have liked this sentiment since I first wrote about it in 2009, but lately it has been bugging me.[4] It is not quite right. It names my very deed of love for our inhuman and disorderly environment but, as Lear's middle daughter might say, it comes too short. Another Serres text, *The Five Senses,* imagines shipwreck as the birth of the soul.[5] Shipwreck modernity seems closer to birth than alert.

Dylan's song solidifies for me a crucial ecological lesson that I have been seeking throughout this project. Shipwreck is not something to prepare for, something that is about to happen. It is happening. Now. We are inside it, not waiting for it. *Castaways,* that name belongs to our present and our future both.

The lush tones of the waltz and gravelly exhaustion in the old man's voice soften this harsh lesson and make it bearable. It turns out that it is not so bad living inside shipwreck. It becomes easier if you stop hoping that there is solid ground somewhere.[6] A central claim of this book has been that shipwreck, the sudden shocking awareness that the vessels that have carried us this far are coming to pieces under our feet, represents an ordinary if painful way to live. My twin stalking horses throughout have been the ecological catastrophes of early modern globalization and today's experience of global warming, but the underlying facts of disruption and disorder exist independently of these historical periods. Humans have been floundering about inside disorder for a long time. We have gotten good at inventing ways to reimagine disorder as order. As I have argued elsewhere, accommodating disorder is one of the things literature does well.[7]

Living inside shipwreck feels even less comfortable than Serres's "shipwreck alert." A key difference involves attitudes toward change. In alert, we are animated by paranoia and fantasies of structure. We are pole-axed with dread, afraid of impending loss, melancholy with nostalgia for things we believe we have now but are about to lose forever. Inside shipwreck, by contrast, as the ship comes apart and water pours in, we have no time to waste and an urgent need to get used to being wet. We must become disorderly workers as well as systematic philosophers.

Several things follow from global shipwreck. Dylan's song unfolds three essential truths: We are all failed watchmen. There is no understanding. The universe opens wide. These three quotations turned maxims employ Dylan's words to transform my historical analysis of premodern culture into a twenty-first-century hymn of ecological catastrophe.

The Watchman

An unnamed figure plays the part of Dylan's Prospero. The watchman appears four times in the crowded song to guide disaster into artistic order. The four moments in which Dylan brings his watchman forward pull his song momentarily up from the raw now-time of disaster, inviting the consolations or transformations of art. But this wizard is not in control. "The watchman, he lay dreaming," goes the refrain: "He dreamed the *Titanic* was sinking" (stanza 6).[8] Four watchman stanzas, out of a total of forty-five stanzas all together, transform disaster into story, distant knowledge into bodily experience, epic possibility into unanswered need. The movement of these four stanzas starts with the basic narrative structure, in which "ballroom dancers" encounter "the underworld" (stanza 6). The scenario distorts itself as the watchman's and ship's bodies tilt together "at forty-five degrees" (stanza 16). Even after he recognizes that "the damage had been done," the watchman still feels a futile desire "to tell someone" (stanza 37). In the concluding stanza, his watch spies out loss and possibility: "He dreamed the *Titanic* was sinking / Into the deep blue sea" (stanza 45). Nothing left for the failed watcher to see in that sea, as the echoing pun lingers.

He watches, but he cannot tell.

In the historical backdrop to the song, the watchman is the one who failed to spot the iceberg. This characterization demotes Prospero from controlling magus to passive dreamer. He sits on the masthead and fails to see. Shakespeare's wizard captures fantasies of power, but Dylan's watchman seals this figure up in an isolated crow's nest. He has nothing to do but watch. His passive position mirrors our own position today amid rapid-fire ecodisasters.

No Understanding

Shipwrecks are hard to narrate. Human meaning-making systems cannot encompass oceanic chaos. As the Shakespearean daughter in the play from which Dylan gets his title bullies her father into acknowledging, the human response to disaster is sympathy: "O, I have suffered / With those that I saw suffer!" (*The Tempest*, 1.2.5–6). Miranda asks her wizard-watchman-father to feel with her and, with us, to attune ourselves to what sailors fear.

Dylan's "Tempest," by contrast, sings Miranda down. Shipwreck creates feeling but not understanding:

> They waited at the landing
> And they tried to understand
> But there is no understanding
> For the judgments of God's hand. (stanza 43)

No understanding. God's hand looms behind the wizard's curse. Listening to these lines in Bob's Jeremiah thunder growl is both ominous and oddly freeing. Might failing to understand mean that we do not have to be on alert anymore? That we can turn, at last, to something else?

Opens Wide

No understanding fixes a dour sentiment at the heart of this long song, but as in Melville's "John Marr" and Donne's maritime lyrics, there is also aesthetic hope in these lines. Despair is not the final force of shipwreck. Against doomed watchmen and broken understanding, Dylan's lyrics present overflowing abundance. Everybody gathers on board the doomed ship. The movie star shows up early: "Leo took his sketchbook / He was often so inclined" (stanza 7).[9] Dylan happily copped to the pop culture reference. "Yeah, Leo," he admitted to *Rolling Stone,* "I didn't think the song would be the same without him. Or the movie."[10]

The star pairs up with rhyming Cleo, who might be Shakespeare's Egyptian queen or Leo's leading lady. They mingle with Wellington and Jim Dandy, Calvin, Blake, and Wilson—the theologian, poet, and American president?—Davy the brothel keeper, Jim Backus, and the bishop, even "the rich man, Mr. Astor" (stanza 24). The story of the *Titanic* unfolds through excess. Who ever heard of a thirteen-and-a-half-minute pop song, much less a waltz? It is too much, too many fragments of story and experience and feeling. But it adds up to something:

> The ship was going under
> The universe had opened wide. (stanza 12)

There is a fundamental ecological point amid the flotsam. Shipwreck, as Dylan sings it, names the core experience, the shock and pressure of the inhuman world on human skin. Being in the world means living inside shipwreck. The disaster is the story we need to explain, cannot explain, and must tell. A direct encounter: ocean liner meets iceberg, human bodies splash into cold salt water. We want and cannot have distance, perspective, narrative, a story that explains and insulates.

We want the source. Tell us the cause, Muse! But we never get it.

The wetness of the encounter, the brute physicality of shipwreck, will not let us understand causes. This song, this disaster, the oceanic histories and snatches of poetry that events like the wreck of the *Titanic* open up resonate without rest. The only stability is on the sea floor, but that distant space is also a churning site of sea changes fast and slow.

Shipwreck ecology need not be a place only of horror or nostalgia. There is ecstasy in the waters too. Not the relief of having survived or the satisfaction of figuring it out: those things do not last. But an intellectual tingle that ripples out into the physical world, a willingness to confront the inhumanity of our environment, and an appetite for experience that does not mind getting wet. In the fall of 2012, Dylan's disaster ballad growled out the stark beauty of shipwreck's global ecology.

The Third Wreck: London, 1703

Meteorologists still describe it as the most powerful storm ever to make landfall in England. On November 26–27, 1703, the Great Storm struck land, destroying massive amounts of property, drowning livestock and dozens of people, and killing an estimated eight thousand sailors on over one hundred navy and merchant ships.[11] Literary historians remain fascinated by this storm in part because of its impact on the career of Daniel Defoe, whose 1704 book *The Storm* provides traces of his emerging literary interests. The future novelist of realism employed empirical reporting to assemble this volume, which largely consists of firsthand accounts that Defoe gathered around southern England. *The Storm* also experiments with narrative structure, and it is the first full-length volume in Defoe's large oeuvre. Robert Markley has treated *The Storm* as a harbinger of changing ecological ideas, noting that Defoe attempts to reconcile Christian apocalyptism with empirical observation. The result is "complex, dialectical, and even incoherent visions of 'Nature.'"[12] Markley persuasively argues that Defoe sees the storm as "part of a natural world that is defined by its volatility" (110). Markley further claims that the Little Ice Age, a climatological anomaly that lasted roughly from 1550 to 1750, represents a particularly disruptive period in English weather: "To live in Shakespeare's or Defoe's England was to experience with some frequency the thunder, lightning, high winds, and flooding that were much less pronounced two centuries later" (111). For my purposes, the Great Storm was not simply a subtropical cyclone that strayed unusually far north and east. It was a landed shipwreck. Numerous critics have suggested that the journalistic methods of *The Storm* provide a foretaste of the realism of *Robinson Crusoe* and the later novels.[13] I further suggest that the Great Storm prefigures the shipwreck around which the life of Defoe's famous castaway turns. Living in London in late November 1703 brought maritime disaster onto land.

Defoe's response to disaster in *The Storm* digs into the entanglements that killing storms produce in Providential thinking. Like Anthony Thacher after the loss of his family, Defoe's narrative attempts to reconcile the conflicting imperative of divine justice and power. His text unfolds this conflict in multiple discourses. Defoe opens with a gesture toward classical meteorology, which considered winds as arising from "a System of Exhalation, Dilation, and Extension."[14] Soon, however, theology trumps Aristotelianism: "There seems to be more of God in the whole Appearance [of winds], than in any other Part of Operating Nature" (1). In such catastrophic events, reasons Defoe, "Nature plainly refers us beyond her Self, to the Mighty Hand of Infinite Power, the Author of Nature, and Original of all Causes" (2). The shift from empirical speculation to theological assertion, however, is not as smooth as these introductory lines imply. The text toggles between human and divine things. As Markley observes, Defoe's book exposes its author's lived incoherence. Defoe's fascination lies directly across this divide. Storms fracture understanding, and it is by breaking existing structures that they reveal hidden truths: "The deepest Search into the Region of Cause and Consequence has found out just enough to leave the wisest Philosopher in the dark, to bewilder his Head, and drown his Understanding" (3). Especially in the third image of the final phrase, drowned understanding, Defoe puts himself in the position of the shipwrecked swimmer, barely keeping himself afloat.

Defoe's text, like Dylan's "Tempest," treats disaster as a symbolic exploration of problems in historical representation. Caught between two ancient systems—Aristotelian meteorology and Christian theology—and two modern developments—empirical reporting and fictional realism—Defoe assembles a hodgepodge volume, full of quotations, citations, and inserted letters from his correspondents. The most difficult task in representing the disaster, as Defoe acknowledges late in his book, is the challenge of "too many Particulars, the Crowds of Relations which he [the Author] has been oblig'd to lay by to bring the Story into a Compass tolerable to the Reader" (270). In literary-historical terms, the solution to this problem of amplitude would eventually be found in the realist novel, with its overflowing capacity and polymorphous form.[15] The intermediary position of *The Storm,* which contains elements of journalism, religious pamphlet, and early modern miscellany, highlights the strain catastrophe puts on existing literary and cultural forms.

The most compact example of how the storm ruptures and rewrites literary forms appears in an inserted pastoral poem, which Defoe claims was sent to him "from a very ingenious Author, and desir'd to be publish'd in this Account" (41). The poem, "A Pastoral, Occasion'd by the Late Violent Storm" (42–45), recalls seventeenth-century controversies around piscatorial subject matter in English verse. In the poem, conventionally named Damon wanders in a familiar landscape, "Where the two Streams their wanton course divide, / And gently forward in soft Murmurs glide" (42). Breaking this pastoral frame, sad Meliboeus tells him a story of catastrophe instead of lovelorn melancholy. "Mine's a publick, nobler Care," says the second swain, "Such in which you and all the World must share" (42). Meliboeus's description of the Great Storm transforms closely observed details into symbolic objects. He begins with a "huge Pine [that] did with the Winds contend" (43) and describes English rivers swollen into destructive mouths, "not like the happy Nile, / To fatten, dew, and fructifie our Ile: / But like the Deluge, by great Jove design'd / To drown the Universe, and scourge Mankind" (43). If piscatorialists such as Diaper and Fletcher had attempted to reframe pastoral harmony in a maritime environment, this poem represents an apocalyptic end stage in which no human habitation remains: "The Waters know no Limits but the Sky" (43). Recalling Shakespeare's Boatswain, Defoe's pastoralist emphasizes the anti-imperial politics of the storm: "What tho' the mighty Charles of Spain's on board, / The Winds obey none but their blust'ring Lord" (44). Eschewing green pastoral, the poem arrives at blue disorder.

The poem's compensating discourse replying to disorder, interestingly, is Virgilian politics. Responding to Meliboeus's long description of an inundated England, populated at last by "hungry Fish . . . [which] quickly seize with greedy Jaws their Prey" (44), Damon leaps to Aeneas. Paraphrasing the opening couplet of Dryden's well-known English translation of Virgil, Damon analogizes flooded land to shipwrecked hero: "So the great Trojan, by the Hand of Fate, / And haughty Power of angry Juno's Hate / . . . Yet safe at last his mighty Point he gain'd; / In charming promis'd Peace and Splendor reign'd" (44). Turning from pastoral to epic and from local to imperial concerns, the poem seeks redemption through shifting genre, scale, and historical circumstances. Turning to Aeneas the imperial conqueror rather than Odysseus the solitary swimmer or Jonah the God-driven prophet indicates Defoe's attempt to suture up a broken polity. Echoing Defoe's complex politics, even though this poem may not actually have been written by Defoe, the disaster pastoral implies that the narrative resources of classical poetry can help Englishmen come to terms with natural disruption.

For this pastoral to serve as partial antidote to or compensation for disaster, its readers must recognize its multiple subtexts—piscatorial, Virgilian epic, Dryden's Augustan classicism—and be able to employ them intellectually. Like Defoe's fictional heroes and heroines who are masters of tool making and negotiation, the implied audience of *The Storm* reads in order to survive. The key virtues that enable partial survival are practical and maritime. England after the storm has become a nation of mariners, powered by metis, and Defoe's pride in seamanlike accomplishments counterbalances his fear of God's wrath. Earlier in the volume, a section clearly written by Defoe contrasts ancient fears of the stormy British Isles with the achievements of mariners in Defoe's time. "I make no question," Defoe writes, "but that our Ships ride out many a worse Storm than that terrible Tempest which scatter'd *Julius Caesar's* Fleet, or the same that drove *Aeneas* on the Coast of *Carthage*" (23). He imagines Britain, which is "open to the Flux of the Sea" (15), as a mariner's training ground and argues that the fears that ancient writers including Horace and Juvenal had of the sea emphasize the relative weakness of classical as opposed to modern British sailors (19). "So that upon the whole it seems plain to me," he concludes, "that all the dismal things the Ancients told us of *Britain,* and her terrible Shores, arose from the Infancy of Marine Knowledge, and the Weakness of the Sailor's Courage" (21). English metis, the complex sets of habits, experience, and embodied knowledge that piloted Jeremy Roch and Edward Barlow around the world's oceans, serves for Defoe as a national marker. Half-quoting Shakespeare's Boatswain, and for the moment glossing over the huge number of ships destroyed by the Great Storm, Defoe insists that English mariners fear no storm if they have space under their lee: "And nothing is greater satisfaction to them, if they have a Storm in view, than a sound Bottom and good *Sea-room*" (21).[16] In a storm-filled world, maritime skills and equipment ensure survival.

The tension between Defoe's celebration of English seamanship and his invocation of divine power underlies a basic split in *The Storm.* In literary terms the solution would seem to be Providential narrative, and with that in mind it seems telling that the last section of the book is a collection of "Remarkable Deliverances" (236–70), stories of people whose lives and sometimes property endured the Great Storm. Defoe as editor displays some anxiety about the contrast between "the sad and remarkable Disasters of this Terrible Night" and the "many remarkable Deliverances both by Sea and Land" (236). The repetition of the word "remarkable" suggests that he sees these two subgenres as equal sharers in the storm story. Of all the deliverances he includes, however, he singles out one in particular to mark his conclusion. Like the hybrid pastoral-piscatorial poem that summed up and commented upon the narrative account of the disaster, the final inset tale looks back across the more than a dozen deliverance accounts that precede it. As the pastoral transforms disaster into epic and political symbol, this final deliverance refashions providential rescue as divine test. On a ship "homeward bound from the *West-Indies*" (271), which transatlantic voyage might be taken to represent England's expanding global reach, a Master and Surgeon despair of surviving the storm. Continuing Defoe's extended meditation throughout *The Storm* on the opening scene of *The Tempest,* these men choose death, after the manner of Sebastian, who would rather "all sink with the king" (1.1.163) than subordinate himself to the Boatswain's prowess. Unlike Shakespeare's ultimately forgiven aristocrats, whose crimes fail to materialize, Defoe's despairing sailors cheat Providence by direct action: "When the Master saw all, as he thought, lost, his Masts gone, the Ship leaky, and expecting her every moment to sink under him, fill'd with Despair . . . they both shot themselves with their Pistols" (271–72). Obedient to authorial and allegorical command, divine hands save the ship after the officers abdicate: "It pleased God the Ship recover'd the Distress, was driven safe. . . . and the Captain just liv'd to see the desperate Course he took might have been spared" (272). Not trusting to the seamanship that Defoe had claimed as the supreme virtue of his own nation, these mariners in committing suicide reject both metis and God. Unlike the Remarkable Deliverances that precede the story, which beg the question of why some people and not others are spared, the final tale provides its own orthodox moral: God and the storm punish the faithless. There is something oddly and ideologically hopeful in Defoe's final recourse to tragedy, as if in this microstory he seeks what he has too seldom found in his reporting on the storm, a narrative scenario whose moral and theological contexts agree. The achieved consonance between things human and divine bears the marks of fiction—Defoe tellingly omits the name of the harbor into which this ship safely comes or other details that might identify the vessel—and it is in fiction, in *Robinson Crusoe,* that Defoe would extend the moral and ecological frames activated in *The Storm.* The image of the dying Captain seeing his ship coming safely to road represents the mismatch between the human need for certainty and the exfoliation of the divine plan through storms. Throughout his career, Defoe would return to shipwreck to consider human responses to this dilemma.

The Last Wreck: An Uninhabited and Imaginary Island, 1719

What happens when *The Storm* becomes all story? Defoe's *Robinson Crusoe* unfurls the definitive first-person narrative of shipwreck in English literature by presenting physical details simultaneously as signs of real presence and tokens of allegorical meaning. The hinge moment in the novel occurs when the hero swims through the surf to make landfall on a deserted island. This brief moment, perhaps a half-dozen pages out of three hundred plus in a typical modern edition of the novel, ends my shipwreck study because it combines the allegorical resources of classical and Renaissance traditions with detailed attention to precise physical experience. While Defoe's novel is conventionally seen as the beginning of a new tradition in English literature, I read it as engaging earlier shipwreck literature, which itself responds to the massive expansion of English interest in and experience of the great waters after the sixteenth century. The hostile waters that drowned Anthony Thacher's family and Edmund Pet's crew, that threaten in the opening scene of *The Tempest* and in Donne's "The Storm," become in Defoe tangible and, to an extent, manipulable. Seaman-like metis collapses into personal and physical abilities, as Crusoe in this crucial moment, uniquely in his tool-filled novel, has no equipment with which he can work or refashion to his use. At the heart of the story is just a human body in the surf.

Living inside this dynamic environment hurts, and if Crusoe's body-surfing represents a physical engagement with the global ocean, as I think it does, the essential point is that the experience is painful and disorienting. If the common insight of the many literary and historical texts this book has explored, from Shakespeare's plays and Barlow's multimedia journal to Donne's lyrics, is that the world in which humans live is not a stable space into which we can project our desires, literary culture imagines ways to endure disorder, not correct it. The essential counterweight to oceanic catastrophe is narrative. Stories, with their structural imperative to bring together unlike things, represent the intellectual infrastructure through which disorderly environments become provisionally legible. By telling stories, literary writers, like other humans, construct ways to make sense of our encounters with disruptive and changing spaces such as the ocean. For our age of ecological crisis, the ancient story of shipwreck tells topical tales.

To unpack *Robinson Crusoe,* I shift back into the seminarrative mode of my chapters on Roch and Barlow and retell the arrival of the shipwrecked sailor at his deserted island as an allegory of human responses to ecological disaster. Reading this famous novel against the realist tradition it is supposed to have founded, I argue that Crusoe's shipwreck points to a symbolic renovation of swimming as a way of responding to ecocatastrophe.

The story begins with the error of going to sea:

> But I that was born to be my own destroyer, could no more resist the offer than I could restrain my first rambling designs, when my father's good counsel was lost upon me. (60)

Responding to the familiar question of causation, Defoe insists upon the self-consuming nature of human longing. Crusoe destroys himself by returning to oceanic "rambling," against the "good counsel" of shorebound stability. Generations of critics, including Karl Marx, have read Crusoe's wanderlust as symptomatic of early capitalist desires for global economic expansion. In an ecological sense, however, Crusoe's rejection of land for sea eschews the pastoral fantasies of stability he inherits from his religious father and instead embraces dynamic, oceanic change. The storm waits for him, but as an ecologist or meteorologist might tell him, it will come whether he goes to sea or not. Venturing on the ocean entails facing rather than avoiding the disorderly and hostile nature of the inhuman environment. The sea voyage always gets interrupted:

> A violent tournado or hurricane took us quite out of our knowledge . . . that for twelve days together we could do nothing but drive, and scudding away before it, let it carry us whither the fate and fury of the winds directed; and during these twelve days, I need not say that I expected every day to be swallowed up, nor indeed did any in the ship expect to save their lives. (61)

Oceanic storms evacuate human knowledge. From a false sense of stability, the storm snatches away the anthropocentric insight Crusoe has claimed about his own habit of self-destruction. He can no longer speak—"I need not say"—and loses all expectations for the future. Like Barlow, he is subsumed by a change too powerful to represent. His language oscillates between attempts to represent extreme experience and allegorical depictions of that experience. Inside the fear of "every day to be swallowed up," a human future can only persist tentatively. Words like "fate" and "fury" gesture toward systems of meaning too remote or violent for comprehension: "It is not easy for any one, who has not been in the like condition, to describe or conceive the consternation of men in such circumstances" (62). Crusoe's immersion, even more than his island stay, represents radical isolation in a nonhuman environment. The project of island survival, from the castaway's first trip back to the wreck to the construction of shelter to the enslavement of Friday, involves assembling or co-opting allies, human and not. The oceanic encounter, by contrast, remains solitary and to some extent beyond representation. Against the accumulation of alliances, shipwreck narrates a stripping away. For a time Crusoe remains on board ship, with his crew-mates and the technological resources of the vessel, but these connections lose potency. The essential ally-antagonist he encounters before he reaches land is the ocean itself:

> In this distress the mate of our vessel lays hold of the boat . . . and getting all into her, let go, and committed our selves, being eleven in number, to God's mercy and the wild sea; for tho' the storm was abated considerably, yet the sea went dreadfully high upon the shore, and might well be called *Den wild Zee,* as the Dutch call the sea in a storm. (63)

Shipwreck takes Crusoe from storm to sea, temporarily connecting him to ten other refugees in the ship's boat. The Dutch phrase links the English hero to the polyglot world of early modern maritime culture, in which the English and Dutch were coexplorers, rivals, and occasionally partners in watery expansion. The wildness of the sea, it seems, can be captured only outside Crusoe's native idiom. Between God's mercy and *Den wild Zee,* it is an uncomfortable place. Crusoe cannot stay there long:

> Nothing can describe the confusion of thought which I felt when I sunk into the water; for tho' I swam very well, yet I could not deliver my self from the waves so as to draw breath, till that

> the wave having driven me, or rather carried me back a vast way on towards the shore, and having spent it self, went back, and left me upon the land almost dry, but half-dead with the water I took in. I had so much presence of mind as well as breath left, that seeing my self nearer the main land that I expected, I got upon my feet, and endeavoured to make on towards the land as fast as I could, before another wave should return, and take me up again. But I soon found it was impossible to avoid it; for I saw the sea again come after me as high as a great hill, and as furious as an enemy which I had no means or strength to contend with; my business was to hold my breath, and raise my self upon the water, if I could; and so by swimming to preserve my breathing, and pilot my self towards the shore. (64)

As Crusoe struggles in the surf, Defoe's precise language, with a particularity that recalls Barlow's technical descriptions of maritime labor, presents the entanglement of human and ocean. The key point is the partial mismatch between human skill—"I swam very well"—and maritime environment. It is not enough to swim well. Crusoe also needs "presence of mind" and patience: "My business was to hold my breath and raise my self upon the water." Rather than struggling against the hostile element, he preserves himself within it. Swimming represents an indirect form of heroic endurance, emphasizing survival and partial control: "So by swimming to preserve my breathing and pilot my self towards the shore." Preserving and piloting: the latter speaks to human efforts to control or influence their situation, but the former lacks direction or even clear agency. In a moment that epitomizes what I have elsewhere called a "swimmer poetics" of accommodation with a hostile environment, Crusoe rides the surf into shore and then slowly extricates his body from its clutches:[17]

> I recovered a little before the return of the waves, and seeing I should be covered again with the water, I resolved to hold fast by a place of the rock, and so to hold my breath if possible, till the wave went back; now as the waves were not so high as the first, being nearer to land, I held my hold till the wave abated, and then fetch'd another run, which brought me so near the

> shore, that the next wave, tho' it went over me, yet did not so swallow me up as to carry me away, and the next run I took, I got to the main land. (65)

The final phase of Crusoe's arrival on the island presents a fully hybrid interaction between human and ocean, body and waves. The essential mediator is "a place of the rock," on which the castaway holds himself while the outgoing surf pours over him. It is likely that Defoe means us to read this rock allegorically as a representation of true faith, as Anthony Thacher doubtless intended his rock in Massachusetts to be read. But it is also possible to interpret these moments as creating a three-part ecological alliance, in which a human connects himself to rock in order to endure watery flows. The ocean cannot be avoided, but it can be passed under and through so that the exile can reach land. Swimming does not represent a permanent solution to environmental catastrophe, only a temporary survival tactic, preserving life until sand appears under our feet, even if that sand may conceal further dangers. Shipwreck ecology clings to that desperate hope.

Three Short Epilogues

To dream of that beach . . .
The absolute singular . . .
Which is the bright light of shipwreck.

George Oppen, *Of Being Numerous*

The Bright Light of Shipwreck

With crisis comes transformative possibilities. Shipwreck writes change and generates tools for enduring change. Something always washes up on the beach.

I borrow the phrase "the bright light of shipwreck" for my first short epilogue to focus on the brilliance and horror of the crisis-instant.[1] The phrase comes from George Oppen's celebrated 1967 poem "Of Being Numerous" about living in New York City during the Vietnam War. For Oppen shipwreck represents pure violent singularity, against which he juxtaposes the collectivity of modern urban experience: "Obsessed, bewildered / By the shipwreck / Of the singular / We have chosen the meaning / Of being numerous."[2] Oppen's bright light proffers a catastrophic clarity that his poem finds bewildering. What he calls "The absolute singular . . . Which is the bright light of shipwreck" (14) represents the experience of being human in an unfriendly world, governed by "unearthly" forces. It is precisely this harsh singularity that shipwreck writers imagine and shipwrecked sailors encounter. Their narratives comprise a tradition in which the bright light of disaster restructures human encounters with a hostile environment. Their stories insist upon being told. As Primo Levi says to his coprisoner Jean when telling his shipwreck story in Auschwitz, "It is vitally necessary and urgent that he listen, that he understand . . . before it is too late" (104). To be singular is to wreck; continuity requires a listening community.

This book has argued that Oppen's singularity is not the only fate of shipwreck. The bright light of catastrophe can be endured, even valued for the stark vision it provides. Stories find audiences. Even disaster stories.

The Bookfish

The final image in this book is from *The Bookfish,* also titled *Vox Piscis,* a slim volume published in London in 1627 (Figure 13).[3] This woodcut picturing a codfish with a book in its belly allegorizes the beating heart of my scholarly practice and my deepest hopes for the blue humanities. The image provides a visual representation of the wisdom that comes up from the sea floor in the human–ocean encounter. The story began off the coast of King's Lynn on Midsummer's Eve 1626. Fishermen caught a codfish in Lynn's Deep, and they brought it to the Cambridge fish market, where it was "cut up, as usually others are for sale."[4] The book's trip out of the fish's belly made a detour into its mouth. According to the printed preface, Ioaccomy Brand, the wife of William Brand, one of the fishermen on the voyage, cleaned the fish to prepare it for sale. After the fish was sold, she "cut off the head, and tooke out the Garbidge" (9). At that point, however, another woman, not named in the preface, "espied in the maw of the fish a peece of canuasse, and taking it up found the Booke wrapped up in it, being much soyled and defaced, and couered ouer with a kinde of slime & congealed matter" (9). The discovered book was taken to Dr. John Goslin, vice chancellor of Cambridge, who examined "the truth of the particulars" before passing the pages on to "Daniel Boys, a Book-binder" to be "carefully washed and cleansed, being shewed unto many both before and after the cleansing thereof" (10).[5] The cod's maw and belly would become, for the three nearly century-old theological tracts that were later printed as *The Bookfish,* an unusual path to publication. The novelty of this conveyance into print served to publicize the new book. If the jests of several undergraduates, three of which are reprinted in the preface to *Vox Piscis,* are to be believed, the book-eating fish caused a sensation in Cambridge in 1626.[6]

In the image the deep-sea manuscript sits squarely in the center of the fish's belly. The preface concludes that divine wisdom "now speaks to thee out of the belly of the fish" (35). The fish, displayed cut open and with its head intact, reveals a "booke in decimo sexto" (8), with no

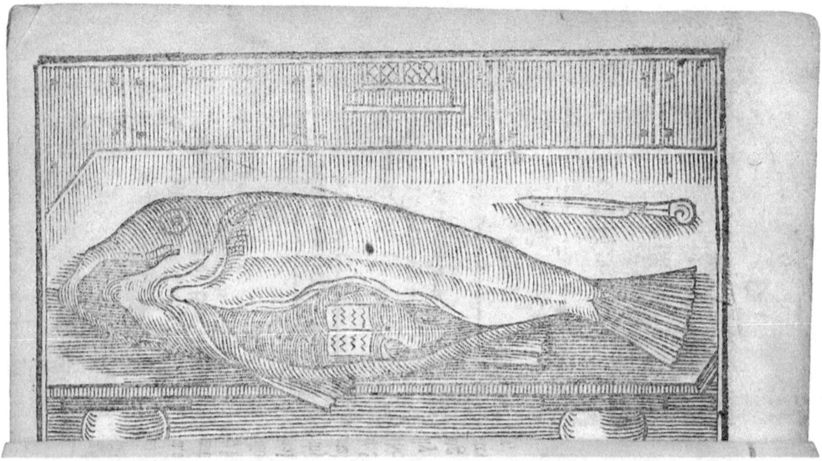

FIGURE 13. From the belly of the cod, a nonhuman voice proclaims divine truth. *Vox Piscis, or the Bookfish.* By permission of the Folger Shakespeare Library.

visible traces of sailcloth or digestive slime. Down at the bottom of the North Sea, amid darkness and ooze, waited a volume of divine wisdom, penned by the Henrician martyr John Frith nearly a century before. The oceanic pedigree of *The Bookfish,* more than its textual contents, underwrites its theological truth. Stories of holy relics returned from the deeps by sea creatures are common in coastal cultures, but the arrival of this fish in the early seventeenth century suggests that maritime symbology intermingled with emerging religious polemic in England. Though the preface is careful to name particulars and provide multiple witnesses, the story seems unbelievable on its face. It may be that the tiny book fell overboard, was swallowed by a scavenging cod, and then discovered at the Cambridge fish market, but it seems at least as likely that the Cambridge doctors associated with its printing, who in 1626 were already engaged in writing about apocalyptic events, invented the cod in order to use the ocean as a powerful and flexible symbol. Who would not want to read God's news straight from the fish's belly? Such wet wisdom bears out the maxim that the preface cites from Democritus: "The truth lies drowned in the deepe" (17).[7] As Julian Yates describes it, *The Bookfish* represents an "oozy underwater archive come topside."[8] In this case, fishermen appear able to recover a small piece of deep oceanic meaning.

The Bookfish provides my favorite oceanic model for scholarly and intellectual practices. While the publication of *Vox Piscis* seems intended to intervene in theological debates in 1620s Cambridge, reconsidering *The Bookfish* today can help frame a nascent "oceanic turn" in literary ecostudies, which I have called a "blue cultural studies" or a "blue humanities." In writing about maritime literature and culture, I suggest that we take *The Bookfish* as a model. The volume from the sea floor represents a gooey and imaginative mixing of scholarly writing and oceanic reality. The prospect of stuffing our manuscripts into the bellies of deep-sea fish as a protest against the crisis in academic publishing has an attractively Quixotic air, though it is worth remembering that *The Bookfish* is, among other things, a masterly bit of marketing. The book's preface names it "a living dumbe Speaking Library in the sea" (17), calling out to England "like another Jonas . . . out of the belly of the Fish" (34). This ocean text captures the alluring fantasy of a truly maritime literary culture. Perhaps we do not want to write from fish's bellies, or even pretend to do so. But real wisdom emerges from human encounters with the slimy deeps, if we are willing to go underwater to bring it back up.

Seven Shipwrecked Ecological Truths

1. Catastrophes are opportunities.
   Out of disasters come possibilities for new order and new ordering systems. The shocking violence of climate change is terrifying, but the chance to reimagine the human relationship with the nonhuman environment is liberating.[9] We will have many chances to ponder the relationship between disaster and opportunity in the coming decades.
2. We must live past "shipwreck alert."
   Being alert is not a bad thing, but it remains too defensive. Shipwreck ecology lets the floodwaters in. We know wrecks are coming and cannot avoid them. We must instead choose to live inside them.[10]
3. Whirlpools may be better than beaches.
   Being on the shore and tracing that liminal space feels familiar. Human beings have been coastal creatures through-

out our history. But the verticality of whirlpools and the lure of the deep ocean open up the possibility of traveling somewhere new. Down into insight and depth, to a cold and lightless place—but also a new place.[11]

4. *Mobilis in mobile.*
   It turns out that Captain Nemo had it right all along.[12] The fundamental truth of the ocean may simply be mobility inside the mobile thing, moving inside motion. All forms of stasis are not so much false as temporary.
5. The ecological future is for swimmers, not sailors.
   Nostalgia for the Age of Sail dominates Anglophone maritime studies, as revealed in scholarly attitudes toward major figures from Hakluyt and Shakespeare to Dana and Conrad. Replacing rippling canvas with steam and diesel engines shattered an ideal relationship between navigation and environment. But amid this lament, too little attention has yet been paid to the growth, mostly in the twentieth century but with deep historical roots, of swimming as a form of popular recreation and site of cultural meaning. Immersion, not sea travel, is now the dominant way humans engage physically with the ocean. Ocean swimming still awaits its Melville, but the difference between being in the ocean and floating in wooden ships atop it has powerful implications for blue literary ecologists.
6. Oceanic reality is distortion.
   Water distorts the senses, changing and diminishing visual perception while muting hearing. The overpowering taste and smell of salt fill our mouths and noses as we pass into the sea. Its fluid touch envelops our skin. Inside this massive body, nothing appears the same.
7. Survival is pleasure!
   What else can it be? If stasis is a dream and stability at best a short-term proposition, what other than pleasure can guide us? To swim in cold water, our senses invigorated by distortion, feeling environmental pressures on our skin and tasting acrid salt in the backs of our throats: what greater pleasure can we ask for?

Acknowledgments

WRITING ABOUT SHIPWRECK means thinking about voyages that never arrive at their destinations. Now that this book has come safely to port, I recall the helping hands along the way more than the rocks narrowly avoided. Books and ships both contain communities.

I am grateful for the support of many great archives and academic institutions. The intellectual seeds of this project germinated at a NEH summer institute in 2006, hosted by the Munson Institute in Mystic, Connecticut, where Glenn Gordinier, Eric Roorda, and my salty coparticipants opened my eyes to oceanic possibilities. The book received further support from a Caird Fellowship at the National Maritime Museum in Greenwich, where I encountered the manuscript diaries that occupy my middle chapters. Spending an academic year with the brilliant global scholars and archival richness of the John Carter Brown Library inspired my turn toward global waters. I thank the generous support of the R. David Parsons Fellowship and the JCB for that opportunity. I owe a special debt to the Folger Shakespeare Library, both for a short-term fellowship and for the invitation to curate a gallery exhibition in 2010, "Lost at Sea: The Ocean in the English Imagination, 1550–1750," that helped me think visually and viscerally about oceanic meanings.

I owe a great deal to the collegial working environment of the St. John's English Department and College of Liberal Arts and Sciences. Department chair Stephen Sicari, Dean Jeffrey Fagen, and my colleagues are ideal cothinkers and supportive interlocutors. I thank the college for supporting my work with two summer fellowships and a research leave.

This project could not exist in its current form without the hospitality and critical generosity of the many audiences who have listened and responded to earlier versions of the arguments. I greatly value the opportunity to have presented various iterations of this material at Hofstra University, the New York Maritime Academy, George Washington University, the University of Alabama, Farleigh Dickinson University, Columbia University, the University of Connecticut at Avery Point, Mystic Seaport, Middlebury College, the John Carter Brown Library, and the Folger Shakespeare Library. I also presented pieces of this project at numerous scholarly conferences, including meetings of the Shakespeare Association of America, the Renaissance Society of America, the Association for the Study of Literature and the Environment, the Group for Early Modern Cultural Studies, and the BABEL Working Group. I particularly valued the opportunity in 2011 to convene a conference at the John Carter Brown Library in Providence, Rhode Island, on "The Hungry Ocean: Literary Culture and the Maritime Environment." Shipwreck's tribulations have been made bearable by the generosity of these audiences.

At these events and other gatherings, colleagues have asked questions and offered insights that have shaped this book. I owe a debt to everyone who has given time, imagination, and attention to this project. It's far too many names to call out the full list!

Working with University of Minnesota Press has been an ideal experience from start to finish, with engaged and sympathetic editors and staff. I also appreciate the labors of the press's manuscript reviewers, whose comments have helped create a better book.

Fathom-deep gratitude goes to those who have been closest to me during the shipwreck years: my dearest voyaging companion, Alinor Sterling, and our children, Ian and Olivia.

Notes

Two Prefaces

1. This term derives from Stephen Greenblatt's prize-winning study of Lucretius, *The Swerve: How the World Became Modern* (New York: Norton, 2012). For a representative summation of medievalist responses, see the recent Book Review Forum in *Exemplaria* 25, no. 4 (October 2013), 313–70, edited by Tison Pugh and featuring essays by Michael Shank, Elaine Treharne, Marjorie Curry Woods, John Parker, David L. Sedley, Lee Morrissey and Will Stockton, David Rundle, Margreta de Grazia, Bruce Holsinger, Suzanne Conklin Akbari, Ruth Evans, Carla Freccero, Karla Mallette, James F. English, and Jeffrey Jerome Cohen.

2. See Jacob Burkhardt, *The Civilization of the Renaissance in Italy,* ed. Peter Murray, trans. S. G. C. Middlemore, int. Peter Burke (New York: Penguin, 1990); Michel Foucault, *The Order of Things: An Archeology of the Human Sciences,* (New York: Vintage, 1994); Thomas Greene, *The Light in Troy: Imitation and Discovery in Renaissance Poetry* (New Haven, Conn.: Yale University Press, 1986).

3. Éduoard Glissant, *Poetics of Relation,* trans. Betsy Wing (Ann Arbor: University of Michigan Press, 1997).

4. William Shakespeare, *Timon of Athens,* ed. Anthony Dawson (London: Bloomsbury, 2009), 4.3.439–45. Further quotations in the text are by act, scene, and line numbers. I previously examined this speech in *At the Bottom of Shakespeare's Ocean* (London: Continuum, 2006), 93–95.

5. I modify this critical maxim from Fredric Jameson's "Always historicize!" in *The Political Unconscious: Narrative as a Socially Symbolic Act* (Ithaca, N.Y.: Cornell University Press, 1982), 9.

6. Jonathan Gil Harris, *Untimely Matter in the Time of Shakespeare* (Philadelphia: University of Pennsylvania Press, 2009), 13.

7. By "blue humanities" I mean recent scholarship that places oceanic and maritime matters at the center of their analysis. I provide a partial bibliography of this subfield in the final chapter of *At the Bottom of Shakespeare's Ocean* (101–12), though many post-2009 titles could be added.

8. Jorge Luis Borges, "The Garden of the Forking Paths," *Labyrinths: Selected Stories and Other Writings,* ed. Donald Yates and James E. Irby (New York: New Directions, 1964), 20.

9. For a recent collection of essays considering the problems inherent in the term *early modern*, see a collection of short essays in *Journal for Early Modern Cultural Studies* 13, no. 3 (Summer 2013), with entries by Jeffrey Jerome Cohen, Helen Cooper, and Nancy Bradley Warren.

10. For a cogent analysis of how Shakespeare gets mapped onto the medieval/early modern divide, see Margreta de Grazia, "The Ideology of Superfluous Things: *King Lear* as Period Piece," *Subject and Object in Renaissance Culture*, ed. Margreta de Grazia (Cambridge: Cambridge University Press, 1996).

11. See Kellie Robertson, "Exemplary Rocks," in *Animal, Vegetable, Mineral: Ethics and Objects*, ed. Jeffrey Jerome Cohen, 91–122 (Washington, D.C.: Oliphaunt Books, 2012).

12. Lee Patterson, "On the Margin: Postmodernism, Ironic History, and Medieval Studies," *Speculum* 65, no. 1 (January 1990), 87–108; David Aers, "A Whisper in the Ear of Early Modernists, or, Reflections on Literary Critics Writing the 'History of the Subject,'" *Culture and History, 1350–1600: Essays on English Communities, Identities, and Writing* (Detroit, Mich.: Wayne State University Press, 1992).

13. Greenblatt's *The Swerve*, to the dismay of many medievalists and some historicists, received a popular and scholarly trifecta of prizes: the 2011 National Book Award, the 2012 Pulitzer Prize, and the 2012 James Russell Lowell Prize, the last awarded by the Modern Language Association.

14. Peter H. Hansen, *The Summits of Modern Man: Mountaineering after the Enlightenment* (Cambridge, Mass.: Harvard University Press, 2013), 293.

15. Francis Bacon, *The New Organon* (London, 1620).

16. While its phrasing courts some of the "epochal claims" that I scrutinize in the previous preface, I employ the term *first age of globalization* for its more objective description of global history during the period roughly between 1450 and 1750 than terms like *Renaissance, early modern, Age of Discovery,* or *Age of Sail.* See Geoffrey C. Gunn, *First Globalization: The Eurasian Exchange, 1500–1800* (Oxford: Rowan and Littlefield, 2003).

17. See, among many others, Dipesh Chakrabarty, "The Climate of History: Four Theses," *Critical Inquiry* 35 (2009): 198–222.

18. For ongoing details of the CO_2 levels measured at Mauna Loa, see the NOAA's Earth Systems Research Laboratory at http://www.esrl.noaa.gov/gmd/ccgg/trends. Melville's vision of "my dear Pacific . . . the tide-beating heart of earth" appears in chapter 111 of *Moby-Dick*, ed. Hershel Parker and Harrison Hanford (New York: Norton, 2002), 367–68.

19. Melville's first voyage on a whaleship left New Bedford, Massachusetts, in 1841. The first commercially viable oil well gushed forth in August 1859 in Titusville, Pennsylvania.

20. For a longer perspective, see Warren Ruddiman, *Plows, Plagues, and*

Petroleum: How Humans Took Control of Climate (Princeton, N.J.: Princeton University Press, 2010).

21. On the cultural consequences of global warming, see Timothy Morton, *Hyperobjects: Philosophy after the End of the World* (Minneapolis: University of Minnesota Press, 2013).

22. Luis vaz de Camões, *The Lusiads,* trans. Landeg White (Oxford: Oxford University Press, 1997), 1.1.7–8. Further citations in the text by canto, stanza, and line number.

23. Josiah Blackmore, *Manifest Perdition: Shipwreck and the Disruption of Empire* (Minneapolis: University of Minnesota Press, 2002), 25.

24. For a brilliant modern novel that makes this precise point, see António Atunes, *The Return of the Caravels* (New York: Grove, 2003).

25. Hansen, *The Summits of Modern Man,* 294.

26. The most accessible and wide-ranging current treatment of the Homogenocene appears in Charles Mann's *1493: How the Ecological Collision of Europe and the American Gave Rise to the Modern World* (New York: Vintage, 2011), which draws extensively on the studies begun in Alfred Crosby, *The Columbian Exchange: Biological and Cultural Consequences of 1492,* 2nd ed. (New York: Praeger, 2003).

27. My focus on the global ocean should not obscure the debt of all modern oceanic histories to Fernand Braudel's magisterial study *The Mediterranean and the Mediterranean World in the Age of Philip II,* 2 vols., trans. Siân Reynolds (New York: Harper and Row, 1972). More recently, Braudel's subject has been compellingly reconsidered as a "new thalassology" by Peregrin Horden and Nicholas Purcell in *The Corrupting Sea: A Study of Mediterranean History* (Oxford: Blackwell, 2000). Their notion of "connectivity" has suggestive implications for the global shapes of oceanic culture from the sixteenth century forward. The tension they identify between exchange and hybridization, the distinctively shared "Mediterranean" flavor that Predrag Matvejevic, in his brilliant analytical memoir *Mediterranean: A Cultural Landscape,* trans. Michael Henry Heim (Berkeley: University of California Press, 1999), sees from each headland and around each crook-shaped point, disperses somewhat across the less quickly spanned spaces of the blue oceans. If I am ambivalent about a full translation of Mediterranean models to blue-water analyses, it may simply be an effort to register the persistent differences that the Homogenocene continues to dissolve.

28. See Jeff Bolster, *The Mortal Sea: Fishing the Atlantic in the Age of Sail* (Cambridge, Mass.: Belknap Press, 2012). Technological advances have repeatedly enabled once-depleted fisheries to become newly productive, as the dragnet revitalized the North Sea cod fisheries in the nineteenth century and as, in a different extractive industry, underground fracking is now revitalizing nineteenth-century oil fields from Pennsylvania to the Dakotas.

29. Hegel, *Phenomenology of Spirit,* quoted in Margaret Cohen, *The Novel and the Sea* (Princeton, N.J.: Princeton University Press, 2012).

30. Peter Sloterdijk, "Geometry in the Colossal: The Project of Metaphysical Globalization," trans. Samuel Butler, *Environment and Planning D: Society and Space* 27 (2009): 29–40; 30.

31. Hans Blumenberg, *Shipwreck with Spectator: Paradigm of a Metaphor for Existence,* trans. Steven Rendall (Cambridge, Mass.: MIT Press, 1996).

32. John Gillis, *The Human Shore: Seacoasts in History* (Chicago: University of Chicago Press, 2012), 38.

33. For more on oceanic poetics, see Steve Mentz, *At the Bottom of Shakespeare's Ocean,* esp. 1–6.

34. Edmund Spenser, *The Faerie Queene,* ed. A. C. Hamilton, 2nd ed. (London: Longman, 2001), 4.12.1.1–2. Further citations given in the text are by book, canto, stanza, and line number.

35. On the "maritime turn" after 1500, see Ulrich Kinzel, "Orientation as a Paradigm of Maritime Modernity," *Fictions of the Sea: Critical Perspectives on the Ocean in British Literature and Culture,* ed. Bernhard Klein (Aldershot, U.K.: Ashgate Publishing, 2002), 28–48.

36. The influential Russian oceanographer Yuly Shokalsky coined the term World Ocean in 1917.

37. Peter Sloterdijk, *In the World Interior of Capital,* trans. Wieland Hoban (New York: Polity, 2013), 43.

38. See also Carl Raschke, "Peter Sloterdink as 'First Philosopher' of Globalization," *JCRT* 12, no. 3 (Spring 2013): 1–18.

39. Jean-Luc Nancy, *The Creation of the World or Globalization,* trans. Francois Raffoul and David Pettigrew (Albany: State University of New York Press, 2007).

40. Gayatri Chakravorty Spivak, *The Death of a Discipline* (New York: Columbia University Press, 2005).

41. Ursula Heise, *Sense of Place and Sense of Planet: The Environmental Imagination of the Global* (Oxford: Oxford University Press, 2009).

42. For visual essays about modern oceanic globalization, see Allan Sekula's 1996 book *Fish Story* (Dusseldorf, Germany: Richeter Verlag, 1996) and his 2010 film, made with Noël Burch, *The Forgotten Space.*

43. Osip Mandelshtam, "Whoever Finds a Horseshoe," *Selected Poems,* trans. James Greene (New York: Penguin, 1991), 47.

44. See Bruno Latour, "An Attempt at a 'Compositionist Manifesto,'" *New Literary History* 41 (2010): 471–90.

45. On swimming as a temporary model for survival in an oceanic world, see Steve Mentz, "After Sustainability," *PMLA* 127, no. 3 (2012): 186–92.

46. I adapt the title of Derek Walcott's famous poem "The Sea Is History"

from *Selected Poems*, ed. Edward Baugh (New York: Farrar, Straus and Giroux, 2007), 137–39.

47. Primo Levi, *Survival in Auschwitz: The Nazi Assault on Humanity*, trans. Stuart Woolf (New York: Touchstone, 1996), 112. Jean, the prisoner to whom Levi narrates this story, spoke French and German but not Italian.

48. On the important southerly dimension to Columbus's voyage, see Nicholás Wey-Gómez, *The Tropics of Empire: Why Columbus Sailed South to the Indies* (Cambridge, Mass.: MIT Press, 2008).

49. Northrop Frye, *The Secular Scripture: A Study in the Structure of Romance* (Cambridge, Mass.: Harvard University Press, 1976), 4. Frye refers specifically to the Greek romances of late antiquity, but I take his joke more broadly to describe a feature of narrative in any maritime culture.

50. Alfred Crosby, *The Columbian Exchange: Biological and Cultural Consequences of 1492* (London: Praeger, 2003).

51. For a somewhat old-fashioned but refreshingly ocean-centric narrative of the Age of Discovery, see J. H. Parry, *The Discovery of the Sea* (Berkeley: University of California Press, 1982).

52. On blue cultural studies, see *At the Bottom of Shakespeare's Ocean*, 96–99.

53. Spivak, *Death of a Discipline.*

54. Aldo Leopold, *A Sand County Almanac* (New York: Oxford University Press, 1949).

55. See Dan Brayton, *Shakespeare's Ocean: An Ecocritical Exploration*, (Charlottesville: University of Virginia Press, 2012); Steve Mentz, *At the Bottom of Shakespeare's Ocean.*

56. See Steve Mentz, "Toward a Blue Cultural Studies: The Sea, Maritime Culture, and Early Modern English Literature," *Literature Compass* 6, no. 5 (September 2009), 997–1013.

1. The Wet and the Dry

1. William Shakespeare, *The Tempest*, ed. Virginia Mason Vaughan and Alden T. Vaughan (London: Arden, 1999). All further citations from this edition given in the text by act, line, and scene.

2. Sir Philip Sidney, *The Countess of Pembroke's Arcadia*, ed. Maurice Evans (New York: Penguin, 1977), 374. For more on this passage and shipwreck in Sidney, see Steve Mentz, "Reason, Faith, and Shipwreck in Sidney's New Arcadia," *SEL* 44, no. 1 (Winter 2004): 1–18.

3. On Gilbert's shipwreck in the context of English settlement of North America, see Steve Mentz, "Hakluyt's Oceans: Maritime Rhetoric in *The Principal Navigations*," in *Richard Hakluyt and Travel Writing in Early Modern Europe*, ed. Daniel Carey and Claire Jowitt (Farnham, UK: Ashgate, 2012), 283–93.

4. See Gerald M. Moser, "Camões' Shipwreck," *Hispania* 57 (May 1974): 213–19.

5. Peter Sloterdijk, *You Must Change Your Life: On Anthropotechnics,* trans. Wieland Hoban (Cambridge: Polity Press, 2013), 10. Sloterdijk first introduced the term "anthropotechnics" in his essay "Rules for the Human Zoo," trans. Mary Varney Rorty, *Environment and Planning D: Society and Space* 27, no. 1 (2009): 12–28.

6. Richard Younge, "The State of a Christian, lively set forth by an Allegorie of a Shippe under Sayle," appears as an introduction to Henry Mainwaring, *The Sea-man's Dictionary* (London: John Bellamy, 1644), sigs. A3–A3v. The passage is included in some copies of Younge's *The Victory of Patience* (London: M. Allot, 1636). It was also published in a single sheet broadside as *The State of a Christian* (London, 1636).

7. On the ecological lessons of the blue world ocean, see Mentz, *At the Bottom of Shakespeare's Ocean,* 96–100.

8. Simon Harris, *Sir Cloudesley Shovell: Stuart Admiral* (Cambridge, Mass.: Da Capo Press, 2001).

9. See *Oxford Dictionary of National Biography,* "Younge, Richard (fl. 1636–1673)," by Ian Greene, first published 2004, http://www.oxforddnb.com/view/article/30287.

10. The marginal notes appear in the upper left-hand corner and reference Proverbs 31:14 ("She is like the merchant's ships / she bringeth her food from afar"); Job 9:26 ("They are passed away as the swift ships: / as the eagle that hasteth to the prey"); Isaiah 23:1 ("Howl, ye ships of Tarshish, for it is laid waste"); and Revelation 8:9 ("And the second angel sounded, and as it were a great mountain burning with fire was cast into the sea, and the third part of the sea became blood"). Authorized Version.

11. Younge's use of the word "insurance" may contain a pun on maritime insurance. For an evocative reading of the early modern insurance business in the context of *The Merchant of Venice,* see Luke Wilson, "Drama and Marine Insurance in Shakespeare's London," *The Law in Shakespeare,* ed. Karen Cunningham and Constance Jordan (London: Palgrave, 2007).

12. "Then the waters had overwhelmed us, / the stream had gone over our soul," Psalms 124:4.

13. Both ecological thinking and empirical science emerge out of the wide range of Providentialist thinking in the early modern period. See, among many others, Keith Thomas, *Man and the Natural World: Changing Attitudes in England, 1500–1800* (New York: Pantheon, 1983).

14. On conceptual parallels between Providentialism and ecological thinking, see Steve Mentz, "Strange Weather in *King Lear,*" *Shakespeare* 6, no. 2 (June 2010): 139–52.

15. Alexandra Walsham, *Providence in Early Modern England* (Oxford: Oxford University Press, 1999), 3.

16. On Providence, accidents, and narrative structure, see Michael Witmore, *Culture of Accidents: Unexpected Knowledges in Early Modern England* (Redwood City, Calif.: Stanford University Press, 2002).

17. Alexandra Walsham has shown that Providentialism in seventeenth-century England was "not a marginal feature of . . . religious culture . . . but part of the mainstream." See *Providence in Early Modern England,* 3–4.

18. A previous version of this argument appears in Steve Mentz, "God's Storms: Shipwreck and the Meanings of Ocean in Early Modern England and America," in *Shipwreck in Art and Literature: Images and Interpretations from Antiquity to the Present Day,* ed. Carl Thompson (London: Routledge, 2014), 77–91.

19. Josiah Blackmore emphasizes the parallels between books and ships: "There is even a similarity between the raw materials of books and ships: each is made of boards and cords, iron (bosses and nails); there is paper and writing in each." *Manifest Perdition,* 103.

20. While incidents of shipwreck peaked in the nineteenth century, which Hans Blumenberg has called the "epoch of shipwrecks" (*Shipwreck with Spectator,* trans. Steven Rendall, [Cambridge, Mass.: MIT Press, 1997], 67), a huge maritime expansion began with the development of square-rigged sails in the fifteenth century. On the early modern maritime, see, among others, Braudel, *The Mediterranean and the Mediterranean World in the Age of Philip II;* Lionel Casson, *Ships and Seafaring in Ancient Times* (Austin: University of Texas Press, 1994); and Daniel Finamore, ed., *Maritime History as World History: New Perspectives on Maritime History and Nautical Archeology* (Gainesville: University Press of Florida, 2004).

21. See Sophocles, *Antigone,* trans. Hugh Lloyd-Jones (Cambridge, Mass.: Loeb, 1994); Plato, *The Republic of Plato,* trans. Francis MacDonald Cornford (Oxford: Oxford University Press, 1959), 195–96; Horace, *Odes and Epodes,* ed. Paul Shorey and Gordon J. Laing (New York: Sanborn, 1919), 1:14.

22. Michel Foucault, "Of Other Spaces," trans. Jay Miskowiec, *Diacritics* 16 (1986): 22–27. Foucault's description of the boat-as-heterotopia is suggestive: "The boat is a floating piece of space, a space without place, that exists by itself, that is closed in on itself and at the same time is given over to the infinity of the sea and that, from port to port, from tack to tack, from brothel to brothel, it goes as far as the colonies in search of the most precious treasures" (27).

23. Simon Schama, *The Embarrassment of Riches: An Interpretation of Dutch Culture in the Golden Age* (London: William Collins, 1987), 15–50.

24. On "weak thought," see Gianni Vattimo, *The Transparent Society,* trans. David Webb (Baltimore, Md.: Johns Hopkins University Press, 1994).

25. On modernity and the radical break, see Frederic Jameson, *A Singular Modernity: Essay on the Ontology of the Present* (New York: Verso, 2002).

26. Margreta de Grazia makes this point when she claims that Shakespeare has come to define modernity for English scholars: "Shakespeare thus comes to mark the passage into the modern age, often serving as a transitional figure between Medieval and Modern, his chronology itself often seen to display the break in the historical continuum, his shift from comedy to tragedy coinciding with the break from old to new (coinciding too with the turn of the century), from feudal collectivity to bourgeois individuality, from manor production to market commodification." "The Ideology of Superfluous Things: *King Lear* as Period Piece," in *Subject and Object in Renaissance Culture,* ed. Margreta de Grazia and Peter Stallybrass (Cambridge: Cambridge University Press, 1996), 17–42, 19.

27. On modernity's ambivalence, see Michael Saler, "Modernity and Enchantment: A Historiographic Review," *AHR,* June 2006, 692–716. For comparable depictions of modernity as a form of "multitemporality" or as a "timeknot," see Lynda Nead, *Victorian Babylon: People, Streets, and Images in Nineteenth-Century London* (New Haven, Conn.: Yale University Press, 2000), 8; Dipesh Charkrabaty, *Provincializing Europe: Postcolonial Thought and Historical Difference* (Princeton, N.J.: Princeton University Press, 2007), 243.

28. As Margreta de Grazia, Hugh Grady, Douglas Bruster, Richard Halpern, and others have recently emphasized, part of the charge of the term "early modern" is its twofold articulation of a rupture with a recent past and connection to our own present day. Medievalists including Lee Patterson, María Rosa Menocal, David Wallace, and Kathleen Davis have helpfully challenged this self-serving depiction of early modernity. See Grady, *Shakespeare and Modernity: Early Modern to Millennium* (London: Routledge, 2000); Bruster, *Quoting Shakespeare: Form and Culture in Early Modern Drama* (Lincoln: University of Nebraska Press, 2000); Halpern, *Shakespeare among the Moderns* (Ithaca, N.Y.: Cornell University Press, 1997); Menocal, *Shards of Love: Exile and the Origins of the Lyric* (Durham, N.C.: Duke University Press, 1994); Davis, *Periodization and Sovereignty: How Ideas of Feudalism and Secularization Govern the Politics of Time* (Philadelphia: University of Pennsylvania Press, 2009).

29. One canonical example is Francis Bacon, who highlights a series of new technologies—the compass, gunpowder, and the printing press—that distinguish early modern from ancient culture. See *Novum Organum* (first published in 1620), 1:119.

30. Glissant, *Poetics of Relation,* 33. On Glissant, see also Ian Baucom, *Specters of the Atlantic: Finance Capital, Slavery, and the Philosophy of History* (Durham, N.C.: Duke University Press, 2005).

31. Rachel Carson, *The Sea around Us,* 2nd ed. (Oxford: Oxford University Press, 1991), 75.

32. Braudel, *The Mediterranean,* 103.

33. "History is the subject of a structure whose site is not homogenous, empty time, but time filled by the presence of the now (*Jetztzeit*)." Walter Benjamin, "Theses on the Philosophy of History," in *Illuminations: Essays and Reflections,* ed. Hannah Arendt, trans. Henry Zohn (New York: Shocken, 1969), 261. On Benjamin's "now-time" as an image of the modernist break, see Jürgen Habermas, *The Philosophical Discourse of Modernity: Twelve Lectures,* trans. Frederick Lawrence (Cambridge, Mass.: MIT Press, 1987), 11–16.

34. Understanding these disasters relies on a Lucretian perspective, a shipwreck-with-spectator vision of rupture that uses rupture to generate a new analytical stance. On Lucretius in the context of the early modern episteme, see Jacques Lezra, *Unspeakable Subjects: The Genealogy of the Event in Early Modern Europe* (Redwood City, Calif.: Stanford University Press, 1997), esp. 1–34.

35. See Blackmore's suggestive comments on shipwrecks as text-producing historical moments: "Out of shipwreck, the poet tells us, come texts." *Manifest Perdition,* 27; see also 29, 102–4.

36. Blumenberg suggests that the notion that shipwreck is the price sailors pay to avoid the catastrophe of permanent calm is an Enlightenment concept, but it is possible to see something like it in historical records like Hakluyt's. *Shipwreck with Spectator,* 29–30.

37. My thinking on how writers respond to disaster draws on Maurice Blanchot, *The Writing of the Disaster,* trans. Ann Smock (Lincoln: University of Nebraska Press, 1995). Blanchot's book also provides this chapter's epigraph.

38. On Lucretius's "shipwreck with spectator" presentation of the philosopher's pleasure in watching shipwreck from the shore, see *At the Bottom of Shakespeare's Ocean,* 19–23.

39. Blumenberg, *Shipwreck with Spectator,* 46.

40. The earliest account of the wreck appeared in Latin in Florence in 1588 (Joannis Petrei Maffeii's *Historiae indicarum libri XVI*), and it was soon followed in Florence by an Italian translation (Francesca Serdonati's *Le istorie dellie Indie Orientali,* 1589); in Lyon by a French translation (Arnault de La Borie's *Histoire des Indes,* 1603); and in Valladolid by a slightly different Spanish version (Fray Antonio de San Román's *Historia general de la India Oriental,* 1603). The epic poem is Jerónimo Corte-Real's *Naufragia de Sepulveda* (Lisbon, 1590).

41. The ordering of the shipwrecks was chronological, as Gomes de Brito notes in his subtitle: "Em que se escreven chronologicamente os Naufragoios que tiveraõ as Naos de Portuga." See Bernardo Gomes de Brito, *História Trágico-Marítima,* 2 vols. (Lisbon: Officina da Congregaçaõ do Oratorio, 1735). See also Josiah Blackmore's recent edition, which reprints C. R. Boxer's English translations but adds his own new version of the *S. João, The Tragic History of the Sea,* ed. and trans. C. R. Boxer, foreword by Josiah Blackmore (Minneapolis: University of Minnesota Press, 2001), viii.

42. The poem mentions neither by name, assuming that the story of the

"Knight" (5.46.2), the "fair and gentle dame" (5.46.3), and their "ill hour' (5.46.5) was well known. I quote from Richard Fanshawe's first English translation, *The Lusiad, or Portugals Historicall Poem* (London: Humphrey Mosley, 1655); further citations given in the text. For a modern English edition, see Luis vaz de Camões, *The Lusiads,* trans. Landeg White (Oxford: Oxford University Press, 1997).

43. Jerry Brotton, *Trading Territories: Mapping the Early Modern World* (London: Reaktion, 1997), 46–86.

44. I quote this narrative from Josiah Blackmore's new translation in *The Tragic History of the Sea,* 1–26. Further citations given in the text.

45. See Blackmore, *Manifest Perdition,* and also James Duffy, *Shipwreck and Empire: Being an Account of Portuguese Maritime Disasters in a Century of Decline* (Cambridge, Mass.: Harvard University Press, 1955).

46. For an influential argument distinguishing between Camões's aristocratic vision and Hakluyt's mercantile one, see Richard Helgerson, *Forms of Nationhood: The Elizabethan Writing of England* (Chicago: University of Chicago Press, 1992), 149–92.

47. As Blackmore emphasizes, part of the attraction of these narratives is their hybrid nature. He writes in his foreword to *The Tragic History of the Sea*: "The resistance of the shipwreck narratives to easy categorization, generic distinctions, or clear-cut historical lessons is precisely what underlies their scholarly appeal" (xi).

48. On causation and the epic tradition, see Susanne Wofford, *The Choice of Achilles: The Ideology of Figure in the Epic* (Redwood City, Calif.: Stanford University Press, 1992).

49. See *Aeneid* 1.8 ("Musa, mihi causas memora"), trans. H. R. Fairclough, rev. G. P. Goold (Cambridge, Mass.: Harvard University Press / Loeb Library, 1999), 262.

50. When clarification seems useful, I refer to the Portuguese from Bernardo Gomes de Brito's edition, *História Trágico-Marítima,* 2 vols. (Lisbon: Officina da Congregaçaõ do Oratorio, 1735). The account of the *S. João* is in vol. 1, pp. 1–38.

51. For more on Shakespeare's technical language in this scene, see Mentz, *At the Bottom of Shakespeare's Ocean,* 6–13.

52. The seasonal monsoon patterns also drastically impacted outward voyages from Lisbon to India, leading one experienced pilot to remark, when asked what time to leave Portugal, "The last day of February is time enough, but the first day of March is late." See C. R. Boxer's introduction to *The Tragic History of the Sea,* 7.

53. Boxer notes that "overloading" was the chief peril of the homeward voyage. *Tragic History of the Sea,* 17.

54. See Boxer, *The Tragic History of the Sea,* 8.

55. Anthony Thacher, "Some part of a Letter . . . ," in *In the Trough of the Sea: Selected American Sea-Deliverance Narratives, 1610–1766,* ed. Donald P. Wharton (Westport, Conn.: Greenwood Press, 1979), 56–64, 57. Further citations in the text.

56. The key term "challenge" reappears in John Greenleaf Whittier's 1858 poem "The Swan Song of Parson Avery," in which the doomed parson prays, "In this night of death I challenge the promise of Thy word!" (line 34). On this poem and the subsequent allusion to Thacher and Avery in T. S. Eliot's "Dry Salvanges," see Steve Mentz, "God's Storms," 87–89.

57. For records of the fatal journey, including a note found on the *Speranza* after Willoughby's death, see Richard Hakluyt, *Principal Navigations,* 12 vols. (Glasgow: James MacMehose and Sons, 1903–5), 2:211–38.

58. The classical parallel, to which Thacher may allude, is Odysseus making landfall on Phaeacia in book 5, during which he clings by his hands to a rock and also requires the river god to help him to shore.

59. On this narrative subgenre, see Julie Sievers, "Drowned Pens and Shaking Hands: Sea Providence Narratives in Seventeenth-Century New England," *William and Mary Quarterly* 63, no. 4 (October 2006): 743–76.

60. For the argument that the retelling of wrecks such as Thacher's would become central to American identity, particularly when paired with representations of virtuous women, see Robin Miskolcze, *Women and Children First: Nineteenth-Century Sea Narratives and American Identity* (Lincoln: University of Nebraska Press, 2008).

61. "The Wreck of the Amsterdam," Palmer Collection, item number BHC 0724, National Maritime Museum, Greenwich, London.

62. See Lawrence Otto Goedde, *Tempest and Shipwreck in Dutch and Flemish Art* (University Park: Penn State University Press, 1989).

63. There is no clear visual evidence that this painting refers to the common practice of "wrecking," or making a living by recovering items from wrecked ships. It was, however, a well-known occupation of coastal communities. For example, see Cathryn Pearce, *Cornish Wrecking, 1700–1860: Reality and Popular Myth* (Woodbridge, UK: Boydell Press, 2010).

64. For an archeological survey of this wreck, see Peter Marsden, *The Wreck of the Amsterdam* (New York: Stein and Day, 1975).

65. For recent curatorial consideration of this painting, see Jenny Gaschle, ed., *Turmoil and Tranquility: The Sea through the Eyes of Dutch and Flemish Masters, 1550–1700* (Greenwich, UK: National Maritime Museum, 2008), 70–71. This note was written by research assistant Sophie Carr.

66. It would not have been possible for this sailor to have furled the sail alone; probably at least three other sailors would have been needed. Perhaps, the pictured sailor is the last of the sailors to descend, and the artist chooses the moment of his solitude for emblematic purposes.

2. Angry Gods

1. John Dryden, trans., *The Aeneid of Virgil,* ed. Frederick M. Keener (New York: Penguin, 1997), 1:1–2. Further citations given in the text by book and line numbers.

2. Authorized Version.

3. For a reading of the Virgilian tradition in terms of an imperial epic theme contesting a romance counterstructure of waywardness and loss, see David Quint, *Epic and Empire* (Princeton, N.J.: Princeton University Press, 1993). By naming the totemic symbol of counterepic the "boat of romance," Quint recognizes the water-bound nature of his counternarrative, although he does not explore its oceanic context.

4. Catherine Keller, *Face of the Deep: A Theology of Becoming* (London: Routledge, 2003).

5. See Christopher Connery, "There Was No More Sea: The Suppression of the Ocean, from the Bible to Cyberspace," *Journal of Historical Geography* 32, no. 3 (2006): 494–511.

6. Epeli Hau'ofa, "Our Sea of Islands," *We Are the Ocean: Selected Works* (Honolulu: University of Hawaii Press, 2008), 39.

7. The first three editions (1597, 1599, 1600) were published in Oxford by Joseph Barnes and sold wholesale in London at the shop of Joan Broome. The final two editions (1611 and 1618) were sold in London by Humphrey Lownes.

8. On King's life, see P. E. McCullough's DNB article, "King, John (*d.* 1621)," P. E. McCullough in *Oxford Dictionary of National Biography,* ed. H. C. G. Matthew and Brian Harrison (Oxford: Oxford University Press, 2004); online ed., ed. Lawrence Goldman, January 2008, http://www.oxforddnb.com/view/article/15568. On court culture and sermon making, see Peter McCullough, *Sermons at Court: Politics and Religion in Elizabethan and Jacobean Preaching* (Cambridge: Cambridge University Press, 1998). King's Deanship of Christ Church, Oxford, continued a Calvinist tradition that had been established there since the start of Elizabeth's reign.

9. I previously used this line from Mapple's sermon as an epigraph for my earliest publication on literary shipwrecks, "Reason, Faith, and Shipwreck in Sidney's *New Arcadia,*" *SEL* 44, no. 1 (2004): 1–18.

10. Timothy Morton, *Hyperobjects: Philosophy and Ecology after the End of the World* (Minneapolis: University of Minnesota Press, 2013), 19.

11. See Timothy Morton, *The Ecological Thought* (Cambridge, Mass.: Harvard University Press, 2012).

12. For my first efforts to think Morton's hyperobjects in oceanic terms, see my blog post "Ocean as (Hyper-) Object," *The Bookfish,* December 4, 2013, http://stevementz.com/ocean-as-hyper-object.

13. John King, *Lectures upon Jonas* (Oxford: Joseph Barnes, 1597), 183.

14. On Lucretius's injunction (*De rerum natura,* 2.1–4), see Mentz, *At the Bottom of Shakespeare's Ocean,* 19–23.

15. For a modern retelling of this tale, see Nathaniel Philbrick, *In The Heart of the Sea: The Tragedy of the Whaleship Essex* (New York: Penguin, 2000).

16. *Lamentable Newes . . . , Reprints of Early English Books,* ed. Joseph Arnold Foster (Claremont, 1948), 2. Further citations in the text.

17. Dryden's translation emphasizes the connection between the sea and the unruly crowd, both of which get tamed by wisdom: "As when in Tumolts rise th' ignoble Crowd'd, / Mad are their Motions, and their Tongues are loud . . . / If then some Grave and Pious Man appear, / They hush their Noise, and lend a list'ning Ear; / He soothes with sober Words their angry Mood" (1.213–14, 217–19).

18. John King, *Lectures upon Jonas,* ed. Alexander Grosart (Edinburgh: James Nichol, 1864), 30.

19. The narrative concludes not with Pet's return to London but by opening outward to describe other disasters as sea and land, including the haunting image of "dead men swimming too and fro between *Graues End* and *London,* being carried by the Tyde" (7).

20. Amy Turner Bushnell, "Escape of the Nickaleers: European–Indian Relations on the Wild Coast of Florida in 1696, from Jonathan Dickinson's Journal," *Coastal Encounters: The Transformation of the Gulf South in the Eighteenth Century,* ed. Richmond F. Brown (Lincoln: University of Nebraska Press, 2007), 31–58.

21. See, for example, the shipwreck narratives collected as *The Tragic History of the Sea.*

22. The most important examples for early American studies are probably the maritime contexts of slaves and ex-slaves, including Equiano and Paul Cuffe. See W. Jeffrey Bolster, *Black Jacks: African American Seamen in the Age of Sail* (Cambridge, Mass.: Harvard University Press, 1998).

23. James Janeway, *A Token for Mariners* (London: T. Norris, 1711), A3. Further citations in the text.

24. Joseph Conrad, *The Mirror of the Sea* (Marlboro, Vt.: Marlboro Press, 1988), 63.

25. Alain Corbin, *The Lure of the Sea: The Discovery of the Seaside in the Western World, 1750–1840,* trans. Jocelyn Phelps (New York: Penguin, 19995).

26. See Mentz, *At the Bottom of Shakespeare's Ocean,* passim.

27. W. H. Auden, *The Enchaféd Flood, or The Romantic Iconography of the Sea* (London: Faber and Faber, 1950). I previously expressed my doubts about Auden's claim, and also about Jonathan Raban's uncritical acceptance of them, in "Toward a Blue Cultural Studies: The Sea, Maritime Culture, and Early Modern English Literature" *Literature Compass* (2009): 997–1013.

3. Isle of Tempests

1. John Donne, Meditation XVII. For an accessible online copy of this well-known text, see the Literature Network website at http://www.online-literature.com/donne/409.

2. Horden and Purcell, *The Corrupting Sea,* 5.

3. Michael J. Jarvis, *In the Eye of All Trade: Bermuda, Bermudians, and the Maritime Atlantic World, 1680–1783* (Chapel Hill: University of North Carolina Press, 2010), 1. Jarvis's study persuasively argues for the "maritime foundation" (1) of early American history, and his treatment of Bermuda as "perhaps the most intensely maritime colony within the British empire" (5) offers an offshore perspective on the spread of British settlement throughout the Americas.

4. On the massive expansion of Bermudan tobacco exports in the 1620s, followed by a devastating crash in 1628, see Jarvis, *In the Eye of All Trade,* 32–38.

5. Simon Pinet, *Archipelagoes: Insular Fictions from Chivalric Romance to the Novel* (Minneapolis: University of Minnesota Press, 2011), 19–20, 22.

6. John R. Gillis, *Islands of the Mind: How the Human Imagination Created the Atlantic World* (New York: Palgrave, 2004), 1. See also Yi-Fan Tuan, *Topophilia: A Study of Environmental Perception, Attitudes, and Values* (New York: Columbia University Press, 1990), and, in a literary context, Laurence Durrell, *Reflections on a Marine Venus: A Companion to the Landscape of Rhodes* (London: Faber & Faber, 1953).

7. For an island-centered history of the British Isles, see Norman Davies, *The Isles: A History* (Oxford: Oxford University Press, 1999).

8. See D. B. Quinn, *Bermuda in the Age of Exploration and Early Settlement* (Williamsburg, Va.: Omohundro Institute of Early American History and Culture Colloquia, 1988), 4–5.

9. For a popular summary of this oft-told tale, see Hobson Woodward, *A Brave Vessel: The True Tale of the Castaways Who Rescued Jamestown and Inspired Shakespeare's "The Tempest"* (New York: Viking, 2009).

10. Jarvis, *In the Eye of All Trade,* provides an excellent overview. The book's opening chapter, "Colonizing Paradise," starts with the *Sea-Venture* wreck and explores the early period of the Somers' Island Company from its formation in 1612 (11–63). The Bermuda motto paraphrases *Aeneid* 5.709.

11. For a parallel history of the Virginia and Bermuda colonies, see Virginia Bernhard, *A Tale of Two Colonies: What Really Happened in Virginia and Bermuda* (Columbia: University of Missouri Press, 2012).

12. See Jarvis, *In the Eye of All Trade.*

13. See Jarvis, *In the Eye of All Trade,* 32–33

14. See Jarvis, *In the Eye of All Trade,* 37–44.

15. Quoted in Henry Wilkinson, *The Adventurers of Bermuda* (Oxford: Oxford University Press, 1933), 23.

16. On the history of interpreting this scene and the play more broadly, see Vaughan and Vaughan, introduction to *The Tempest.*

17. For an authoritative summary of this scholarship and a defense of the traditional sources, see Vaughan, "William Strachey's 'True Reportary' and Shakespeare."

18. For an attack on the relevance of Bermuda to the play, motivated by the Oxfordian aim of redating *The Tempest,* see Roger Stritmatter and Lynne Kositsky, "'O Brave New World': *The Tempest* and Peter Martyr's *De Orbe Novo,*" *Critical Survey* 21, no. 2 (2009): 7–42. Stritmatter and Kositsky argue that much of the New World discourse in *The Tempest* was available in mid-sixteenth-century Spanish works by Peter Martyr, Oviedo, and others, translated into English by Richard Eden starting in 1555, and further that these humanist writers often drew on classical sources, especially Ovid and Virgil. These points are perfectly valid, and the full name of the Spanish historian Gonzalo Fernández de Oviedo y Valdés does seem suspiciously *Tempest*-like. Their argument, however, does not require an earlier date for the play, and it seems very likely that Shakespeare knew both the midcentury Spanish histories and the very recent Bermuda pamphlets when he wrote the play around 1610–11.

19. On maritime features in the play and in Shakespeare, see Mentz, *At the Bottom of Shakespeare's Ocean,* esp. 1–13.

20. In a richly suggestive line, Ariel notes that he would forgive the captured Neapolitans "were I human" (5.1.19).

21. See Strachey, "A True Reportary of the Wrack," in Wright, ed., 5, 7. Further citations in the text.

22. Quoted in *The Tempest,* 288–89.

23. On storms in Ovid, see Teoman Sipahigl, "Ovid and the Tempest in *Othello,*" *Shakespeare Quarterly* 44, no. 4 (1993), 468–71. Erasmus's colloquy on shipwreck appeared in *Colloquia Familiaria* (1518) and was widely influential throughout the century. For Alberti's humanist shipwreck essay, see David Marsh, ed. and trans., *Dinner Pieces (Intercenales)* (Tucson, Ariz.: Medieval and Renaissance Texts and Studies, 1987).

24. Interestingly, he does not use the New World word "hurricane" to describe this storm, though the storm's date, June 24, falls within modern hurricane season, and the word had come into English from the West Indies via Richard Eden's translations of Peter Martyr's *Decades of the New World* (1555). For brief consideration of Shakespeare's use of this word in *King Lear,* see Steve Mentz, "A Poetics of Nothing: Air in the Early Modern Imagination," *Postmedieval* 4 (2013): 30–41.

25. Wilkerson, 24.

26. See Quinn, *Bermuda in the Age of Exploration and Early Settlement,* 2.

27. See Quinn, *Bermuda in the Age of Exploration and Early Settlement,* 3.

28. See Quinn, *Bermuda in the Age of Exploration and Early Settlement,* 6–7.

29. Wilkinson, *The Adventurers of Bermuda,* 25.

30. See Quinn, *Bermuda in the Age of Exploration and Early Settlement,* 10–11.

31. For an excellent reading of Norwood's map, see Smith, *The Cartographic Imagination in Early Modern England.*

32. Job Hortop, *The Travailes of an English Man* (London: William Wright, 1591), 26. See also Purchas, 16:3;

33. On humanism and English colonization, see Armitage, *The Ideological Origins of the British Empire,* and Fitzmaurice, *Humanism and America.*

34. See Jourdain, in Wright, ed., 108. Further citations in the text.

35. Norwood, *Journal of Richard Norwood,* lxviii.

36. See Sarah Bendall, "Norwood, Richard (1590–1675)," *Oxford Dictionary of National Biography* (Oxford University Press, 2004), http://www.oxforddnb.com/view/article/20365.

37. Richard Norwood, *The Journal of Richard Norwood, Surveyor of Bermuda,* introduction by Wesley Frank Craven and Walter B. Hayward (New York: Scholars Facsimiles & Reprints, 1945), 54. Further citations in the text.

38. Wilkinson, *The Adventurers of Bermuda,* 25–26. See also *Archive of Indies,* 78.3–9, vol. 5:57.

39. See Rich, *Newes from Virginia.* Further citations in the text.

40. Wilkinson, *The Adventurers of Bermuda,* 35–37.

41. D. K. Smith, *The Cartographic Imagination in Early Modern England: Rewriting the World in Marlowe, Spenser, Raleigh, and Marvell* (Aldershot, U.K.: Ashgate Publishing, 2008), 160–65.

42. John Smith, *The General Historie of Virginia, New England, & The Summer Isles,* 2 vols. (Glasgow: MacLehose and Sons, 1907), 1:335.

43. Edmund Waller, "The Battell of the Summer Islands," *Poems* (London, 1645), 52–59. Further citations given in the text by canto and line numbers.

44. Reading *Moby-Dick* as a valorization of Ahab's quest requires minimizing Ishmael's place in the novel or, at least, assuming the bow oarsman's subordination to his captain. That interpretation has dominated Melville criticism since the twentieth-century Melville revival, but it leaves open a more ecological, oceanic, and Ishmael-driven interpretation of the novel.

45. See Bruno Latour, "An Attempt at a Compositionist Manifesto" *New Literary History* 41 (2010): 471–490.

46. See Smith, *Cartographic Imagination,* 163–64.

47. Smith writes, "Despite Marvell's claims of peace and comfort . . . it turns out there were storms aplenty, and a good many other problems as well." *Cartographic Imagination,* 163.

48. See, for example, Rosalie Colie, "Marvell's 'Bermudas' and the Puritan Paradise," *Renaissance News* 10 (1957): 75–79; Annabel Patterson, "*Bermudas* and *The Coronet*: Marvell's Protestant Poetics," *ELH* 44 (1977): 478–99.

49. Andrew Marvel, "Bermudas," *The Complete Poems,* ed. Elizabeth Story

Donno (New York: Penguin, 2005), 116–17. All further citations given in the text by line number.

50. Smith, *Cartographic Imagination*, 168.

Interchapter

1. On these pearl fisheries, see Molly A. Warsh, "Enslaved Pearl Divers in the Sixteenth Century Caribbean," *Slavery and Abolition* 31, no. 3 (September 2010): 345–62.

2. On the history of Spanish pearl diving in the Caribbean, see Enrique Otte, *Las Perlas del Caribe: Nueva Cádiz de Cubagua* (Caracas, Venezuela: Fundaciíon John Boulton 1977).

4. Metis: Jeremy Roch

1. The richest line of analysis of maritime labor in the Age of Sail appears in the "red Atlantic" Marxist historiographies influentially promulgated by Marcus Rediker, Peter Linebaugh, and others. See, for example, Marcus Rediker, *Between the Devil and the Deep Blue Sea: Merchant Seamen, Pirates, and the Anglo-American Maritime World, 1700–1750* (Cambridge: Cambridge University Press, 1989); *The Slave Ship: A Human History* (New York: Viking, 2007), *Villains of All Nations: Atlantic Pirates in the Golden Age* (Boston: Beacon, 2004), and, with Peter Linebaugh, *The Many-Headed Hydra: Sailors, Slaves, Commoners, and the Hidden History of the Revolutionary Atlantic* (Boston: Beacon, 2000).

2. For my previous reading of the Boatswain's technical language through the term "yar," see *At the Bottom of Shakespeare's Ocean*, 10–13.

3. For an idiosyncratic defense of Shakespeare's maritime knowledge, see Alexander Falconer, *Shakespeare and the Sea* (London, 1964).

4. For an influential reading of metis in classical context, see Marcel Detienne and Jean-Paul Vernat, *Cunning Intelligence in Greek Culture and Society*, trans. Janet Lloyd (Chicago: University of Chicago Press, 1991).

5. Hesiod, *Theogeny*, trans. Dorothea Wender (New York: Penguin, 1973), 34, 52.

6. Margaret Cohen, *The Novel and the Sea* (Princeton, N.J.: Princeton University Press, 2010), 15–58.

7. Cohen writes that her primary sources are Samuel de Champlain's *Traitte de la marine et du devoir d'un bon marinier* (1632), Captain's Cook's journals, and Conrad's *Mirror of the Sea* (1906), but she draws widely on many primary sources, including the narrative of the great galleon *S. João* that I explore in chapter 1 (17, 23).

8. For an excellent analysis of "expertise" in Elizabethan England, which

includes but is not limited to maritime skills, see Eric Ash, *Power, Knowledge, and Expertise in Elizabethan England* (Baltimore, Md.: Johns Hopkins University Press, 2004).

9. On Latour's actor–network theory, see, among his other works, *Reassembling the Social: An Introduction to Actor-Network-Theory* (Oxford: Oxford University Press, 2005). For a helpful analysis of Latour in philosophical context, see Graham Harman, *Prince of Networks: Bruno Latour and Metaphysics* (Melbourne, Australia: re-press, 2009). Harman's earlier study *Tool-Being: Heidegger and the Metaphysics of Objects* (Chicago: Open Court, 2005) provides perspective on the often deeply emotional relations between sailors, ships, and other tools.

10. For a study of collective action and cognition in a modern naval vessel, see Edwin Hutchins, *Cognition in the Wild* (Cambridge, Mass.: MIT Press, 1995).

11. Hugo Grotius, *The Freedom of the Seas,* trans. Ralph van Deman Magoffin, ed. James Brown Scottz (New York: Oxford University Press, 1916), 22. Further citations from this edition.

12. Stuart Elden notes that the *Mare Liberum* was a small part of Grotius's larger work, which explores territorial concerns. See *The Birth of Territory* (Chicago: University of Chicago Press, 2013), 239–41.

13. On forming networks, or work-nets, for which Latour employs the metaphor of the fisherman and his nets, see *Reassembling the Social,* 128–33.

14. In this context Latour's fascination with terms such as "fluid" seems meaningful. *Reassembling the Social,* 65.

15. See Cohen, *The Novel and the Sea,* 42. Smith's *Sea-Grammar* has the unusual distinction of being the first published but second-written mariner's dictionary in English. Sir Henry Mainwaring's *Seaman's Dictionary* was written around 1620 but not published until 1640. On the evidence that Smith cribbed from Mainwaring's manuscript, see P. L. Barbour, "Captain John Smith's *Sea-Grammar* and Its Debt to Sir Henry Mainwaring's *Seaman's Dictionary,*" *Mariner's Mirror* 58, no. 1 (1972): 93–101.

16. James Muldoon, "Who Owns the Sea?," *Fictions of the Sea: Critical Perspectives on the Ocean in British Literature and Culture,* ed. Bernhard Klein (Aldershot, U.K.: Ashgate Publishing, 2002), 13–27, 16. Further citations in the text.

17. Of these two, only Barlow appears in the *DNB.*

18. Several other sailors, including Henry Teonge and Moses Bathurst, did include poetry in their journals, quite a lot in the case of Teonge. In this they were not unlike landsmen, though I also suggest that poetic form might have had special resonance at sea.

19. On the *outis/metis* pun in Homer's Greek text, see Ann Bergren, "Odyssean Temporality: Many (Re)turns," in *Approaches to Homer,* ed. Carl Rubio and Cynthia Shelmerdyne (Austin: University of Texas Press, 1983), 38–73.

20. Spenser's *The Faerie Queene* provides a familiar example of the poem-as-ship topos; see Jerome S. Dees, "The Ship Conceit in *The Faerie Queene*: 'Conspicuous Allusion' and Poetic Structure," *Studies in Philology* 72 (1975): 208–25.

21. Holles, who lost his arm in the Battle of the Four Days, was also a critic of Buckingham's naval policies. He died in combat during the Third Dutch War and is buried in Westminster Abbey. See the entry by J. D. Davies in the *DNB*.

22. Macaulay's famous phrase appears in the first volume of his *History of England from the Accession of James II* (1849–61). For recent reconsideration, see Robert E. Glass, "The Image of the Sea Officer in English Literature, 1660–1710," *Albion* 26, no. 4 (1994): 583–99.

23. J. D. Davies lists Roch as one example of the well-known class of "tarpaulin lieutenants" in the Restoration navy, accomplished sailors who served as nautical aids to the less-seaworthy "gentlemen" captains. Davies, however, sees the split between these two figures in less stark terms. J. D. Davies, *Gentlemen and Tarpaulins: The Officers and Men of the Restoration Navy* (Oxford: Clarendon Press, 1991), 38.

24. The manuscript is broken into five separate journals, each describing Roch's voyage on a particular ship: (1) the naval vessel *Antelope,* on which he saw action in the Second Dutch War; (2) the private little boat *Neptune,* which Roch sailed from Plymouth to London; (3) the yacht *Mercury,* which was wrecked on a shoal off Holland under Roch's command; (4) the *Charles Galley,* another naval vessel from which Roch was dismissed from the service; and (5) the private merchant man *Tamer,* which was captured by the French during Roch's last voyage. The title page of the manuscript also mentions a journey before the first, on the man-of-war *Preston,* which would later be renamed the *Antelope* when Roch rejoined her in the long voyage narrated in the first journal.

25. Roch's journal is bound but not paginated consecutively. Roch, or some previous owner, paginated each voyage separately by leaf.

26. I cite Roch's journal from Bruce S. Ingram's edition, *Three Sea Journals of Stuart Times* (London: Constable and Co., 1936), though at times I also refer to original spelling or pagination from the original manuscript, "Journal of Jeremy Roch," Caird Library, National Maritime Museum, IGR/17.

27. See Muldoon, "Who Owns the Sea?," 17, 26n.

28. On Barlow, see chapter 5 and also Patricia Fumerton, *Unsettled: The Culture of Mobility and the Working Poor in Early Modern England* (Chicago: University of Chicago Press, 2006).

29. See *DNB* entry on Holles, J. D. Davies, "Holles, Sir Frescheville (1642–1672)," *Oxford Dictionary of National Biography* (Oxford University Press, 2004); online edition, January 2008, http://www.oxforddnb.com/view/article/13551.

30. Cohen, *Novel and the Sea,* 38.

31. Ingram's edition indicates this pause with a period after "undertake it," but Roch's manuscript contains only a comma at this point.

32. Davies, *Gentlemen and Tarpaulins,* 38.

33. Roch's version reads "had gain'd" for "did gain," and Roch transposes "act" and "write" in the second quotation. See John Dryden, *Selected Poems,* ed. Steven Zwicker and David Bywaters (New York: Penguin, 2001), 51, 67.

34. For background on the science of early modern astrology, see Anthony Grafton, *Cardano's Cosmos: The Worlds and Works of a Renaissance Astrologer* (Cambridge, Mass.: Harvard University Press, 2000), and Tara Nummendal, *Alchemy and Authority in the Holy Roman Empire* (Chicago: University of Chicago Press, 2007). For consideration of English astrology, see also Alison Chapman, "Marking Time: Astrology, Almanacs, and English Protestantism," *Renaissance Quarterly* 60, no. 4 (2007): 1257–90.

35. The journal's "Astrological Appendix" analyzes Roch's four other voyages. The *Antelope* receives the most analysis (five "schemes," 75–83), but each of the other voyages—the *Mercury* (83–84); the *Charles Galley* (84–86); and the *Tamer* (86–87)—has its own scheme.

36. Bruce Ingram, the editor of Roch's journals, speculates that his unceremonious departure from the *Antelope* at the war's end in 1667—Ingram terms it "French leave" (74n)—may have kept Roch from further navy employment before 1678, when he joined the *Mercury.* We have no record, however, of Roch's doings between 1667 and 1677, though it seems very likely he was somewhere employed at sea, if not in the Royal Navy.

37. The more recent fascination with solo sailing, given canonical expression in Joshua Slocum's *Sailing Alone Around the World* (New York: Penguin, 1999; first published 1900), seems not to exert much pull on Roch. Oceanic solitude may be a Romantic phenomenon, as figures including the Ancient Mariner and Ishmael suggest.

38. Roch's phrase "I was forced to steer by the Breach of the shore" employs the technical term "breach," meaning "surf made by the sea heaving over rocks." Ingram cites the *Shorter Oxford English Dictionary,* 91n.

39. Roch also notes that "20 sail of ships great and small" (83) were wrecked along with the *Mercury.*

40. Roch notes in passing several voyages on "the *Mary* yacht to St. Malo, Marlaix, and other parts of France, and also diverse coasting voyages along the English shore . . . upon the account of trade and merchandise" between 1680–84, but passes over these because he met "no cross adventures or any other disaster" (111).

41. The journal is never clear about what accusations are made, but the "Astrological Appendix" notes that he has been entrusted with "40,000 pounds of cash for the Army" (84), and in the course of getting his ship off the rocks, he left

the ship "for a few hours" (86), which was seen as dereliction of duty, "though no damage came to the ship or money, but all delivered and returned safe" (86).

42. Admiral Shovell would later become famous for losing his life in the Scilly Islands disaster of 1707, which occasioned the naming of a prize for the computation of longitude at sea.

5. Metis: Edward Barlow

1. On Barlow's drawing of this moment and his self-representation as "wandering," see Fumerton, *Unsettled*, 63–83. Fumerton sees this drawing as the key to Barlow's self-image, and she uses it on the cover of her book.

2. Edward Barlow, *Barlow's Journal, of His Life at Sea in King's Ships, East & West Indiamen & Other Merchantmen from 1659 to 1703*, ed. Basil Lubbock, 2 vols. (London: Hurst and Blackett, 1934). Further citations in the text.

3. Fumerton quotes the 1954 notes of a Royal Naval College archivist that "it is more probable that the record of each voyage was written up during the intervals between voyages" (66).

4. Fumerton asserts that these two illustrations were made while Barlow was imprisoned in various ships and prisons during 1673 (166).

5. Since Lubbock does not print this poem, I cite it directly from Barlow's manuscript, JOD 4 in the NMM catalog. Further citations given by signature in the text.

6. Here, the unanswerable question of timing seems particularly important. I associate this poem with Barlow's decision while in captivity in Batavia to start the journal, but it could plausibly have been added when he made a fair copy sometime later, perhaps on shore. Lubbock's dramatic claims for Barlow's neat handwriting despite "the foul air of the foc's'le, crowded to suffocation by tired-out, heavy-breathing seamen" (1:12) seem overwrought, but in all likelihood at least some of Barlow's writing was done on board a traveling ship. The journal's loose pages do not provide any clear evidence about when or where they were collected.

7. On Barlow's reticence on this subject, see Fumerton, *Unsettled*, 74–82.

8. See Fumerton, *Unsettled*, 108–27. She notes that Barlow is "more interested in the *practice* [of pilotage] than the state of hydrographical knowledge" (117) and thus represents something of a "throwback" to an earlier age of marine illustrations. On the rivalry between practical pilots and academic navigators, especially in the Spanish context, see Alison Sandman, "Spanish Nautical Cartography" in *The History of Cartography*, vol. 3, *Cartography in the European Renaissance*, ed. David Woodward (Chicago: University of Chicago Press, 2007), 1095–142; and Surekha Davies, "The Navigational Iconography of Diogo Ribeiro's 1529 Vatican Planisphere," *Imago Mundi: The International Journal for the History of Cartography* 55 (2003): 103–12.

9. All the interruptions in this chapter draw on the *Oxford Dictionary of National Biography,* accessed online.

10. This poem appears in Barlow, *Barlow's Journal,* ed. Lubbock, 34.

11. See also Philip Edwards, ed., *Last Voyages: Cavendish, Hudson, Ralegh: The Original Narratives* (New York: Oxford University Press, 1989).

12. See Barlow, *Barlow's Journal,* ed. Lubbock, 81–83.

13. Fumerton, by contrast, suggests that these pages present a "God-sanctioned I" or devotional self, because Barlow's poem resigns itself to God's will. By contrast, I see a more vexed triangular relationship among the devotional poem, the depiction of seamanship in crisis, and the visual emblem. See *Unsettled,* 106.

14. See Barlow, *Barlow's Journal,* ed. Lubbock, 195–97, esp. the illustration on 196–97.

15. Picturing men working in the rigging became standard in the Dutch, and Dutch-influenced, tradition of maritime painting as it evolved in the seventeenth century. On this tradition, see Lawrence Otto Goede, *Shipwreck and Tempest in Dutch and Flemish Art* (College Park: Penn State University Press, 1989).

16. On Chapman's Homer, see also the scholarly edition by Nicole Allardyce, *Homer: The Odyssey* (Princeton, N.J.: Princeton University Press, 2000).

17. Hesiod, *Works and Days,* trans. Dorothea Wender (New York: Penguin, 1973), 66. See also Christopher Connery, "*There Was No More Sea*: The Suppression of the Ocean, from the Bible to Cyberspace," *Journal of Historical Geography* 32 (2006): 494–511.

18. *The Odysseys of Homer,* trans. George Chapman, ed. Richard Hooper, 2 vols. (London: John Russell Smith, 1857), 5:155–56. Further quotations in the text by book and line number.

19. Robert Fagles's more recent translation reads "man of misery." See Homer, *The Odyssey,* trans. Robert Fagles (New York: Penguin, 1996), 167.

20. On early modern swimming, see Mentz, *At the Bottom of Shakespeare's Ocean,* 35–49.

21. On Barlow's cartography, see Fumerton, *Unsettled,* 108–27.

22. The loose sails include a lateen on the mizzen, the top and mainsails on the mainmast and foremast, and a spiritsail off the bow.

23. Barlow, *Barlow's Journal,* ed. Lubbock, 442–43.

24. See James McDermott, *Martin Frobisher: Elizabethan Privateer,* (New Haven: Yale University Press, 2001), esp. 407–23.

25. Barlow, *Barlow's Journal,* ed. Lubbock, 552–53.

26. Daniel Defoe, *The Storm* (London, 1704).

27. Fumerton provides a transcription, which I cite parenthetically in the text. *Unsettled,* 174–76.

28. See Fumerton, *Unsettled,* 99, 202n.

Interchapter

1. *Moby-Dick,* 133.
2. *Moby-Dick,* 133.
3. *Moby-Dick,* 136.
4. *Moby-Dick,* 136.

6. "We Split"

1. Collections of sea poetry are myriad, but my favorites include the wonderfully multilingual *The Sea! The Sea!,* collected by Peter Jay (London: Anvil Press, 2005); Jonathan Raban's wide-ranging prose and poetry collection *The Oxford Book of the Sea* (Oxford: Oxford University Press, 2002), and J. D. McClatchy's collection *Poems of the Sea* (London: Everyman's, 2001).

2. For a compilation of maritime work songs by the last working shantyman, Stan Hugill, who sang work chanteys on a commercial sailing ship in the 1920s, see *Shanties from the Seven Seas* (Mystic: Mystic Seaport Press, 1994). I am grateful for the working shantymen and women at Mystic Seaport for my own introduction to the practical pleasures of maritime work songs.

3. It seems possible, perhaps likely, that Melville is thinking of the last voyage of Odysseus, as described by Tiresias in book 13, to a "land that knows nothing of the sea" where an oar is mistaken for a winnowing fan. According to Tiresias's prophecy, Odysseus will sacrifice to Poseidon in this sealess space, after which his wanderings will be over and he can die peacefully at home. Many continuers of this story, from the author of the *Telegony* to Dante, have imagined more violent or watery endings for the master mariner.

4. I omit Ahab intentionally, though in this space I will not elaborate a full anti-Ahabic reading of *Moby-Dick.*

5. Emily Dickinson, "Exultation Is the Going," *Final Harvest: Poems,* ed. Thomas Johnson (Boston: Back Bay Books, 1964), 8.

6. For a compelling reading of this stage direction and its comparable moment in *Pericles,* "Enter . . . a-shipboard" (3.2.0SD), see Lowell Duckert, *Enter, Wet: Composing with Water in Early Modern Drama and Travel Literature* (Minneapolis: University of Minnesota Press, forthcoming).

7. Not coincidentally, the following scene (1.2) contains over five hundred lines, all in verse, including Ariel's first two songs. The contrast between disaster in prose and artistic redemption by verse could not be clearer.

8. G. Wilson Knight, *The Shakespearean Tempest, with a Chart of Shakespeare's Dramatic Universe* (London: Methuen, 1960).

9. For a more sustained reading of the "sea" in Ariel's sea change, see Mentz, *At the Bottom of Shakespeare's Ocean,* 1–11.

10. While most of Theocritus's extant lyrics are traditional "bucolics" or

landed pastorals, several poems mention the sea, including number 11, about the Cyclops Polyphemous's love for the sea nymph Galatea, and number 21, in which two fishermen debate whether they should continue in the difficult profession. Some scholars have argued that 21 is a later imitation, not by Theocritus.

11. Mentz, *At the Bottom of Shakespeare's Ocean,* 44–47, and also " 'Half-fish, half-flesh': Dolphins, Humans, and the Early Modern Ocean," in *The Indistinct Human in Renaissance Literature,* ed. Jean Feerick and Vin Nardizzi (London: Palgrave, 2012), 29–46.

12. For a fine study of eighteenth-century controversy over piscatorialism, see Nicholas D. Smith, "Jacopo Sannazaro's *Eclogae Piscatoriae* (1526) and the 'Pastoral Debate' in Eighteenth-Century England," *Studies in Philology* 99, no. 4 (2002): 432–50. Smith's conclusion, that discussions of the piscatorial eventually shift into canonization of Walton's *Compleat Angler* (1653), glosses over my own interest in the oceanic pull that occasionally peers forth within piscatorial poetry. Walton, a freshwater fisherman, stands outside this maritime tradition.

13. Quoted in Jacopo Sannazaro, *The Piscatory Eclogues of Jacopo Sannazaro,* ed. Wilfred Mustard (Baltimore, Md.: Johns Hopkins University Press, 1914), 24–25. Further citations in the text.

14. On Spenser's presentation of marine excess, with sources in Pliny and elsewhere, see Mentz, "Half-fish," 33–34.

15. On Fletcher's piscatorial poetry, see Gary M. Bouchard, "Phineas Fletcher: The Piscatory Link between Spenserian and Miltonic Pastoral," *Studies in Philology* 89 (1992): 232–43.

16. This allegorical/anatomical poem, in praise of which Fletcher has called "the Spenser of this Age" in an adulatory poem by his friend Frances Quarles, continues to interest modern critics. See Mark Bayer, "The Distribution of Political Agency in Phineas Fletcher's *The Purple Island,*" *Criticism* 44 (2002): 249–61.

17. Phineas Fletcher, *Piscatory Eclogues, with other Poetical Miscellanies* (Edinburgh: A. Kincaid, W. Creech, and T. Cadet, 1771), sig. a3v. Further citations in the text.

18. For excellent exploration of this frustration in Marlowe, Shakespeare, and others, see Robert Watson, *Back to Nature: The Green and the Real in the Late Renaissance* (Philadelphia: University of Pennsylvania Press, 2006).

19. Joseph Addison, in *The Oxford Book of the Sea,* 80.

20. On the Romantic vision of the sea, see W. H. Auden, *The Enchaféd Flood, or the Romantic Iconography of the Sea* (London: Faber & Faber, 1951).

21. William Empson, *Some Versions of Pastoral* (New York: New Directions, 1960), 23.

22. On the distinction between blue and green ecologies, see Mentz,

"Shakespeare's Beach House: The Blue and the Green in *Macbeth*," *Shakespeare Studies* 39 (2011): 840–94.

23. Auden, *Enchaféd Flood*, 2.

24. Moses Brown, *Piscatory Eclogues: An Essay to Produce New Rules, and New Characters into Pastoral* (London: John Brindley, 1729), 31. Further citations in the text.

25. On Browne's devotion to Walton, see Smith, "Pastoral Debate," 445–47.

26. On "Lycidas" as oceanic poem, see Mentz, "Toward a Blue Cultural Studies," 1002–4.

27. William Diaper, *Oppian's Haleuticks* (Oxford, 1722). Diaper died in 1717, and this posthumous publication includes his translation of the first two books of Oppian's poem and the remaining three as translated by John Jones. Citations in the text by book and line number.

28. See Mentz, "After Sustainability," 589–90.

29. William Diaper, "To Mr. Congreve," *The Nereides: or, Sea-Eclogues* (London: E. Sanger, 1712), iii. Further citations in the text by eclogue and page numbers.

30. On the paradoxical image of fish in trees in classical and Renaissance poetry, see A. D. Nuttall, "Fishes in the Trees," *Essays in Criticism* 24 (1974): 20–38. Smith notes that this trope of inversion was important to many piscatorial poets (435).

31. Donne did not live long enough to know Sir Richard Fanshawe's 1655 translation of Camões's epic into English, but he may well have known the poem, first published in 1572. For a cogent argument about the influence of Camões on late-Elizabethan writers, including Shakespeare, see Shankar Raman, *Framing "India": The Colonial Imaginary in Early Modern Culture* (Stanford, Calif.: Stanford University Press, 2001).

32. For an overview of Donne's role in Cadiz and the Island Voyage, see Albert C. Labriola, "Donne's Military Career," in *The Oxford Handbook of John Donne*, ed. Jeanne Shami, Dennis Flynn, and M. Thomas Hester (Oxford: Oxford University Press, 2011), 424–34.

33. For a reliable and detailed summary of the voyage, see Julian S. Corbett, *The Successors of Drake* (New York: Burt Franklin, 1990), 181–211. Primary sources from Monson and Gorges given in notes 36 and 38, respectively.

34. John Stubbs speculates that Donne's motive in volunteering for both Cadiz and the Islands Voyage was dissatisfaction with his active love live, as documented in his early lyric poems. See John Stubbs, *John Donne: The Reformed Soul* (New York: Norton, 2006), 63–66.

35. See Stubbs, *Reformed Soul*, 67.

36. For details, see Sir William Monson, *Naval Tracts*, vol. 2., ed. M. Oppenheim (London: Naval Records Society, 1902), 21–83, esp. 22–24.

37. Brooke would later, in 1601, serve as witness to the secret marriage

between Donne and Ann More, and he would be briefly imprisoned for so doing (DNB).

38. Monson, *Naval Tracts;* Sir Arthur Gorges, *A Larger Relation of the Iland Voyage,* in *Purchas his Pilgrimes,* 24 vols. (Glasgow: MacLehose, 1905–7), 20:44–112.

39. On the literary history of the voyage narrative, see Robert Foulke, *The Sea-Voyage Narrative* (London: Routledge, 2001).

40. See also Corbett, *The Successors of Drake,* 189, for Essex's message to Elizabeth explaining his leaving Ferrol for the Azores.

41. All quotations from "The Calm" and "The Storm" are from John Donne, *The Complete English Poems,* ed. A. J. Smith (London: Penguin, 1971), 197–200. Citations given in the text by line number.

42. On humanist tropes of friendship, see Kathy Eden, *Friends Hold All Things in Common: Tradition, Intellectual Property, and the Adages of Erasmus* (New Haven, Conn.: Yale University Press, 2001).

43. He indicates his sympathy with the biblical castaway by wishing to "curse those men / Who, when the storm rage'd most, did wake thee [Jonah]" (33–34).

44. Blackmore, *Manifest Perdition,* 22.

45. The most famous of these disasters, the wreck of the *S. João,* which stranded the nobleman Manuel de Sousa Sepulveda along with his wife on southern Africa, gave rise to multiple literary texts, including pamphlet histories, verse epics, and stage plays. See Blackmore, *Manifest Perdition,* 25–27.

46. David Quint, *Epic and Empire* (Princeton, N.J.: Princeton University Press, 1993), 113–30.

47. Richard Helgerson, *Forms of Nationhood: The Elizabethan Writing of England* (Chicago: University of Chicago Press, 1992), 149–91.

48. Quoted from the *Hatfield Papers,* vii.361, in Corbett, *The Successors of Drake,* 185.

49. See OED 1, "calenture, n.," OED Online, March 2015, Oxford University Press, http://www.oed.com/view/Entry/26323?rskey=oSnyFd&result=1&isAdvanced=false.

50. Wallace Stevens, "Sea Surface Full of Clouds," *The Palm at the End of the Mind: Selected Poems and a Play,* ed. Holly Stevens (New York: Vintage, 1972), 89–92. Further citations given in the text by section and line number.

51. See Wallace Stevens, "Adagia," in *Opus Posthumous: Poems, Plays, Prose* (New York: Vintage, 1990).

52. Roy Neil Graves notes, in his witty exploration of sexual imagery in the poem, that the shape of each stanza on the page, with its vertical number, two short lines, and larger concluding line underneath, resembles "a rudimentary sinking ship." "Hardy's 'The Convergence of the Twain,'" *Explicator* 53, no. 2 (1995), 96–100.

53. Thomas Hardy, "The Convergence of the Twain," *Collected Poems of Thomas Hardy* (London: Macmillan, 1932), 288–89. Citations given in the text by stanza number.

7. Castaways

1. Northrop Frye, *The Secular Scripture: A Study of the Structure of Romance* (Cambridge, Mass.: Harvard University Press, 1978). The fruit of my work on early modern Greek romance is *Romance for Sale in Early Modern England* (Aldershot, U.K.: Ashgate, 2006).

2. Mikhal Gilmore, "Bob Dylan on his Dark New Album, *Tempest,*" *Rolling Stone,* August 16, 2012, http://www.rollingstone.com/music/news/bob-dylan-on-his-dark-new-album-tempest-20120801.

3. As Dylan and many other people do not seem to know, Shakespeare wrote or cowrote at least a few more plays after *The Tempest,* though all our dates for his plays are unreliable.

4. See Mentz, *At the Bottom of Shakespeare's Ocean,* 98.

5. Michel Serres, *The Five Senses: A Philosophy of Mingled Bodies (I),* trans. Margaret Sankay and Peter Cowley (London: Continuum, 2008) 17–21. I thank Jeffrey Cohen for this reference.

6. This distinction marks my dissent from the Lucretian model, in which visible disorder served to buttress higher intellectual order. See Mentz, *At the Bottom of Shakespeare's Ocean,* 19–23.

7. See Steve Mentz, "Tongues in the Storm: Shakespeare, Ecological Crisis, and the Resources of Genre," in *Ecocritical Shakespeare,* ed. Lynne Bruckner and Dan Brayton (Aldershot, U.K.: Ashgate Publishing, 2011), 155–72.

8. Since I have not found a published text for Dylan's song, I am relying on my own transcription, with help from fan-annotated websites such as Rock Genius, at http://rock.rapgenius.com/Bob-dylan-tempest-lyrics.

9. The Rock Genius website notes that Leo Zimmerman was a historical passenger on the *Titanic* and that Bob Dylan's given name is Robert Zimmerman.

10. Gilmore, "Bob Dylan on Dark New Album."

11. See Robert Markley, "'Casualties and Disasters': Defoe and the Interpretation of Climatic Instability," *Journal of Early Modern Cultural Studies* 8, no. 2 (Winter 2008): 102–24. Markley quotes Stanford University's Risk Management Systems modern report on the 1703 storm; see the RMS website at www.rms.com/publications/1703_windstorm.pdf.

12. Markley, "'Casualties and Disasters,'" 109. Further citations in the text.

13. See, for example, Everett Zimmerman, *The Boundaries of Fiction: History and the Eighteenth-Century British Novel* (Ithaca, N.Y.: Cornell University Press, 1996); John Richetti, *The English Novel in History, 1700–1780* (London:

Routledge, 1999); Lorna Clymer and Robert Mayer, eds., *Historical Boundaries, Narrative Forms: Essays on British Literature in the Long Eighteenth Century in Honor of Everett Zimmerman* (Newark: University of Delaware Press, 2007); and many others.

14. Daniel Defoe, *The Storm* (London, 1704), 1. Further citations in the text. For a modern edition, see *The Storm,* ed. Richard Hamblyn (London: Penguin, 2005).

15. On the novel defined through eighteenth-century empirical realism, see Richard McKeon, *The Origins of the English Novel, 1600–1740* (Baltimore, Md.: Johns Hopkins University Press, 2002). For a partial rebuttal of McKeon and a defense of a longer history of prose fiction, with ancillary bibliography, see Steve Mentz, *Romance for Sale in Early Modern England* (Aldershot, U.K.: Ashgate, 2006), 9–15.

16. The Boatswain also craves nothing but sea room, as he shouts to the storm, "Blow till thou burst thy wind, if room enough!" (1.1.7–8).

17. See Mentz, "Swimmer Poetics."

Three Short Epilogues

1. I thank my colleague Lee Ann Brown for first pointing me toward Oppen's poem.

2. George Oppen, *Of Being Numerous* (New York: New Directions, 1967), 13. Further citations in the text. For a reading that explores Oppen's Marxist and collectivist tendencies, see Marjorie Perloff, "The Shipwreck of the Singular: George Oppen's *Of Being Numerous,*" *Ironwood* 26 (Fall 1985).

3. This image is visible as the header to my personal website, www.stevementz.com, and is also part of the online exhibition of my summer 2010 gallery exhibition at the Folger Shakespeare Library, "Lost at Sea: The Ocean in the English Imagination, 1550–1750." The image is used with the permission of the Folger Library.

4. John Frith, *Vox Piscis, or the Bookfish* (London: Boler and Milbourne, 1627), 8. Further citations in the text.

5. Alexandra Walsham has found evidence that Dr. Joseph Mede, fellow of Christ's College, was also involved in the authentication of the work. See Alexandra Walsham, "*Vox Piscis or the Bookfish*: Providence and the Uses of the Reformation Past in Caroline Cambridge," *English Historical Review* 114, no. 457 (June 1999): 574–606. She cites a letter from Mede to Sir Martin Stuteville, dated June 16, 1626, BL MS Harley 390, fol. 81t-v (Walsham 575n).

6. Walsham adds another jest to the three included in *Vox Piscis,* later reprinted in Thomas Fuller's *History of the Worthies of England* (576n).

7. The more usual version of Democritus's saying is, "Truth lies at the bot-

tom of a well." The authenticity of this and other sayings of Democritus are controversial.

8. Julian Yates, "Wet?," in *Elemental Ecologies,* ed. Jeffrey Jerome Cohen and Lowell Duckert (Minneapolis: University of Minnesota Press, 2015). Yates's earlier exploration of *The Bookfish* and *The Tempest* appears in Yates and Richard Burt, *What's the Worst Thing You Can Do to Shakespeare?* (New York: Palgrave, 2013), 75–110.

9. That radical cultural change often parallels climatological change is the thesis of Geoffrey Parker's recent study of world history in the early modern period, *Global Crisis: War, Climate Change, and Catastrophe in the Seventeenth Century* (New Haven, Conn.: Yale University Press, 2013).

10. For a fuller elaboration of this point, see my essay "Shipwreck," in *Inhuman Nature,* ed. Jeffrey Jerome Cohen (Brooklyn: Punctum, 2014), 1–15.

11. On the aesthetic possibilities of the deep ocean, see Stacy Alaimo, "Violet-Black," in *Prismatic Ecologies: Ecotheory beyond Green,* ed. Jeffrey Jerome Cohen (Minneapolis: University of Minnesota Press, 2013), 233–51.

12. Captain Nemo's motto, "mobilis in mobile," appears in Jules Verne's celebrated science-fiction novel *Twenty Thousand Leagues under the Sea,* ed. Peter Costello (London: Everyman, 1992), 41. Verne's novel was originally published in French in 1870. For some early thoughts about this phrase as ecological model, see Steve Mentz, "Swimmer Poetics," in *O-Zone: A Journal of Object-Oriented Studies,* ed. Eileen Joy and Levi Bryant (2015), http://o-zone-journal.org/short-essay-cluster.

Index

STEVE MENTZ is professor of English at St. John's University in New York City. His work in oceanic and environmental criticism includes the edited collection *Oceanic New York,* the book *At the Bottom of Shakespeare's Ocean,* and the Folger Library exhibition "Lost at Sea: The Ocean in the English Imagination, 1550–1750." He has also written *Romance for Sale in Early Modern England* and coedited two collections of essays on narrative fiction in the early modern period.

www.ingramcontent.com/pod-product-compliance
Lightning Source LLC
LaVergne TN
LVHW100024310826
846742LV00012B/32
* 9 7 8 0 8 1 6 6 9 1 0 6 7 *